The Collaborative Podcast Series; Book 3

The 10 Essential Steps

By David B. Savage

Table of Contents

Guests on the Collaborative Podcast Series

In order of appearance on the podcasts, I thank these friends, mentors and collaborative leaders:

Chuck Rose, Denise Chartrand, Kathy Porter, Duncan Autrey, Jeanne McPherson, Allan Davis, Patricia Morgan, Don Loney, David Gouthro, Ken Cloke, Cheryl Cardinal, Ryan Robb, Esther Bleuel, Jeff Cohen, Joan Goldsmith, Amy Fox, Richard Schultz, Laura Hummelle, Colin Campbell, Donna Hastings, Rob McKay, Art Korpach, Tara Russell, Linda Matthie, Viki Winterton, Stephen Smith, Dee Ann Turner, Doreen Liberto, Dana Meise, Teresa de Grosbois, David Milia, Don Simmons, Bruce McIntyre, James Armstrong, Michael Hill, Johanne Lavoie, Atul Tandon, Prabha Sankaranarayan, Bob Anderson, Ginger Lapid- Bogda, Dan Savage, Sarah Daitch, India Sherri, Kevin Brown, David Milia, AnnaMarie McHargue, Bob Acton, David Mitchell, Tristen Chernove, Martin Parnell, Mike Thompson, Stephen Hobbs, Julie Murray, Doreen Liberto, Chuck Rose, Elisabeth Delaygue Bevan, Florian Wackermann, Lance Kadatz, Cliff Wiebe, Amy Schabacker Dufrane, Japman Bajaj, Kate McKenzie, Shawn Anderson, Martin Parnell, Jim Gibson, Jeff Cohen, Barry Wilson, Doreen Liberto, Jeff Cohen, Deva Premal and Miten, Klara Fenlof, Robert Stewart, Sara Amos and Quinn Amos, Ken Cloke, and Duncan Autrey.

This is Break Through To Yes: The Collaborative Podcast Series by David B. Savage

Book 3: The 10 Essential Steps of Collaboration provides you with 16 podcasts originally aired on Voice America in 2015 and 2016. We cover the 10 Essential Steps plus Leadership, Assessment, the Next Generation of Collaborators and more.

Let's work together better for our shared future.

Imagine the peaks we will reach together.
Collaboration is the path.

Foreword

If You Want to Go Fast, Go Alone. If You Want to Go Far, Go Together- African proverb

I've been asked many times, why have I done this podcast series. Why have I written Break Through to Yes: Unlocking the Possible within a Culture of Collaboration? Why is collaboration so important?

I'll tell you why. We need it. I need it. Our future needs it. Business is forced into silos and must give up to an open and agile system that better suits today's world and our shared future. We must create shared value. We must think critically. The costs of command and control leadership are getting higher.

During my 42-year career in business, I've held titles including director, president, and chief operating officer. I have seen many and repeated failures, sometimes with the cost of billions. These failures affect organizations and their capital projects and operations. When a company starts making mistakes, tries to force its agenda on others, or is in conflict with its own stakeholders, the consequences are significant. People revolt and profit margins are destroyed. Projects get delayed in regulatory and community review for extended lengths of time. Employees simply don't give their best because they do not trust the systems they work in especially when they have little influence in the processes or programs in which they are involved.

The cost to organizations can be both internal and external disengagement, rejection by regulatory bodies and governments, rejection by impacted communities, and damage to the environment. Add to that a wide range of negative human impacts including everything from depression, conflict, suicide, marital breakdown and career paralysis to the loss of intelligence and vision of the brightest people in your business, simply because they mentally and spiritually check out when they come to work.

All this means lost productivity, lost opportunities to grow and prosper, and distracted leaders and workers who no longer feel able to do good work. Leaders and organizations however can gain a strategic advantage by avoiding all this energy and revenue-zapping negativity simply by working together to build a culture of collaboration.

The soul killing command and control, also, damages families. What if you mattered? What if we mattered. And it was more valuable to explore together than be seen to be right.

Collaboration is not an event, it's a culture. It's the way we work together. I am a lifelong student of how to get the right people in the right place with the right information in the right mindset to figure out how to conquer challenges and solve conflicts together.

Collaboration is a new field of study and success. Collaboration must evolve. Let's learn together and make our world, communities and families better.

Google collaboration in 2012 and you will get 278 million results. Google collaboration today and you will get 550 million results. We are seeking wisdom, skills and systems for collaboration. With this series, I want to build that together.

This is a quote from an OpEd article By THOMAS L. FRIEDMAN in the New York Times September 27, 2017:

"When work was predictable and the change rate was relatively constant, preparation for work merely required the codification and transfer of existing knowledge and predetermined skills to create a stable and deployable work force," explains education consultant Heather McGowan. "Now that the velocity of change has accelerated, due to a combination of exponential growth in technology and globalization, learning can no longer be a set dose of education consumed in the first third of one's life." In this age of accelerations, "the new killer skill set is an agile mind-set that values learning over knowing."

Today's increasing speed of change and increasing complexity make collaboration more important now than ever before. No one person can know it all, solve it all or be it all. Together we are better. Together we go far.

Welcome. I am David B. Savage. This compilation of my podcasts is created to provide you, in one source, the deep look at how we work together and how we can do that better. I offer you this compilation of 41 podcasts for your enjoyment, education, and leadership.

When I started writing my book Break Through to Yes: Unlocking the Possible within a Culture of Collaboration, I realized in 2012 that there were few books on collaboration and none of them were collaborative books. This series of podcasts, 41 podcasts, is not about me. It's about "we". It's about "we" and how to create shared value.

In my books and podcasts, I offer you insights from my 42+ years of business leadership, plus the wisdom from over 175 leaders from eight countries around the world. Yes, my book and podcasts have over 175 other voices.

I hope you'll add yours. You may email me at David@DavidBSavage to share your learning and insights. Let's collaborate. I believe that through leadership, excellence and collaboration, we can make our personal and professional lives far better together.

In this compilation, you will experience many perspectives and dreams. It's divided in four easy to listen to or read books.

I)   Book 1: The Foundations for Collaboration

offers you eight 15-minute podcasts originally aired on the Tenacious Living Network, a quick hit, a series of eight 15-minute podcasts.

II)   Book 2: The Collaborative Guest Podcasts

offers you three podcasts where I had been a guest on Barry Wilson, Bob Acton and Duncan Autrey's podcasts. The subjects are collaboration and negotiation, leadership and cumulative environmental effects on our landscape.

III)   Book 3: The 10 Essential Steps of Collaboration

provides you with 16 podcasts originally aired on Voice America. In addition to the 10 Essential Steps, this Book includes the Next Generation of Leaders and our Shared Future.

IV)   Book 4: Unlocking the Possible with Collaboration

provides you with a further 14 podcasts originally aired on Voice America. These podcasts feature collaboration and Disruptive Technology, Organizational Assessments, Critical Thinking, Sports, Leadership and combating human Sexual trafficking with collaboration.

Plus, there's a bonus in our podcasts. You will hear the beautiful music of Chuck Rose, Deva Premal and Miten, and Led to Sea.

Note; The chapters and books are transcripts from the podcasts. These are minimally edited and are not rewritten for the Collaborative Podcast Series. These are the brilliant unpolished conversations.

Here is a quote from the podcasts by my friend Ken Cloke, founder of Mediators Beyond Borders and author of many books including The Dance of Opposites.

"The first thing that's misleading is that there is a single thing that is known as collaboration. We can certainly think of it as singular but we can also think of it as having a kind of infinite number of manifestations. There are small- scale collaborations, which we engage in every time we have a conversation. There are larger collaborations that we engage in in communities and families. "What we have a hard time I think imagining is how far exactly this can go. What is the deepest level of our collaboration? What's the highest achievement that we can make in this field? I think when we begin to think in those terms, we begin to see all of life completely differently,"

Welcome to our Collaborative Podcast Series. Let's collaborate for a better shared future for our people, planet, and communities. You matter. We matter. We are better together.

What is Creating Shared Value, Critical Thinking and Collaboration?

In my talks, writing and consulting, I focus on Creating Shared Value and Critical Thinking. Along with collaboration, critical thinking and leadership, Creating Shared Value is our path to our shared future.

What is Creating Shared Value?

The Harvard Business Review says it best in the January – February 2011 issue How To Fix Capitalism, Michael E. Porter and Mark R. Kramer write;

"The capitalist system is under siege. In recent years business has been criticized as a major cause of social, environmental, and economic problems. Companies are widely thought to be prospering at the expense of their communities. Trust in business has fallen to new lows, leading government officials to set policies that undermine competitiveness and sap economic growth. Business is caught in a vicious circle.

A big part of the problem lies with companies themselves, which remain trapped in an outdated, narrow approach to value creation. Focused on optimizing short-term financial performance, they overlook the greatest unmet needs in the market as well as broader influences on their long-term success. Why else would companies ignore the well-being of their customers, the depletion of natural resources vital to their businesses, the viability of suppliers, and the economic distress of the communities in which they produce and sell?

It doesn't have to be this way, say Porter, of Harvard Business School, and Kramer, the managing director of the social impact advisory firm FSG.

Companies could bring business and society back together if they redefined their purpose as creating "shared value"—generating economic value in a way that also produces value for society by addressing its challenges. A shared value approach reconnects company success with social progress.

Firms can do this in three distinct ways: by reconceiving products and markets, redefining productivity in the value chain, and building supportive industry clusters at the company's locations. A number of companies known for their hard-nosed approach to business—including GE, Wal-Mart, Nestlé, Johnson & Johnson, and Unilever—have already embarked on important initiatives in these areas. Nestlé, for example, redesigned its coffee procurement processes, working intensively with small farmers in impoverished areas who were trapped in a cycle of low productivity, poor quality, and environmental degradation. Nestlé provided advice on farming practices; helped growers secure plant stock, fertilizers, and pesticides; and began directly paying them a premium for better beans. Higher yields and quality increased the growers' incomes, the environmental impact of farms shrank, and Nestlé's reliable supply of good coffee grew significantly. Shared value was created.

Shared value could reshape capitalism and its relationship to society. It could also drive the next wave of innovation and productivity growth in the global economy as it opens managers' eyes to immense human needs that must be met, large new markets to be served, and the internal costs of social deficits—as well as the competitive advantages available from addressing them. But our understanding of shared value is still in its genesis. Attaining it will require managers to develop new skills and knowledge and governments to learn how to regulate in ways that enable shared value, rather than work against it."

What is Critical Thinking?

"Critical thinking is self-guided, self-disciplined thinking which attempts to reason at the highest level of quality in a fair-minded way. People who think critically consistently attempt to live rationally, reasonably, empathically. They are keenly aware of the inherently flawed nature of human thinking when left unchecked. They strive to diminish the power of their egocentric and sociocentric tendencies. They use the intellectual tools that critical thinking offers – concepts and principles that enable them to analyze, assess, and improve thinking. They work diligently to develop the intellectual virtues of intellectual integrity, intellectual humility, intellectual civility, intellectual empathy, intellectual sense of justice and confidence in reason. They realize that no matter how skilled they are as thinkers, they can always improve their reasoning abilities and they will at times fall prey to mistakes in reasoning, human irrationality, prejudices, biases, distortions, uncritically accepted social rules and taboos, self-interest, and vested interest. They strive to improve the world in whatever ways they can and contribute to a more rational, civilized society. At the same time, they recognize the complexities often inherent in doing so. They avoid thinking simplistically about complicated issues and strive to appropriately consider the rights and needs of relevant others. They recognize the complexities in developing as thinkers, and commit themselves to life-long practice toward self-improvement. They embody the Socratic principle: The unexamined life is not worth living, because they realize that many unexamined lives together result in an uncritical, unjust, dangerous world." Linda Elder, September 2007 as reported by the Critical Thinking Community website.

"A well cultivated critical thinker:

- ✓ raises vital questions and problems, formulating them clearly and precisely;
- ✓ gathers and assesses relevant information, using abstract ideas to interpret it effectively comes to well-reasoned conclusions and solutions, testing them against relevant criteria and standards;
- ✓ thinks open-mindedly within alternative systems of thought, recognizing and assessing, as need be, their assumptions, implications, and practical consequences; and
- ✓ communicates effectively with others in figuring out solutions to complex problems.

Critical thinking is, in short, self-directed, self-disciplined, self-monitored, and self-corrective thinking. It presupposes assent to rigorous standards of excellence and mindful command of their use. It entails effective communication and problem-solving abilities and a commitment to overcome our native egocentrism and sociocentrism."

Richard Paul and Linda Elder, The Miniature Guide to Critical Thinking Concepts and Tools, Foundation for Critical Thinking Press, 2008

What is Collaboration?

Here is an except from Break Through To Yes: Unlocking the Possible within a Culture of Collaboration.

"When you Google "collaboration" you get at least 278,000,000 results. [Note if you searched Collaboration on Google in October 2017, you would have received 530,000,000,000 results. This is almost a double in just two years. Will we reach a billion in 2018? There is a significant and growing interest in collaboration.]

Seems there is a lot of interest in learning about collaboration. But what is collaboration represented as?

Merriam Webster defines collaborate as "to work with another person or group in order to achieve or do something." This could be the definition of a meeting or what a football team does. I prefer this definition:

"Collaboration is highly diversified teams working together inside and outside a company with the purpose to create value by improving innovation, customer relationships and efficiency while leveraging technology for effective interactions in the virtual and physical space."

Let's make a joint proclamation that we value collaboration as a powerful way of leading. Collaboration isn't an act, it is the way we lead. To collaborate isn't simply to work together, it is an organizational culture."

And from What Is Collaboration at Work? By Bruce Mayhew, HuffPost July 24, 2014;

"Collaboration is the successful structure of the future - not a single conversation between two employees. A diverse and collaborative culture is a powerful competitive advantage. A well-implemented, trained and supported high-performance team will better align their outcomes around both their objective and company mission.

Tomorrows successful organizations recognize that in today's complex professional environment that collaboration is critical.

Collaborative leaders recognize there will be challenges and that their greatest responsibility is to guide change and future success by preparing their employees to overcoming these challenges in a respectful and mindful way."

Define Your Personal Values as a Successful Collaborative Leader

Name five values: (for example, integrity, transparency, fairness, innovative, inclusive, curiosity, accountability, intelligence, courageous, perfection, altruism, loyalty, respect, family, humility, truth, determination, independence, ...

1)
2)
3)
4)
5)

How do you choose to lead?

_____
_____
_____

What resources do you need (human, technology, networks, financial, environmental, social)?

_____
_____
_____

What do you choose to let go of to make this so?

_____
_____
_____

What else?

_____
_____
_____
_____

Chapter 1 Why Collaborate featuring Chuck Rose and Denise Chartrand

David: Now is our time to lead more powerfully, consciously, and collaboratively in ways that make our world a better place today and in the future. Leaders in companies will make this essential shift now. Welcome to Break Through to Yes with Collaboration. I'm David B. Savage.

Why are we doing this? Well, I've seen too many bad examples of collaboration; bully bosses, manipulation in the name of working together. Think about the saying, "A camel is a horse designed by a committee." Yes, a camel is a horse designed by committee. Have you seen that? Doesn't look like a thoroughbred. It's not what they planned but it was a compromise.

Too often leaders seek people that think like them and see the world like them. Too often collaboration is at best little steps when so much is possible. We are fixing this now with this radio show, Break Through to Yes with Collaboration, my book, "Break Through to Yes" and with you. Thank you, listeners for tuning in and sharing and collaborating with me.

Well, who am I? I am a Canadian. I am a negotiator, an executive coach. I do organizational development work. For the first 35 years of my career, I was involved as a leader in the Canadian oil and gas industry. My focus was bringing people together creating synergy groups, creating profound discussions and conversations where all the stakeholders had a view where we got to the underlying interest.

In the last eight years, I've been writing. I've been doing professional speaking, workshops, etcetera hoping that we could work together far better. There are many books on negotiation, conflict management, communication, and marketing. There are very few books on collaboration and how to work together better.

This book and this show will actually be the first collaborative show and collaborative book. Through my book, "Break Through to Yes," I'll have over 100 experts from five countries who've added their voice and their wisdom. I will bring as many as I possibly can during this weekly radio show. I will interview them; seek their advice, and their current knowledge.

This is for business. This is for collaborative leaders. This is for our planet. On this show today, our first in the series, I am delighted to introduce you to Chuck Rose, a friend, a great musician and an organizational development specialist. I, also, introduce you to another great friend, Denise Chartrand, of Collaborative Engagements. We will talk about collaboration and how do we work together better.

Near the end of the hour-long show, each week we'll bring the Outrage of the Week. Outrage of the Week will be what are we angry about today and what might we learn from essential collaboration. I always seek your (listeners') insights either by e-mail or by call in.

The key messages today:

why this show serves you because it is all about you, the listener;

what collaboration is and is not;

why we need a break through to yes with collaboration.

What does collaboration mean to you? Why does it matter? Each week I'll also bring you a story about collaboration and how leaders, brave leaders, visionary leaders are making this change.

Too often we suffer bully bosses and managers who fail to stand up, we have secret shame and group think where fitting in are the standard. All are diseases too prevalent in today's business world. Today's corporate cultures allow a few to put themselves above values, ethics, and their own people. That's not leadership.

The person in the organization that stands up and stands out takes significant risks of being ostracized, ignored, shamed, and even terminated. "You are not one of us. You don't play by our rules." I submit to you, in fact those that stand up and stand out and say what's their truth (it doesn't have to be my truth or your truth but it's important to them), they are some of the most valuable team members.

Today is an example. I wish to recognize two leaders who I've had conversations with in the last couple of days. I want to recognize them for standing up and taking the risk. The fact situations are examples of standing up and taking the risk with the intention of making your team stronger. I do not know the details of these events, only the highlights through conversations with both leaders. Let's go.

Firstly, I wish to recognize Donna Hastings, Chief Executive Officer for Heart and Stroke Foundation, Alberta, Northwest Territories in Nunavut. Donna saw a major problem happening in the organization. She found there were many people that were afraid to talk about it. She brought in the right people to analyze it and start coming up with not only solutions but more importantly, ways to encourage Heart and Stroke employees and executive to ensure they will speak up and stand up when similar situations arise.

Also, I recognize Rob Mardjetko, a negotiator in the oil and gas industry. Faced with an extremely challenging economic environment for energy companies this year, his company, like most, has a mandate to sell assets, reduce costs, and pay down debt. When Rob and his company were completing negotiations with another company to sell a significant block of assets, the price kept falling.

After a sleepless night, Rob went to his boss recommending that they walk away from this deal. The outcome was not what they needed and he would commit himself to finding negotiating a better deal in the next year. Fortunately, the executive of his company honored Rob's insight and agreed.

Walking away (the theme song that you'll be hearing shortly) is what Rob did, what Donna did -- stand up. How will you stand up? What serves you? What serves your intention and your values and ethics as a leader? Collaboration is not compromise. Collaboration is not getting along. Collaboration is diversity of perspective. Collaboration is truth telling.

We need Break Through to Yes because, well simply, it is our time to lead more powerfully and consciously in ways that make our world a better place. In this time of emotionally triggered, self-centered, and divisive broadcast from media, politicians, business, environmentalists, aboriginal organizations, this is our time to come together with all of them. We are one.

We need a new space for innovation, for listening, and creation. We will create a new dialogue, a new space, a new mind, a new heart, and a shared spirit. "You cannot go throughout a single day without having an impact on the world around you. What you do makes a difference and you have to decide what kind of difference you wish to make." That's last quote is from Jane Goodall. I'll say it again; "You cannot go through a single day without having a major impact on the world around you. What you do makes a difference and you have to decide what kind of difference you wish to make."

Now we'll listen to "Win, Win, Win or Walk Away" by Chuck Rose.

<music>

David: This is David B. Savage, Break Through to Yes with Collaboration. Before the break, we were talking about collaboration, what it is and what it isn't. You've, also, heard for the first time "Win, Win, Win or Walk Away" by Chuck Rose.

Chuck, I'm looking at these amazing words that you wrote for this show. They include, "I have a dream. There's enough for everyone." It goes on, "Find a win-win-win or walk away. Confrontation is a mistake that we have outgrown. We will break through to yes."

Chuck Rose, I'm so grateful because you've incorporated your spirit, your belief, and your leadership into this.

Chuck is a team-building and customer service consultant. He helps leaders to get their teams to buy into their vision and mission. Chuck does this through stories, songs, humor, activities that get people up and moving. Chuck believes in abundance. There is enough for everyone if we can just choose love over fear.

Chuck, the music of this show as we've just mentioned and before the break we've just heard for the very first time is how we collaborate. Even this music is a collaboration. Tell our listeners about our conversation and what you did with a request from me and that piece of the story.

Chuck: Well, David when you approached me to provide music for your show several months ago, I immediately thought of a song I did that I'd had probably five years ago. I wrote down the title five years ago, which was called "Win, Win, Win or Walk Away."

I read your introduction to your book and I saw so many areas where you and I are on the same wavelength in terms of people working together and not having to have a loser in any situation. How if we can't find a win for everybody then we're going to change the rules of the game.

I saw so many similarities there. Then you and I sat down and we actually ran over some lines together and we found lines that were actually right out of your book that were already in the ideas for the song that I had. We were able to collaborate on that and come up with something, again, that was better than it would have been if I had just worked on my own. That's what collaboration is all about is finding a way that is better for everybody, not finding a win-lose situation.

Then of course I collaborated with my son on recording it. It was a collaboration in a number of areas. It was great. I'm very happy with the results. It's going to wind up on an album that I'm in the process of recording right now. It should be available fairly soon.

David: Your song, Win, Win, Win or Walk Away, contains so many of the elements of the work that you and I believe in. It's in my book. It's in your music. It's in your coaching and training of teams where it's getting brave enough to step forward and find their own voice, express it, really realize that there's actually nothing I or you or any of our listeners do that is on its own. We are one. Ideas are out there. Who stands for those ideas?

I am just so impressed with what you've created and gratefully allowed me to share it with our listeners and to the world.

Chuck: You know, David I firmly believe that the world is on the verge, humanity is on the verge of realization that the incredibly competitive win-lose mentality and I think of it as a mentality of fear because people are afraid there's not enough.

When we break through that and realize that there is enough if we lead from love, if we love each other and look for the best in each other and look for win-win-win situations instead of "I win, you lose," when we get to that point, there's going to be enough for everybody.

There already is. It's just a matter of right now people are protecting their turf because of fear. I'm seeing people like that. They're kind of dinosaurs. People who can't get through to the new realization are dinosaurs. In my opinion, well, they're having a reptile dysfunction.

David: "A reptile dysfunction," that's a new one, Chuck.

Chuck: That's the reptilian brain that tells us we are a world where there isn't enough for everybody so "I got to get mine and it doesn't matter what happens to you." That's ancient thinking. That's past. We've got to get to the future.

David: That reptilian brain, the fight or flight immediate response that we have to know then we have to judge. In this weekly radio show, I'm providing in segment Outrage of the Week where in social media and politics, in whatever, in conversations around the coffee table, we tend to jump and emotionally engage without actually informing ourselves.

That reptilian brain, it's useful. Can't live without it but two things happen. Our pre-frontal cortex where our logical brains are and mostly as Chuck says, our heart...lead from our heart in recognition of "together we are better."

Chuck: Yes.

David: Chuck, what's the most important requirement for getting teams to buy into the program? What's your wisdom around that?

Chuck: Well, the first requirement is trust. If a team doesn't trust the leader and there's only one way to get the team to trust the leader and that is the leader has to put the team first. I heard a wonderful piece on CBC Radio just the other night. A professor was talking about how in individual situations, you can win if you're the aggressive bad guy but in team situations, in social situations, in cultural situations, altruism wins over selfishness.

When the team works together, they're going to have a better result than if each member of the team is out for themselves; if the leader sets the example by putting the team first. I've got a program that I do called "Love Them or Lose Them." It's about staff retention.

If you don't love your staff and I mean that as actively loving. It's not an emotional thing. It's what you do -- putting their needs ahead of your own. If you don't do that, they're going to see it. They're going to say, "Well, what's in this for me?" However, if you do put their needs first, they're going to put your needs first.

David: Yes. They need to be able to trust you enough that they can speak up and you also have their backs.

Chuck: Yes. Yes, absolutely. In this atmosphere of trust where people know that they can voice their concerns without fear of reprisals, without fear of it coming back to punish them and they don't have to agree with the leader. If the leader is strong enough and confident enough that they can handle people not exactly agreeing with them, that's a much better way to get buy in because people would buy in as long as they've had their voice heard.

They don't have to agree. If they feel like they've been heard, listened to, and that their opinion has been taken into account, then they're willing to say, "Okay, at least they heard me. I'll get behind the program."

David: Yes. It's so important to recognize that listening, having empathy, understanding...doesn't mean you have to agree with them.

Chuck: Right. Exactly. When you delegate leadership, as a business owner, I've delegated leadership to my key people and when you delegate it you have to also delegate the authority to get the job done. It's not just responsibility. It's also authority. Then you've got to be willing to say, "Hey, it's not exactly the way I would have done it but the results are what's important." The team is also more important than the individuals.

David: And that building of trust that you've also highlighted.

Chuck: Exactly.

David: Donald Trump, in the Republican Party, in the race to the American Presidential nomination, there's an amygdala, a reptilian brain, somebody that seems to be more and more popular that seems to segregate and judge and reject so many, doesn't it pay to be a jerk, Chuck? Doesn't it just pay to be a jerk?

Chuck: I think this is exactly what we're talking about a minute ago where in an individual level yes it can pay. On a social level, on a team, on a national level, it doesn't work. Putting the team first, being altruistic and saying, "I'm not just in this for me. I'm in this for my team, my city, my country, my race."

When I say race, I mean the human race. I don't mean...there are no individual people who have racist ideas. There is only one race. It's the human race.

David: Yes. Break through to yes. We've got Chuck Rose, the creator, performer, author, organizational development speaker, and someone that leads from the heart. Chuck, as we're about to finish this interview, what's one more thing that you'd like to share with our listeners?

Chuck: Well, the most important choice we can make is between fear and love. As far as I'm concerned that's the only two choices we have. If we choose love, we're always going to put the team first and we're always going to have better results ourselves because of it. It's a no-brainer to me. Fear is not faith.

David: All right. Thank you so much, Chuck Rose. Beautiful wisdom, leadership and love.

David: This is David B. Savage, Break Through to Yes with Collaboration. Before the break, we were talking with Chuck Rose, the creator, performer of "Win, Win, Win or Walk Away" the theme song for this show. He was talking about trust, love, and being complete. For more about this show, my book, and my services, my website is davidbsavage.com.

Now, we are going to go into an interview with another great leader, Denise Chartrand, project manager in Alberta's energy sector, trained in negotiation, mediation, facilitation, and conflict management. She's managed numerous projects in Western Canada and more recently at international levels creating an integrated solution for her customers.

Working with multiple and diverse stakeholders, Denise appreciates the wisdom of others as she assists them to explore solutions from their varying perspectives. Denise is skilled at creating safe spaces where everyone is encouraged to participate. Denise believes that the best solutions are those that are reached together.

Hi, Denise. Thank you so much for joining us.

Denise: Thanks for having me, David.

David: I just want to launch into some questions so we can take best advantage of this limited time we have. What is about what people call collaboration that is misleading, Denise?

Denise: Well, I found out many people look at the idea of collaboration the same way they look at compromise where you win some and you lose some. That isn't actually what collaboration is all about. Collaboration essentially means working together towards achieving mutually beneficial results where all parties win.

If you think about it, there really isn't any other solution that is sustainable. The only sustainable outcomes must have the agreement and input of all parties. Otherwise, you are under the constant threat of retaliation because honestly if I'm not happy, I'm going to keep looking for ways to become happier. If on the other hand all parties have the opportunity to have a voice, they will likely be excited by and accepting of the resolution because it will be beneficial to them as it is to everyone else.

David: Thank you. So why collaborate? Where's the value?

Denise: The value in collaboration is everything. If you take the time to step back and look around you, you'll see that everything beautiful, everything good is a work of collaboration. For instance, my daughter used to ask me what my favorite color was. I would say, "It's all the colors of the rainbow." There's so many beautiful colors in existence but none would be as beautiful without the contrast of all the others.

As another example, I once had the opportunity a few years back to go to an incredible midsummer gala out in the mountains. At one point as we were waiting for the presentations to happen on the outside stage, a beautiful trumpet burst out and started playing this beautiful song.

We couldn't see where it was coming from but a few moments later other instruments started to chime in. Whether it was flutes or violins or whatnot, before long we had this whole beautiful symphony playing from rooftops of all these buildings out in the mountains.

Even though that first trumpet on its own would have been absolutely beautiful and stunning based on the setting, I can't even explain what the energy and the impact was to have this whole symphony just playing out in the mountains. It created such fantastic energy and only was possible because of a collaborative effort between all of the people playing the instruments.

David: Fantastic metaphor. You are one of the many that have contributed your wisdom to my book, "Break Through to Yes" and part of what you wrote for me and thank you so much for that, Denise is...I'll just read it and just ask if you can talk about that.

"Collaborative leadership is the process of creating an inclusive environment, opening up space for all stakeholders to be a part of an expansive solution. The goal of collaborative leadership is to create positive new futures by working together. There is no room in collaborative leadership for heroes as every person is an integral part of the solution." Tell us more.

Denise: When I was younger, I studied leadership. I was excited about the idea of becoming a great leader one day, a leader who could inspire others to accomplish big ideals. I wanted to be that person who people could look up to somewhere along the way. I realized that was a somewhat narcissistic viewpoint. Who am I to lead others to accomplish great things?

Since then as I've explored, I realized there's a big difference between great leaders and collaborative leaders. Great leaders lead the process to complete a task that they assert as the ideal whereas collaborative leaders facilitates a process that brings people together to solve tough problems together in a way that's mutually beneficial.

It's nobler to me and it takes the individuality out of the equation. There's not only one person who is intelligent enough to have all the answers. We all come together and build an integrated and inclusive solution with many different viewpoints. I think that is the strength of a collaborative leader rather than a leader who has great ideas. It brings together a whole bunch of people with great ideas instead of just one.

David: Thank you so much, Denise Chartrand of Collaborative Engagements, President of Collaborative Engagements.

Denise: Thank you for having me, David.

David: All right. We've just heard from Denise. From my book "Break Through to Yes, Unlocking the Possible within a Culture of Collaboration" we've got over a hundred leaders from around the world, I think there's six countries represented, who have added their own wisdom about collaboration. Here's a little more about what Denise Chartrand, collaborativeengagements.com has illustrated, provided wisdom for my book.

I quote now. "Collaborative leaders must be both humble and courageous. Humble because they know that they alone do not have all of the answers. Courageous because they must trust." There's that word again.

"It takes the knowledge of many to create meaningful and sustainable results. They work towards consensus knowing that any solution will fail unless there is agreement between all. For collaboration to work, people must be accountable and responsible to look collaborative process doing what they say and saying what they do while acting with integrity. This process takes time but the results are amazing and well worth the investment."

That is one of the quotes from "Break Through to Yes" that Denise Chartrand has provided to me. What I want to invite the listeners to contact me. Provide me with your insights with respect to your collaboration; when it's bad, when it's great, and how do you make that difference, make that difference yours.

Going forward in this weekly radio show, we will be coming back and I commit to respond to everybody that sends me an e-mail or makes that contact. I commit that where we can, I will actually read portions of your wisdom and where you allow me to, I will add that to our collaborative leadership, collaborative cultural knowledge base through my blog and through quotes in future books. We are all in this together.

I'm not the expert. Oftentimes people are looking for heroes. I'm just a man who's lived an abundant, healthy, happy, and creative life, lived the life I choose and I've surrounded myself with amazing people. In this radio show I invite you in. I invite you to provide your wisdom and your insights.

I think with that we will build a world community of collaboration. With that we will build a world community where we can electronically, digitally connect and in person. We can learn these tools and learn how to clean up prior messes that the heroes make. We can also understand that when we look for heroes, sometimes we're looking for ourselves.

When a company or a culture or a nation where young people look for rock stars, rock stars in business as well, we're giving away our own power. We have power. Rock stars in business especially, they can be rock stars for a while but too often when they become human in our eyes, when they fail, when they don't meet our expectations that we've set for them unilaterally then we kill them.

Very few business leaders, corporate leaders, political leaders actually survive. Some survive for months, sometimes for decades but oftentimes we give away our power and then we punish them. Let's stand up. Let's break through to yes together. Let's be seen.

How can you do this? Well, one of the ways you can do this is you simply bring it to yourself. Create a personal board of directors just like a corporate board of directors. Hire a coach. Do whatever it requires to allow you to become yourself, to make your world a better place, to be courageous. Like Denise says, "Collaborative leaders must be both humble and courageous."

Trust as Chuck Rose says. Love and through that, through that oneness, that connection, that access to a network of amazing people and resources around the world that we now have. We have all the resources we need. Just like the song "Win, Win, Win or Walk Away," we have enough. Let's connect. Let's innovate and create and serve.

David: We're back. This is David B. Savage, Break Through to Yes with Collaboration on Voice America. Before the commercial breaks, we've talked to Denise Chartrand, of Collaborative Engagements; and Chuck Rose. We're talking about trust, about courage, about integrity. I'm encouraging connection with the listeners, with you to provide your insights.

Sometimes we go the opposite way and sometimes that's fine and sometimes that's horrific, I will say. I even stutter on that word "horrific." In social media whether it's Facebook, whether it's whatever and in media, too often we have outrages where everybody gets angry all of a sudden at one thing.

Today our hearts break for the little three-year-old, Alan Kurdi. Alan, his brother, Galib, mother, Rehana, and father, Abdullah were escaping from the madness that is Syria today. For years, Syrians have been plagued with a civil war in the Islamic State and chaos. We saw recently the lifeless bodies of Alan, his brother, and mother washed up on the shores of Turkey on the beach, on a tourist beach.

For years there's been this humanitarian crisis. For years the world has turned a blind eye to violence, hatred, and murder. For years we, the world has ignored the millions of refugees in camps. Europe is now under huge pressure from tens of thousands of refugees desperately seeking a safe place to live, work, and be in a healthy community. We have ignored them because most of us have a safe place to live, work, and live in healthy communities until...until a picture.

A picture often is the catalyst for the world to understand differently. A photograph, a picture of little Alan Kurdi, a picture of his dead three-year-old body on a tourist beach in Turkey. The world woke up. On September 3rd, 2015, there was a worldwide shock and outrage. How can this happen? Who is responsible?

Around the world television commentators, journalists, radio hosts, social and political activists, families of the dead and the refugees, Facebook, Twitter, Instagram, politicians, all joined in the chorus of shock, sadness, outrage, judgment, and anger. Who can be punished for this? Well, we might punish ourselves. Instead of brutal internet and social outrage, what might we learn? How will we learn and break through to yes?

Well, let's be curious. Reach out. Learn. Integrate. Form a new perspective and your own perspective. Be in the world, not judging others or sitting idly by. What might each of us do to combat the chaos in Syria to provide an opportunity for safe, healthy, and prosperous, loving communities for all of us to live in? There is enough, as Chuck says.

What can we do as communities? What can we do as companies, as nations, as a global collaborative movement? Where is love? Where are collaborative leaders? Where are the allies? Where is the United Nations? Most importantly, where am I? What do I choose now? Now is our time.

According to Post Media on September 4th, the dead boy's weeping aunt, Tima Kurdi said in a news conference from Vancouver there is one thing that should be done. "End the war. That's all I can say." Think about Chuck's song, "Win, win, Win or Walk Away." "I have a dream. There's enough for everyone. Find a win-win-win or walk away. Confrontation is a mistake that we've outgrown. We'll break through to yes."

Key messages for this show: why does this show serve you? Let me know. What is collaboration and what isn't it? What do we need and why do we need Break Through to Yes? I think we desperately need that connection. I think we desperately need a way of integrating to yes, to innovation.

I often tell people in some organizations one plus one equals one. In the organizations that we dream of, that we envision, one plus one can equal 11. We are better together when we listen, when we innovate, when we serve, and when we have the strength of leadership.

Too often people that believe they're collaborating, I would say they are manipulating. They are not collaborating. They have an idea. They have a route. They have a goal. They have a method. They call a meeting. Calling a meeting isn't collaboration. Oftentimes it's a waste of everyone's time because only one person is actually showing up.

Here's a brief excerpt from my book, "Break Through to Yes." "Hatred and violence is fuelled by ignorance and isolation. Canada, my country used to be an internationally respected world leader in peacemaking. Today, Canada is not seen as a trusted neutral to engage warring factions and peacemaking and peace building and nation building."

"America is not seen as a trusted party and certainly not neutral to make peace. America has seen both admirable leadership in stopping the bad guys in the world and self-centered leadership in a blind dedication to getting its own way with the world. Think about that 2004 animated movie, 'Team America World Police.' The only thing standing between order and chaos is us. Ah, America is order or is America chaos?"

Let's come together. Let's connect in new ways. Let's break through to yes. We can get beyond the reptilian archaic structures that have served us in the past. What are nations? What are companies? Let's evolve to a new way of connection.

I look through my career where I started doing business in 1975 and what's most important is the people I trust, the people I turn to when things are challenging, the people that I can work effectively together honoring each other's differences, different perspectives, different skills and finding ways. This is a break through. I can wear many hats, political, economic, social, corporate. I'm always me and I'm looking to discover me every day in every way.

Thank you, listeners today.

Chapter 2 Collaboration Gone Bad
featuring Kathy Porter and Duncan Autrey

David: Now is our time to lead more powerfully, consciously, and collaboratively in ways that make our world a better place today and in our shared future. Leaders in companies will make this essential shift now. Welcome, listeners. This is our second episode in Break Through to Yes. I'm David B. Savage. I'm the Founder and President of Savage Management, Think Sustainability Consultants, and the Collaborative Global Initiative.

Savage Management was founded 1993 and we provide consulting, negotiation, conflict management, organizational development, stakeholder engagement, coaching, and collaborative leadership services. The Collaborative Global Initiative (CGI) founded in 2013, at that time, with Ron Supancic in Los Angeles, California has evolved. We're going to focus on CGI for a good part of our show today with our guests Kathy Porter and Duncan Autrey.

The Collaborative Global Initiative is a global community of collaborative and dispute resolution professionals located in Canada, the United States, France, and Spain. CGI is committed to addressing and embracing conflict and supporting the more peaceable and healthy sustainable living environment in families, communities, business, and our world.

Now, I do this show thinking about the future. I do this show for you, my listener. I do these shows and my book, "Break Through to Yes: Unlocking the Possible Within a Culture of Collaboration" for my grandchildren - - for Quinn, for Sara, for Owyn, for Bailey, for Charlie, for Jack and all those that have yet to be born.

Quinn is the oldest at eight right now. Owyn's the youngest. There are more grandchildren to come, I know and great-grandchildren; and for your family and for your future and how our businesses and organizations create that. That is my Why for this series.

This show is for entrepreneurs, shareholders, and innovators. This show and book are for our shared sustainable, healthy, and profitable future. This is on the Business Channel Voice America for a reason. What's the title and theme for this show? Collaboration Gone Bad and What We Need Now. Sounds like a Hollywood title, doesn't it? Often collaboration does go bad. We fail at it miserably. We pretend we're collaborating when we're really not. We're manipulating or just doing things badly.

We're going to talk about how to be much more effective as collaborative leaders and what is the Collaborative Global Initiative and how can we move forward. As I've mentioned, Kathy Porter is one guest. She lives and works out of British Columbia, across Western Canada and the world. Duncan Autrey who has just recently moved back to California and he's lived for six years in Ecuador and prior to that, Argentina.

The key messages for our show today:

1) collaboration has been a dream and a dirty word.
2) we need to work together not just on projects and in our silos, but as the way we do our work.
3) the Collaborative Global Initiative is ready to consult, build capacity, and resolve conflict with you.

A quote from my "Break Through to Yes" book, it will be published February 2016, "I've been a businessman since 1975. My undergraduate degree is in Economics. I have seen repeated failures in organizations and their capital projects and operations. The monetary cost of such failures is in the billions. When a company makes mistakes, tries to force its agenda on others, or is in conflict with stakeholders, stakeholders revolt. Projects get delayed in regulatory and community review for extended lengths of time.

And employee simply don't give their best because they do not trust the systems they work in. They do not trust their leaders. The cost can be disengagement, rejection by regulatory bodies and governments, impact the communities, damage the environment, and more.

The human cost ranges from depression, conflict, suicide, marital breakdown, career paralysis, and the loss of the intelligence and vision of bright people in your business because they check out when they come to work. They're not themselves. They are drones. They are messengers. They are doers as opposed to innovators and entrepreneurs.

Engineering bridges, practicing law, designing buildings, raising money, and other professional activities are hard aspects of business, are executed much more efficiently and cleanly than the work it takes to get stakeholders, professionals, politicians, and in many more work to work together effectively. It's building a culture of collaboration based on leadership, negotiation, and conflict management capacities is what is needed most, produce meaningful results within organizations."

Hey, remember Monty Python's John Cleese? He had a series of great videos on training. Those videos, if you were in my demographic, you remember them. "Meetings, Bloody Meetings." Well, we can now do the same with Collaboration, Bloody Collaboration.

Too often, the boss has a task he wants others to buy in to. The task is narrow and pre-determined. The boss at times is afraid of making decisions alone. That boss calls a meeting. "We must collaborate to succeed," the boss begins oblivious to the yawns, sideways glances and grimaces. You've been in meetings like that. I have.

Stop wasting time and resources and people on poorly managed projects. Break Through to Yes promises to deliver a method to make collaboration work for you and your company while creating the conditions, yes, the conditions that promote innovation and Break Through within and across your business and network. Seize this opportunity to join this movement of progressive, principled, and successful leaders.

I think that's where we are with respect to Break Through to Yes. I really want to show and tell you where you can get help, and where you can help me. The bottom-line that we have left to deal with is how to break through, how to get beyond collaboration, bloody collaboration. We just see that manipulation. Maybe we should have a Clint Eastwood type movie, "The Good, The Bad, and The Ugly." That's an idea for a future episode of Break Through to Yes with Collaboration.

I was delighted after our very first show. Camille Nash, Executive Producer of this show kindly offered me an extra episode in December. Perhaps it will be "The Good, The Bad, and The Ugly of Collaboration." I think that could be fun. Send us your feedback. Maybe we can do an episode simply on your feedback, simply on what we need to better collaborate.

Today we are also going to look at ways -- how do you know; how do we actually start? One of the things that we do is, within Collaborative Global Initiative and the work that I do and Kathy Porter does is do an assessment of the Collaborative Competency and Capacity of your organization. What are the things that you need? What are the tools that you can have? Is your network as strong and connected in caring, as you believe?

David: Hey, listeners before the break, we heard Chuck Rose's "Win, Win, Win or Walk Away." It's a beautiful theme song for Break Through to Yes with Collaboration. Just love that collaboration. I asked Chuck if he would help me out to create a theme song for me. As a Professional Consultant, organizational development speaker, and performing artist, it led Chuck to record his very first album. chuckrose.ca. Thank you so much, Chuck.

We were talking about collaborations, bloody collaborations, take off on "Meetings, bloody meetings" of Monty Python. That's the way it usually goes -- wasted resources, wasted time, lost opportunities, disconnected people. Let us know your ideas.

Today, I'm also very delighted to introduce our listeners to my good friend and wise woman, Kathy Porter of British Columbia. Kathy Porter is a BPE, PBDE, and is a chartered meditator and specialist in stakeholder consultation and decision-making. Kathy began working in the mediation field in 1998 primarily in multi-stakeholder disputes. She has worked extensively in the resource sector, mining, oil and gas, fisheries, health and social services, and the labor management disputes.

Her work in public consultation led her to combine her facilitation expertise in group dynamics and decision processes with her experience as a mediator. She conducts public policy mediations where the outcomes include science settlement agreements in instances where the dispute might otherwise have been settled in court or not.

She has successfully mediated terrestrial and aquatic environmental management frameworks and infrastructure development and transportation. Kathy has joined us as part of the Leaders Circle within the Collaborative Global Initiative.

Welcome, Kathy. What else would you like to say about yourself? I'll blow your trumpet anytime but I'll let you introduce yourself a little more.

Kathy: Thanks, David. Thanks for having me. It's just delightful to be here today and to talk to you about collaboration, something that I'm quite passionate about. It was interesting when I was listening to the introduction, not so much about me but the "Meetings, bloody meetings" part because collaboration is similar.

I think partly because we talk about it a lot but we really don't understand what's involved and how to go about collaborating because in some ways we have to step out of our normal, as a businesswoman, competitive approach to working with others, going after contracts.

I think that we're on the cusp of having to break into a deeper understanding of collaboration and what it really takes to do that because we have to both be assertive to our positions and something I'm actually good at because I'm passionate about a lot of things. We also have to be cooperative. We have to listen to those other voices as well. I certainly had to learn to listen to those other voices over the years. Yes, it's such an interesting topic to me if you can maybe tell.

David: It's an interesting topic for me because as you say, oftentimes we in the dispute resolution negotiation practices, we seem to be very competitive amongst ourselves as opposed to saying what is in the best interest of the client, what is in the best interest of the community, what is in the best interest of the planet and start from there. I really appreciate your work in trying to work together with those various groups that are often in conflict or just don't understand each other.

Kathy: I think you're right that we don't understand each other and certainly in my work. I'm often working with engineers or planners or architects or environmental scientists, all professional people but they all have a particular language, a particular jargon that they speak.

Certainly, when we first come to the table particularly on some of these big environmental decisions...I spent five years working up in oil fields region of Northeastern Alberta and just getting started and learning what one person means about some particular topic is really the critical first step to build collaboration.

David: If that's the first step, why is it so hard for us to take that first step? We tend to jump ahead all the time.

Kathy: I think we jump ahead because we're very good at making assumptions. We assume that because we know intimately what we're talking about, we just assume that everybody else understands and speaks the same language because we happen to be all speaking in English. Sometimes I think it might be easier if we were all speaking, understood that we are in fact speaking a bunch of foreign languages together.

We don't, so people do jump in and they're passionate about their professions or their choices that they make as volunteers or in other ways that they participate in society to protect the environment, to protect economic interests, to even to protect democracy.

We have to sort of slow the process down and explain. At least, what I do is I take the time to explain to people how this process is going to work, that there's going to be a lot of divergence in our thinking and in our views.

That can take a significant amount of time just to sort of put all of that out making very sure that what do you mean when you say sustainability, for example. What do you mean when you say collaboration? We have to have those almost basic conversations before we can get into the meat and potatoes part.

David: Kathy, what do you mean by collaboration?

Kathy: I break it down in to two components as I sort of briefly mentioned earlier. We have to be able to assert our perspectives, our views, our knowledge, our expertise into the conversation and we need to make sure that as we're asserting that that we take the time to make sure that other people understand and then to sort of clarify back and forth. I actually use that word "collaboration" a little bit differently and this is what it means to me just as you're doing right now.

Then once we've gotten through that then we actually have to cooperate. It's really sort of almost a minute scale sometimes, a system of making little trade-offs and adjustments. We can't make those trade-offs and adjustments until we understand what the trade-offs might need to be.

I think the other thing with collaboration is that the group is involved in making the decision. This is an interesting conversation that I often have with the stakeholders that I'm working with because often I'm asking them to make consensus decisions and at the end of the day they'll say, "But we don't get to make the decisions." That's true but you're still making a consensus recommendation as something that's going to government.

Let's work to make sure that we're all on the same page and we can put forward a strong recommendation rather than what has often happened and given stakeholder engagement a bad name. It ends up some sort of watered down thing that doesn't really say anything. It's hard work.

David: The watered-down pieces are really meaningful. I'd like to really stress what you're saying, Kathy. I think of it as the math of working together. When I hear the word "compromise," I hear subtraction. Less than.

Kathy: Yes.

David: When I hear the word "collaboration," I hear addition, greater than what the sum of the parts are.

Kathy: Absolutely, right. Certainly, I didn't invent some of this stuff. I just kind of picked up on some of the ideas. There's a synergy that comes from a well-functioning group that is very powerful. I often use that example from that movie of many years ago of "Apollo 13" when they were stuck up there and they had to get these guys in a room and said, "Here's what you've got. Figure it out." They had to work together to find a solution.

Often it is a stressful situation. You've got issues that need to be resolved. Water and drought, these are certainly coming to the forefront now. We're going to have to work together and we're better off for it. Human beings are in fact by nature collaborative but we've forgotten that. We need to bring ourselves back to that, our earlier history. We're here as human beings because we collaborated; we worked together to protect ourselves, to raise our families. We need to remember that I think.

David: Yes, remembering again and again and again. Kathy Porter, how do people get a hold of you? We've got only about 30 seconds left on this portion of the show in this interview. How do people get a hold of you to follow-up with you and your ideas?

Kathy: I have a personal e-mail at porterkath@gmail.com. That's probably the easiest way. I have several company e-mail addresses but they're very long-winded and not very collaborative.

David: Wonderful. One of the things that you and I and Duncan Autrey, our next guest and Charalee Graydon, Jeff Cohen, and Sara Daitch are doing is creating the Collaborative Global Initiative. We're representing people from Spain, the United States, Netherlands and we hope to include more. We really welcome everyone's input, insights, and collaboration.

Kathy, in the brief seconds we have left is there a challenge that you'd put out to our listeners today before we sign off?

Kathy: I think reflect on ways that you can collaborate even if it's with your neighbors. In the workplace, investigate what's really involved there and ask good questions -- what do you mean by collaboration as you asked me great questions.

David: Thank you so much, Kathy Porter of British Columbia and founder of the Collaborative Global Initiative.

David: Welcome back, listeners. Before the break, we were talking with Kathy Porter and her wisdom with respect to slowing down and remembering and being one looking at what's needed now, truly listening to each other. Now, what I'd like to do is we'll talk a little more, a lot more I hope about the Collaborative Global Initiative. I'm really excited about my next guest, Duncan Autrey.

Duncan is a kindred spirit. He's a conflict transformation consultant with experience in both North and South America. To find out more about Duncan Autrey, go to duncanautrey.com. Duncan and I first met I think it was six or seven years ago, Duncan at the Omega Institute in Upstate New York.

We were working with our mutual friend and best-selling author, Erica Ariel Fox. She's penned and promoting and doing great work with "Winning from Within." We were also working with great people like Emily Gould and David Gould and others.

We've evolved ourselves. Duncan and I have stayed very close. We've collaborated, coached one another, and dreamed together. Duncan works with Mediators Beyond Borders and has worked in the United States, Argentina, Ecuador, Turkey, and other places. Duncan's now back in California and doing great work there.

Duncan, thank you so much for joining us. What else might you say about your introduction and your vision around collaboration?

Duncan: Thank you, David. Thank you for the introduction and it's a pleasure to be speaking with you. I wanted to actually just touch on that transition that I've been...the reason that I returned to the United States after many years abroad. It's been interesting to realize the importance of doing network both locally and internationally. It's really important.

It's been really interesting to connect with conflicts that are more local whether they be conflicts about the local drought in California or to be paying attention to conflicts that are happening in collective houses or just between neighbors. It's been interesting to connect to a community level again. I think that's a great introduction, so thank you.

David: One of the things that I will tell our listeners and then you can correct me, Duncan.

Duncan: Sure.

David: One of your most recent contracts has been in Ecuador dealing with boundary disputes dealing with what happens when satellites give you different boundaries than 20 steps from the old oak tree type of survey system.

It's my recollection, my judgment that while you're really initially focused on resolving boundary disputes, the majority of your success there was actually building skills and capacity within the people that you were working with so "Teach a man to fish" type of metaphor. Can you tell us a little bit more about that experience?

Duncan: Absolutely. I was working in Ecuador with the provincial government to help them resolve a series of border disputes. They were basically just historical accidents based on maps that were done in the 1500's not corresponding to maps done in the 1980's. It was interesting.

The idea of the work was to help the communities really communicate with each other to help decide where the borders would be but what ended up becoming more important was the realization. Because of the political situation in Ecuador where it's just a very divisive politics, the work of getting people to work with each other and realize just the value of including the voice of the other side became, I would say the main focus of the work.

It was always easy to say, "We don't want to include the voices of our enemies. We just want to include the voices that agree with us." Unfortunately, I would say a rule of conflict is if you try to not include someone then they're going to find a way to be included later.

David: Whether it's positive or otherwise.

Duncan: Whether it's positive or otherwise. Whether you have any control over the situation or not. When you have a culture that has people protesting and so forth, that becomes a really relevant situation.

It was really interesting also just the importance of working with the team, coordinating people who are taking legal perspectives with people who are taking a geological perspective and people who are taking a cultural perspective and a historical perspective and a political perspective.

Those are four very different ways to try and decide where the borders are going to be. Giving those voices to communicate to each other is also very interesting. It's very easy for us to sort of focus on whatever our sort of field of work is and say, "This is the main focus." I think that's a lawyer's job is to defend the law but in the same way the scientist's job is to defend science. I was looking at people whose job is to defend the voices of the people.

David: In that situation, what's your job, Duncan?

Duncan: I think part of the job is to make sure that each of those voices actually recognize that they have a voice that they're trying to communicate and then from there helping them to communicate that to each other. It can be even as simple as, "It sounds like you're trying to say X," and hoping the person realize what they're trying to say and realize the importance of what they're trying to say.

Then there could just even be a little coaching about how can you communicate that. I would say on a bigger level, I think that you need to create spaces where all those voices do have a space or that are acknowledged as being important. I think that that's just something you build into the systems; you build into the way you present the concept.

David: In another way I'm thinking nobody gets to be wrong and your right doesn't have to be my right but together we can figure out what works better.

Duncan: I love the example that Kathy brought of the "Apollo 13" because oftentimes that's what happens. You could say, "Look, we have this bit of law that says this. We have this historical pact that says this. We have this request. This is this." We have to figure out how to move forward from here. I think just a reminder of that was always important.

Oftentimes people would say, "Wait a minute. We don't agree. We're stuck." I say, "Of course we don't agree. That's why we're here in the first place. That's why we came together. The question is how do we find an agreement?"

I think another thing that was always really important was to help people realize that they're the ones that get to make the decisions. It's very often that people feel like when we get stuck in conflict that we want to hand that decision up to a higher power. I think that's why we want to go in to the police or going to a judge or whatever.

With the realization that those of us who are in the situation are the ones that are going to have to come to the solution or help people come to that realization. I think it's super important that there's no way they can move forward without moving forward with the other.

David: Moving forward it means buy in and it's theirs not the mediators' or the lawyers' or the governments'.

Duncan: Absolutely.

David: I wanted to spend some of our time talking about the Collaborative Global Initiative that you and Kathy and Jeff Cohen, Charalee Graydon, Sarah Daitch and I have been working on. I'll just read a little bit of our text for our listeners.

"We live in an increasingly complex and interconnected world. Humanity faces global, environmental, economic, and human-based challenges of all kinds. Lasting solutions to these challenges require effective communication and learning how to cross perspectives, cultures, and sectors.

At CGI, we believe humans are by nature collaborative. When people work together allowing space to capture collective wisdom, we achieve great things. Forward thinking people and communities recognize the need for widespread collaboration. They will need a unique toolbox, a tool kit and skills to collaboratively navigate the future of our increasingly complex and diverse world and work."

Tell me more about that, Duncan.

Duncan: I would say that the greater complexity that we start seeing in the world and I would say as just the process of globalization and interconnectedness moves forward that things will always be more complex. As we become more complex our need for greater collaboration increases in pace.

The reason for that is in a way the best way we can find true solutions or the...I guess the best solutions will always come from the most perspectives but this only is true if those perspectives are working collaboratively toward a shared goal or shared understanding.

Of course, the trick is turning people from enemies into people who want to collaborate with each other. It's that new vision of the world that's going to get us through this next stage.

David: Yes. Oftentimes as facilitators, coaches, mediators, we can help people get unstuck by focusing on the future -- where do we want to end up together? In the intro to this show, I mentioned my grandchildren and this show and my book and our work with CGI as being for them. How does that work for you? How do you bring that in to your clients?

Duncan: This is a work around affirmation. It's an affirmation of the world we want to move towards. The choice to be collaborative is often an affirmation. It's an affirmation that our collective wisdom is greater than our individual perspectives. When we choose to say, when we ask what is the world we want to live in, almost all of us start finding the same answer at that point.

David: It's different than the world we live in today. Listeners, you can find out more about Duncan Autrey at duncanautrey.com and more later about our Collaborative Global Initiative which is collaborativeglobalinitiative.com.

Duncan, as I asked Kathy earlier and I'm asking all of my guests, if there was one thing in this moment that you'd like to challenge our listeners to do or be aware or think about, what would it be?

Duncan: I would say conflict is a normal thing. It happens to everyone at all skills. It can either be positive or negative and there are people who can help you with it. Reach out to them.

David: Thank you so much, my friend. Listeners, this has been Duncan Autrey. Thank you.

David: Welcome back, listeners. Before the break, we were talking with Duncan Autrey about the Collaborative Global Initiative and about his work. Remember, he was talking about aspiration, about intention, about future focus, about how do we move forward together and create great. Let me just use that phrase. We'll create great together.

In this portion, this final segment of our episode number two, what I'm doing is the Outrage of the Week. This is to cover the emotional, the amygdala, reptilian brain where so often we see in journalism, politics, social media, people get outraged. Often, they get outraged. Their amygdala gets outraged before they actually start asking questions.

Duncan talked about complexity. Complexity is increasing. There is so much information available to us. How do you get through it with this world, this digitally connected world? I've seen estimates that by 2016 there should be about four billion people on the planet connected to the internet. That's a blessing and it's a curse.

Last week, we talked about the outrage related to Syrian refugees. We talked about the poor little Alan, his body on the beach and how a picture changed the world's heart, how we started to pay attention. Unfortunately, all of the world isn't paying attention. They aren't incorporating all the perspectives. We can do far better. Since that broadcast, the world is starting to do better.

This week, it's an outrage that's really been going on for years. I think about four years. Let's talk about Uber, the taxi service. My son and daughter have used it in Los Angeles. It's very popular in many cities and it's very hated in many sectors. For several years now, this service or app, as they claim themselves to be continues to be in the news and on social media. People have firm positions on all sides. They are not affirming or even listening.

Here's a quote from Inc. Magazine by journalist Christine Lagorio-Chafkin. Here's the quote: "In most major US cities and many around the world, there's an alternative to standing on a street corner flailing an arm for a taxi. Typically, this is phone in a local car service or within the past couple of years, opening an app on your phone.

Open the Uber app which is the first car service app available in most US cities, American cities and you'll see a map, your location replete with nearby vehicles for hire and their estimated times of arrival. One can usually reach you within five minutes and a ride will carry a minimum cost of about $7 but you can't do this in South Florida.

Regulations in Miami -Dade County dictate that a car service or limo ride must be booked at least 60 minutes before the ride begins, in cost at least $80. That's US$80. Huh. Unless the Miami-Dade County

Commission changes the law, Uber is locked out of a multi-hundred million-dollar market.

As it expands, Uber often meets legal complications, cease and desist orders, court injunctions, and the impounding of cars. Uber is no stranger to complaints from public utilities commissions, from city councils, and from taxi and limousine commissions all of which have constituents clamoring for protection from the likes of Uber."

Wow. That's the end of that quote. Every city that Uber attempts to do business in is in turmoil over regulations protecting taxi drivers and their families, insurance, liabilities, safety, etcetera. This turns into conflict and angry words. People get in to their positions very easily. Instead of internet outrage, die-hard proponents and political and taxi federation fear mongering, what might we learn?

What if we step back and went really slow as Kathy Porter encourages us to do and listen and think about what our intention, what our dream for the future is. What may we learn about business that some delivery models and business practices are not in tune with our new technology-driven age and expectations? Autonomous drivers, internet, text messaging, all of those things, they just come to a place where we are changing. Technology has allowed us to be different, to do different things.

What I will say is instead of fighting those good fights or bad fights, let's look at where we are going in the future and maybe we can capitalize on that as entrepreneurs, organizations, leaders. In the past 40 years, cost differentials, reduction of trade barriers, and low-cost shipping meant the loss of most of the garment industry, manufacturing industry in North America and Europe.

Technology algorithms, big data, and demand for on-the-spot performance is changing how we shop, work, and how we travel. The taxi business fights against Uber. That is a battle but the war has changed. Are you really warring against evolution and transformation? It needn't be a war.

What are the signs? How as a leader can you listen, reach out, embrace all perspectives and come up with something greater? What are the evolutions that you can take advantage of as a businessperson and a leader in the coming year? In other words, get out of the trenches. Just get out of the trenches. Think about the trends. What's the future you want to be part of creating?

Be curious. Reach out. Learn. Integrate. Form a new and your own perspective and be in the world this way. That will be part of your break through to yes. Contact me about this work and how we may collaborate.

Collaboration is not, it is not, I can't say that strongly enough, it's not an event. It's not a project. It's not a to-do. It's the way we are. It is the way we are together.

Today we've explored the wisdom of Duncan Autrey and Kathy Porter and the evolution of the Collaborative Global Initiative. We've looked at Uber as our Outrage of the Week and talked about let's look at the trends. What do we want to create as opposed to defend from the old world?

In this show, Collaboration Gone Bad and What We Need Now, our key messages have been: collaboration has been a dream and a dirty word. Two, we need to work together not just on projects or in our silos but as the way we do our work together. Three, the Collaborative Global Initiative is ready to consult, build capacity, and resolve conflict.

Next week's show and guests come together today for our future with Alan Davis of British Columbia and Jeanne McPherson of Washington State. We will also explore Rotary International and Youth Leadership programs. Future shows will go through my Ten Essential Steps to Collaboration. Listen every week.

We will also feature the Heart and Stroke Foundation, the Enneagram, the Center of Excellence for Collaborative Leadership and we want to work with you. Let's work together. Let's be aware of how you engage and how you may be more effective.

Thank you for your time and your collaborative vision. Send us your thoughts. Thank you, listeners.

Chapter 3 Our Global Campfire featuring Jeanne McPherson and Allan Davis

David: Now is our time to lead more powerfully, consciously, and collaboratively in ways that make our world a better place today and in our shared future. Leaders in companies will make this essential shift now. Welcome, everybody.

Through Voice of America we're speaking to up to 3.6 million listeners in 160 countries. I don't know how many we actually have because this is our third show. We have a channel. Thank you for listening in whether you're listening in live or through the podcast.

Today's show is titled Our Global Campfire. How are you today? What are you searching for? What are you looking for? I'm searching for ways to connect, encourage, and challenge you to work together even more powerfully to serve your interests and our global interests. We are making the future a better place.

In our first episode I talked a little bit about my corporate business background. Second episode, I talked a little more about the consulting and writing that I'm doing. For today's episode, our conversation I want to introduce you a little more in to some of the ways that I serve because with our guests today Jeanne McPherson and Allan Davis they take service above self seriously.

Here's some of the ways I serve. I'm really interested in hearing more from you. E-mail me David@savagemanage.com and tell me more about you and what you need, what do you think.

Here are some of the ways I serve. I'm a co-founder of the Global Collaborative Initiative, the Company to Company Dispute Resolution Council, the Alberta Energy Regulator Dispute Resolution program, and the Global Negotiation Insight Institute and Synergy

Alberta. All those places that I've either founded or co-founded are ways of working together better.

Synergy Alberta brings oil companies, landowners, environmentalists, first nations, and next generation leaders together to talk about issues, not to decide, but talk about issues.

The Company to Company Dispute Resolution Council is very similar. We formed that with about 100 volunteers and we found that rather than just getting enraged, engaged in wanting to beat the other company, if we could sit down and have a situation assessment meeting, we could actually hear each other, understand each other. It doesn't mean you need to reach agreement, but understanding the other side and then setting a process on how do we work together to resolve this dispute. This worked very, very well.

After 32 years in the Canadian petroleum industry and some in the United States, since 2007 I've focused on developing and engaging collaborative leaders in sustainable business development.

What I'm doing now is important volunteer activities with aq'am, that's the St. Mary's Indian band; Community Enterprises, that's economic development within the Ktunaxa Nation of Southeastern British Columbia. I'm an active volunteer in the Provincial Advisory Board for the Heart and Stroke Foundation of Alberta, Northwest Territories, and Nunavut.

I'm also a volunteer for the TransCanada Trails BC, Rotary; we'll talk more about that with Allan and Jeanne today and the Canadian Association of Professional Speakers.

I do this work, like I said last week for you. I also do this work, my radio show and my book for my grandchildren, for Quinn and Sara, Bailey, Charlie, and all those yet to be born. Equally so I do it for you as a leader, as a shareholder, as an innovator, an entreprensure, as a businessperson trying to get beyond the cultures of top down messenger leadership.

This show today is Our Global Campfire. We're featuring Rotary International and two leaders who collaborate for youth leadership in the world. Those leaders are Allan Davis of British Columbia and Jeanne McPherson in Washington State.

The key messages, here are the three things that I really want us to focus on today, the three things that I'm going to loop around when we close: mediots make us ignorant, cold, and disconnected. Mediots make us ignorant, cold, and disconnected; secondly, how to light our global campfire and form our circle; thirdly, third key message is Rotary International does great work locally and globally, "Service Above Self".

I'm a Rotarian. I'm very proud. Whether it's Lions, Shriners, whatever service club organization that you wish to serve or create, do it. That is such a powerful opportunity to make our world a better place and make ourselves a better place.

Recently, like many of you, you've probably listened to political debates. In the last few weeks, I've listened to the Republican Party in the United States and the three major political parties in Canada. I got to tell you, I'm really sad. What I hoped to hear is leadership, collaboration, integrity, and vision.

Instead, what I hear over and over and over is fear, isolation, blame coming mostly from wealthy, grouchy, old, white men. Where's the love? Where's our future? Where do we serve? It is beyond time to reinvent democracy around the world. Democracy isn't something that's run by a reptilian brain out of fear. It's out of vision, commitment, service, and leadership.

Let me tell you a quote from my book, "Break Through To Yes: Unlocking the Possible within a Culture of Collaboration."

"I coined the term 'mediots'. They are those in the media and the world who subscribe to narrow, exclusive, one-dimensional thinking who cast fear, separation, and misunderstanding in their pronouncements on current events and issues."

Here's how we can show our leadership to take charge in solving many challenges: a circle. Instead of that reactive blame game, shame game that we are subjected to on social media -- Twitter, Facebook, from the political leaders, form a circle. Come together, listen, speak, connect, solve, learn, and be a community. Our Earth is a circle. Our life is a circle, a circle in collaboration.

When my son, Dan was, I think he was about four years old in Kindergarten; he did a project. I still have this poster he developed. "Life is a circle." It's just fantastic. He knew then. A circle includes all of us. We are one.

Consider that all the expertise and experience we have may not be enough effectively and to successfully deal with the great challenges we face today. As individuals, families, organizations, professions, and nations consider the collective wisdom that is possible from a circle of listening, speaking, and understanding and co-creating solutions, this is an invitation to engage people who care about subjects and questions that matter to you and your organization.

Your circle will be most successful in solving significant challenges when you bring in others whose opinions and experiences are very different from yours. We can't let the grouchy old white guys to continue to form our platform. We can no longer afford groupthink or yes men. The stakes are too high. We must invite in the first nations, the environmentalists, the Americans, the Chinese, the Koreans, the Malaysians, the Spanish, the Serbians, the Syrians. How do we light our global campfire?

These are the principles of great circles:

1) our intention must be authentic
2) we build relationship and trust first
3) we invite and respect diversity of opinion, yes, diversity; invite and respecting those that disagree with you;
4) we establish key questions that matter;
5) we listen deeply.
6) we seek new ideas from the collective wisdom.

I believe that one plus one can equal 11. Through compromise, one plus one often equals one-half.

7) we're open to unexpected outcomes. This is so critical to me. When we collaborate, when I'm open, when I realize that I don't have the truth, I don't have your truth and you don't have my truth, brilliance comes.
8) we take as long as it takes.

In our radio show, you'll hear from aboriginal leaders. You'll hear from business leaders. It just takes time. You must go slow before you go fast.

9) the ninth consideration or characteristic of great circles, we commit to action and hold accountability.

What are the questions that matter to you?

From the list of significant challenges, we face, choose with courage and vision. Remember not to sell or attempt to convince. Listen first. Understand what the underlying interests are and be open to what arises. Let it come. Let it percolate. Let it evolve. Through listening to that collective wisdom, as leaders let's work with all the diversity of opinions and perspectives we can while rounded.

Let's create outcomes that we never believed possible. Let's move from mediot division to an inclusive vision. A wonderful outcome is that business may do far better. Business and create better bottom lines. We have seen too much of the fear-based mentality that serves select interests.

Select interests. Fear-based politicians. Where are the visionaries? Who are the visionaries? Think about your nation, your country; who are the leaders that you say, "I understand. I want to be with them. I support them." Instead, we castigate and we blame and we shame.

Let's light our global campfire. Let's come together within your business, within your team. Let's start over. Let's start by listening first, by setting intention in serving the other. Interestingly enough, through my 40 years in negotiation and dispute resolution and collaborative leadership development, I know that if I go to your side first and understand, not agree but understand, then it allows you to come to me, then it allows us to collaborate.

David: Today's guest is Jeanne McPherson. She has a Ph.D. Organizational Communication and provides customized workforce development that emphasized collaborative leadership skills. With a Master's degree in French and Spanish, she draws out the best from cross-functional and multi-cultural, multi-ethnic groups.

This is so important, Jeanne is all about the diversity and embracing collaborative leadership. Jeanne is a former professor. She's developed a model for making leadership choices in moments of interaction. It's in the moment as opposed to you got to refer to a book.

For collaboration, her career has evolved from technical editing/writing in areas of nuclear waste management to consulting in change leadership, conflict management, and interactive skills development. Her current project brings together 30 year of career expertise and her newest program and book "How Do You Do Leadership? Collaboration for our Multi-Stakeholder Workplaces."

Jeanne, thank you so much for joining us today and thank you, Allan Davis for introducing us a few months ago. We're going to be doing some work together on conflict management and Rotary Youth Leadership Program. Jeanne, tell us a little more about your book and the work that you do.

Jeanne: Thank you, David. I appreciate this opportunity to do that. My model and my book are directly an outcome of requests from participants in my classes and seminars. I think that we mostly can agree on what collaboration looks like, what leadership looks like, but in my programs, people say, "Well, what do I say when somebody does X? Or what do I say when there's a blocker? Or what do I say when?"

It's those things that trip us up. I evolved to a focus on the interaction in a moment. Sometimes we can plan. Sometimes, we can get everybody on board, but then in the moment, things just fall apart. I'm very interested in process in the moment of interaction. That's what my model is and that's what my book is.

David: Yes, it's a very holistic approach, Jeanne where you must be present and ready to interact and at the same time look at the complete system. Jeanne, what's the value of collaboration? Why would we do this thing? We often talk about it, but why would we actually want to do it?

Jeanne: We want to do it and mainly we want to do it when things are important enough that whoever's at the table realizes that we're all going down or we can work together and come up with something we haven't thought of yet. In my experience, if you've got any one person that thinks they can block something, the collaboration is going to be very difficult.

The value is research is compelling to say that the longest-term solutions, the most buy in, the most commitment are when people come together and collaborate. Even great ideas rolled out from the top often are not well accepted. Collaboration really is our future salvation in my mind.

David: Wonderful. Just a beautiful vision. Jeanne, help me and our listeners across the world to think about what's in the moment coaching that you might do. Could you give us an example? Just one example where I'm hearing something from my boss or my workers, whichever way you want to go and the hair on the back of my neck goes up when I hear the word "collaboration" and/or "let's have a meeting."

Can you give us an example of the in the moment coaching that you're bringing forward in your new book?

Jeanne: If you don't mind, I'll go about that in slightly different way. I have a nice example where I talk about an engineering manager. They told me this story not long ago that he had the best, brightest engineer. He had him for about two years, hired right out of the university and was in a performance review meeting that went very well. He got top marks for everything. This young engineer asked, "How can I get a job?" It was three or four levels above the one he was in.

This manager was just dumfounded, didn't know how to respond and he just blurted out, "Well, that's impossible. You don't just go from a level one to a level three or four. You've got a process. You've got steps to take." This engineer, the best and brightest quit the next week. The end of that particular story was he started his own engineering firm and 15 years later he had a multi-million-dollar firm.

The interesting thing in the coaching part was we don't have to blurt out the first thing that comes to mind. Collaboration would be affirming what you hear. That would be one step you could take. What if this manager had just said, "Wow. Your talent and drive are really important to our organization."

In my way and my model, that's the collaborative opening. That gives you time, buys you time to think and it encourages another person to continue talking so you can look for some place where you might have some overlapping values. There are other steps along the way, but I felt that was very interesting. In 15 years, this manager was dumbfounded and could not see why this particular person quit.

David: That's a tremendously powerful example where it cost that manager and that company a lot of opportunity. What you're telling us is if they had just taken that moment, they could turn from that error phrase, that curiosity to saying, "If that was possible, what steps might we design together to make this happen?" and turn it into a powerful empowered future leader.

Jeanne: Yes, and there are other steps in my model, too. After you affirm in a collaborative way that says you're open, maybe, given the response, you would have three other choice points in my model. Maybe you would choose something to empower this individual. Maybe you would coach or if there was resentment for an unfair system, maybe you would deal with conflict management.

The point is collaboration means staying open to whatever happens. In this instance I agree. I think this young engineer might have stayed longer at least.

David: Yes. There's a real value proposition underneath your example, Jeanne where I'm thinking about it and thinking, "Wow. The manager may have just been too busy, but for the sake of five minutes, look at the cost. For the sake of awareness, just look at what he's lost and the opportunity he's never actually become aware of simply because of he didn't take your first step."

Jeanne: Think about how that multiplied throughout our organizations.

David: Yes. Jeanne, if you could, could you spend a little bit as we close, I'd like you to do two things. Could you talk a little bit about Rotary and how you see your role as helping collaboration in Rotary International? Then the last thing is what would be one challenge for our listeners around the world to think about that you can put in front of them?

Jeanne: Thank you for those questions, David. I'm very excited about Rotary and what I'm doing right now. I'm a facilitator in the Rotary Leadership Institute and that's an international development program. I was asked to develop a half-day graduate program on conflict management for our club.

I have developed a program based on this model, this interactive model, "What Do You Say To Win?" and practiced for people in Rotary that goes through Rotary Leadership. Rotary is wonderful. And yet, we all have, as human beings tension or conflict or different points of view. I'm very excited to be able to bring this model to Rotary International.

I guess the challenging closing for people that may be listening is what everybody's saying is stay open to the moment. The hardest skill that I see that people have difficulty grasping is just to affirm what they hear as a default interaction, not judging it.

Just like the previous example I gave, if the manager had just said, "Your talent and drive are important to this organization." That doesn't promise a promotion. It's just an acknowledgement of affirming the value that this person was expressing. My challenge is listen for value and affirm value. I don't want to give a lecture so maybe I should stop there. Thank you, David.

David: That's such a gift, that one response, that one pause, that one opening. Jeanne McPherson, your next book, I'll look for it. I'll be collaborating and encouraging you to look for it, "How Do You Do

Leadership? Collaboration for our Multi-Stakeholder Workplaces." Thank you so much, Jeanne McPherson.

Jeanne: Thank you. It was a pleasure, David.

David: Before the break we talked about mediots, about how to light our campfire, our global campfire, service above self. We offered you the opportunity in your organization to think about what are the ways that you can light your campfire. Change your leadership style. Change your organization.

I offer these ten steps, which I'll talk about later, and the characteristics of great circles in the hopes that there will be something for you wherever you are in an organization and in the world to move forward. E-mail me at David@savagemanage.com and let me know your thoughts. I will respond.

Today I'm really delighted. Another good friend and someone I have the deepest appreciation for is Allan Davis. Allan has been a member of the Rotary Club of Cranbrook Sunrise since 1997. I'm a member of that in the last three or four years.

Allan served as its President in 2001-2002 and as District Governor in 2008-2009. He has held several positions in Rotary both at the District and the Zone level. I know Allan's respected globally. He has attended a leadership conference in San Francisco just a few weeks ago. He has a lot of wisdom and a lot of heart.

Allan was born in Ottawa, Ontario, Canada and educated in Ottawa, Vancouver and Spokane. He has a Masters of Education and he's taught Chemistry and Computer Studies. He's retired in 1998. He continues his love of education in retirement in the role of District and Divisional Chair of the Rotary leadership Institute.

Allan, welcome. What would you like to share with our listeners, a little more about yourself, your life, and your purpose?

Allan: Thanks for the welcome, David. I think one of the things about what you had just finished saying about me and it was kind words were that I've been gifted to be able to continue my love of education and sharing information with Rotarians through the Rotary Leadership Institute.

Following my years as Governor, we needed and I took on the role of District Trainor. It was there that I found a place where I could fit and I could work with Rotarians in a way that has become incredibly meaningful to me. I'm thankful for that opportunity very much.

David: Tell me a little more; tell us a little more about why it's incredibly meaningful to you.

Allan: One of the things I really loved when I was teaching in high school and in the junior high and I see it with the Rotary Leadership Institute is that learn light when it comes on in people's eyes. You look at that and you see that they really understand what's going on. Then they start talking with other people.

The lovely thing about the sessions that we do with the RLI is that we have people from many different clubs. We have people who have not perhaps even met each other before that day. They start talking together. They talk in a way that is very different than what they would actually encounter in their own club I think.

They share information. They discuss ideas. They come to a point where they really understand that working together is an amazing thing. When that light comes on and it's there at the end of the day, it's a thing they could carry you on wings back home at the end of the day.

David: I love that metaphor, the learning light, the light of learning. It's when the light bulb comes on.

Allan: Oh, yes.

David: I've also, through some of your work, I've had an opportunity to hear and meet some of the participants in the Rotary Youth Leadership. Young people who live across the international border between British Columbia and Washington, Idaho, Montana actually learning not only about themselves for the first time.

While they might live within 500 miles or 800 kilometers of each other, it's really the first time they get to know the experience of this is what it is to be young in America or young in Canada and then they turn to our opportunities in the world.

Allan: It's true. In my early experience within Rotary, I was deeply involved with the Rotary Youth Exchange Program. I chaired the district committee for four years. That's a program that my wife and I have become deeply in love with and are participating in different ways, as our lives get more mature.

The Leadership Institute we're talking about does more than just touch young people. It touches people who are into their 80's, believe it or not. That's another aspect of it that you see both the young and the old or older, shall we say coming together and sharing things and going, "Ah! Now I see. Now I understand." It's like all of a sudden shifting position of viewpoint and the bear that was hiding behind a tree now becomes visible.

David: Yes.

Allan: It's wonderful.

David: It is a gift that you bring and listening brings. Allan, you've recently done some of your leadership work and participated in a Rotary Conference in San Francisco. What were the accomplishments? What did you walk away from that conference with?

Allan: Probably the biggest thing was my head was so crammed full of information and feelings that it's taken me several days to really begin to sort it out and put it into a framework. It was called Young Professional Summit where we had district leaders and young professionals, all Rotarians by the way; gather together at the Haas School of Business and Innovation at UC Berkeley campus. It was an amazing event.

We started off by the district leaders and the young professionals meeting in two separate locations on the campus discussing some of the things that we felt needed to be addressed or even examined that could be barriers to young professionals joining Rotary and being accepted.

When we got together, the progress that we made, the things that we discussed, sometimes I felt, "Gee, we've actually known these things, but we didn't have the courage to say, 'Yes, let's do something about it here.'"

However, the ability to work together, these two apparently disparate groups was an amazing thing. It just left me and still in many ways it leaves me reeling with the possibilities that can be brought back into our own Rotary district to work with the young professionals in our Rotary clubs.

David: Yes. I've got a judgment. I'll self-confess that in the days of my father and before, mentorship and championing the next generation of leaders seems to be a common thing. All too often today the business of our companies and our organizations turn the youth into messengers as opposed to innovators.

When I hear about your experience and the innovation center, that's really exciting where the next generation and I'm thinking whether that next generation is one year old or 60 years old, but those who are about to take control of the organizations have an opportunity to say yes to what their visions are.

I hear you, Allan talking about things that you knew before but together they came to the surface and you set some plans and some initiatives to act globally and locally.

Allan: Yes, we did. It was interesting. The 23 Rotary districts that were represented there and that was everyone in the district in the two zones, each one of them had a slightly different take on which initiative they wanted to tackle first.

The overlaps, if you put them all together, the overlaps were incredible; but each one of the districts realized that they were slightly different. Perhaps not even being totally conscious of the fact that they had acknowledged that. They looked at different solutions.

The main thing was that they felt that they could treat each other, the two different age groups, very same, the very same. You didn't have to say, "Oh, Pat the young ones on ahead. Treat them like a pet."

When it comes to saying, "Okay, here's what you can do." You give them all the hard stuff that the older folks didn't want to do or you can turn them into small slaves. No. You treated them as equal partners. That was the key thing that we needed to have reinforced.

Your comment about the mentoring from a previous generation, our parents; yes. I think we need to get back to saying, "We need to do that again."

David: Yes. There's an opportunity there to realize and I know you know this. I look around at the next generation whether they be 50 years old, whether they be my children and grandchildren and their friends and I think, "Oh. This is the most amazing generation." Wow. While we're so globally aware, we're so disconnected. We're so left alone.

Allan: It's a huge irony, isn't it? Being connected but being so separated in so many ways. I don't know what the cause is. I'm not sure that even knowing what the cause is will be a big help.

I think what we have to simply say is, "We need to get back together in whatever ways we can get together through collaborative work." That seems to be the sensible way to do it. It uses up very little time if you do it efficiently and it gets to the point where you want to be. You, as you say, you want to say yes.

David: Yes. I want to make sure our listeners around the world have an opportunity to realize that while we're talking about Rotary, there are many service clubs, many opportunities to connect, to collaborate, to work together, to have courage together.

Getting back to Rotary specifically, Allan, for our listeners if they wanted to learn more about leadership, about Rotary, about how to be involved and serve, tell us some ideas, something that they might do, some places online that they might visit, anything that you can provide an invitation to our listeners.

Allan: Sure. The easiest spot would be to go to the Rotary International website www.rotary.org and there you'll be able to find a lot of information just about what Rotary happens to be. The other thing is almost every town in Canada and America has a Rotary club, not everyone but almost everyone. The Chambers of Commerce will be able to tell you exactly where those Rotary clubs meet.

t's an interesting thing that Rotary does this and we've talked about it. I have used that collaborative work that we've been talking about specifically in Rotary. I've used it in so many other ways and stuff that I've been fortunate to take advantage of; with BC Games or with planning a national golf tournament. It's been incredibly helpful.

David: Wonderful. Allan Davis of Cranbrook, British Columbia, you and I and Jeanne McPherson who we'll talk to later on this episode are working on youth leadership and conflict resolution skills. As we close, what's one thing you might wish our listeners to be more aware of?

Allan: I think what we have to do is listen to what other people are saying, making sure that it doesn't have to be our way. It has to be a way to get to the goal. You talked about one plus one sometimes equaling a half.

I think what we have to do is realize if we want to get to the same goal, there's all sorts of different ways. Listening to other opportunities and ways to get there, we might find a better way. We need to do it together because we all want to get to that final goal.

David: Thank you so much, Allan Davis, Cranbrook Sunrise Rotary, British Columbia.

Allan: Thanks, David for the opportunity.

David: This is David B. Savage. Before the break we were talking about conflict resolution, leadership, Rotary Youth Leadership, and how to light our global campfire. Our guests, Jeanne McPherson and Allan Davis are great examples of service above self as they offer their wisdom to those that are making our world a better place.

Now in our weekly show, I want to engage your amygdala, your reptilian brain because this is a time for Outrage of the Week. Outrage is how we get thing so wrong too often.

In our first show we talked about the Syrian refugee and the little boy Alan whose body, there was a picture of his body washed up on the Turkish seashore. It changed the world, created empathy. Last week we talked about Uber and the conflict that just continues to go around Uber.

This week we started our show with mediots. Mediots being those in the media and the world and politics who subscribe to narrow, exclusive, one-dimensional thinking, who cast fear, separation, and misunderstanding in their pronouncements on our current events and issues.

Too often our reptilian brains take charge. On social media we rage against whatever sparks our reptilian brain. So often, this shaming, blaming we actually destroy without knowledge, empathy, learning or accountability, without accountability. If you're face-to-face, what would the conversation be in person versus sitting at your keyboard and shaming and blaming?

This week's example and I'm not going to use names. I don't want to go into the people. I want to go into the message about Outrage of the Week. There's an example of a professional woman participating in a conference in Winnipeg a couple of years ago, Winnipeg, Manitoba, Canada.

She was annoyed that her experience of the conference was challenged by two professional men sitting in a row right behind her. They were talking about sex, about who they would like to take to bed, and the size of their "dongles." Imagine that, professional men, a professional woman. How would you feel? Each plays into one of those three people.

What happened and this is a true story, the woman turned, took a cellphone photo of the two men and sent a tweet to the conference organizers about her disgust and asking them to deal with it. She was uncomfortable and she was not there in the conference to hear this nonsense. Good news. The organizers did. They talked with the men and the woman. The men were asked to leave the conference.

That got on to social media -- Twitter feed and then Facebook. Here's a very brief history of what apparently happened. Hundreds of people around the world reacted, it could have actually been thousands of people, and stated on social media their positions and favored the women and against the men. You can imagine.

Then a few days later, a few weeks later, one of the men apologized on Twitter. He said he was sorry for doing that but wanted the woman to know that he'd been fired from his work because of this. Of course, the next thing that happened is hundreds and thousands of people around the world reacted and stated on social media their support of the men. Further, they condemned the woman. It was her fault. How dare she!

Then a while later, yes, this is true, the woman was fired from her work. Yes, according to a report that I heard last night, two years later the woman is still looking for work. What did she do? She wanted to stop sexual harassment. She wanted to stop two men interfering with her experience of a professional conference.

This went way, way overboard. Can you imagine that; at least two people unable to find work because of momentary conversation; tweets that just went global? How will we learn and break through to yes? Well, we could be curious, reach out, learn, integrate, and form a new perspective. Be in the world this way. Be in the world. Form your own perspective.

Recently, the flip-flopping, I've talked about shaming and blaming. In politics recently, there's a lot of talk about flip-flopping politicians. I say, instead of exposing yourself as a leader or a politician in your family, your community; on the platform nationally, globally by taking a position before you actually know the ground, know the environment, know the people involved.

Why don't you talk to people? Listen. Form an opinion that's fully informed. Be prepared as you learn more. As time goes on, as your knowledge, as the light of learning turns on, as Allan had shared with us, be prepared to continue to learn. Now we condemn our leaders, our politicians for flip-flop. They take a position and then they have to change it. Well, they are weak. My goodness. My goodness.

In my book, what you'll find is the ten steps, ten essential steps to collaboration. What we'll find in the coming series, the next ten episodes, I'm going to go through these ten steps. You can see the ten steps on my website.

Today, we've talked about how things go wrong, we've talked about lighting our own campfire.

Very quickly I will share the ten steps and they will be the subjects of these next weeks' shows.

1) Set intention.
2) Be aware.
3) Embrace conflict.
4) Seek diversity.
5) Design the collaboration.
6) Come together. Notice that come together is actually step number six. That's where most people start to collaborate is when they call a meeting. Meetings, bloody meetings.
7) Listen deeply.
8) Collaborate with vision. Where's the vision of the Donald Trumps of the world, the Angela Merkels of the world? Where's the vision? Lead from there.
9) Now Lead. Too often collaboration is manipulation or avoidance. We need strong leadership -- purposeful with accountability.
10) Make it so. Positively change the energy and the future together.

Today we have talked about our key messages. They are mediots make us ignorant, cold, and disconnected. Two, how we can light our global campfire and form our circle. I've given you those nine considerations, characteristics. We've learned about

Rotary International. We've learned about the great work and service above self. We've learned from Allan and Jeanne.

Next week, we will be featuring Set Intention. It's the theme of the show. We'll be featuring the Canadian Association of Professional Speakers and their expertise as collaborators. We'll have our guests next week, Patricia Morgan of Calgary and David Guthrie of Vancouver. Future shows will go through each of my ten essential steps to collaboration.

Please listen every week. Listen and we'll talk about the Heart and Stroke Foundation. We'll teach a little more about the Enneagram. We have so much work to do together. Be aware. Light your campfire.

Thank you so much for joining me today. See you in the next episode. Thank you for your time and collaborative vision.

Chapter 4 Set Intention featuring Patricia Morgan, Don Loney, and David Gouthro

David Savage: Hello, listeners. Now is our time to lead more powerfully, more consciously, and more collaboratively in ways that make our world a better place today and in our future. Leaders in companies are making this essential shift right now.

Through Voice America we have access to up 3.6 million listeners in 160 countries. Welcome. It could be my brother and my sister and my wife and my friend, Linda Matthie only listening to this but I don't believe that's true.

This is the fourth show in our series. Today's show is titled Set Intention, which is the very first step of collaboration. So important, perhaps the most important step in my Essential Ten Steps. In my book, "Break Through To Yes" I set out ten steps that are essential to successful collaboration. During the next ten shows, I will walk you through each one of these ten steps. Each step will be the theme of an episode.

The ten steps are

1) Set intention.
2) Be aware.
3) Embrace conflict.
4) Seek diversity, seek diversity. Think about that for a second.
5) Design the collaboration, really carefully design it. Put it together like a puzzle that's beautiful together.
6) Come together. This is the place where most people start their collaboration. They just call a meeting. "Let's talk about..." That doesn't really work.
7) Listen deeply. Listen to what's underneath the words and the emotions. Watch the energy in the room. Really find out what's underlying.

8) Collaborate with vision. Be brave. Be audacious.
9) Now lead. Just because you collaborate doesn't mean you're not a leader. Take charge. Lead.
10) Make it so. This is where the energy, the accountability, the continual improvement works.

In this show, Set Intention, we feature a leader in publishing in North America and the Canadian Association of Professional speakers with two of its most respected leaders to collaborate and make that association the best place for professional speakers in Canada to learn network and lead. Our featured guests today are Don Loney at Toronto, Patricia Morgan of Calgary, and David Gouthro or Vancouver.

The key messages for today:

1) the very first step when you collaborate is to set and declare your honest and authentic intention;
2) when you work together, you may create something that is better than you can by yourself. Most often you will.
3) participate in a professional, technical or social entrepreneurial or community organization. Get together. Make it work.

For speakers, that includes CAPS, Canadian Association of Professional Speakers that I'm a member of or the National Speakers Association in the United States as part of your service, network, and professional development. As Patricia told me a long time ago, "We are better together."

Where do we go with all of this? We take the ten steps. We take the advice of people like Don Loney, Patricia Morgan, David Gouthro and we declare our honest intention. Declaring that honest intention in fact leaves us to the point where we together decide what do we really want to accomplish here and what's possible.

Don, I'm really excited to introduce you, my listeners to mentor and a challenger of mine and a champion of mine, Don Loney. Don is the President of Loney Publishing Group in Toronto, Ontario. When we first met, he was the Executive Editor for John Wiley and Sons Canada in Toronto. Since that time, he's...well, I'll describe him as a high-energy critical thinker with a talent for recruiting subject matter experts, developing their ideas into book-length works, and publishing to a global market.

How I met Don Loney was in Calgary at a Canadian Association of Professional Speakers' meeting. He offered to come to Calgary and have a book pitched to him by a number of us. Don was brutal to me. He cut me to threads, this beautiful, amazing book that I was writing on collaboration. Don spent a lot of time telling me I better sharpen up. I better be more critical. I better be more concise.

That's the moment a few years back when I said, "I want Don Loney as my mentor in this publishing world so people can hear me, people can come together." About nine months ago now, Don and I reconnected, talked about, "Okay, Don. I think I'm ready. I've got the improved product. Will you help me out?"

He's been there with me all along the ride, mentoring me, challenging me, helping me, and introducing me to excellent people in my collaborative network now. Don, thank you for that. I think it's been a real gift to me.

In a prior interview, we've had tough talk. One of our subjects in our book is about embracing conflict. I think I want to lead into that is to say when I saw that you're being so hard on me, I knew that that was a sign that this was important to you. Can you tell me about how you find those subject matter experts and then mold us?

Don: Well, thank you, David. I really appreciate your kind words. It's an honor to be part of the development of the book. It's an honor to be invited to the table to discuss ideas, to bring the book ideas to a global audience, to educate, to coach, and train and give people the creative space to think about what collaboration can do.

It's something that's part and parcel what we do every day. It's seldom articulated as collaboration. I think that technologies today have tended to move us away from the idea of collaboration into little bits of sound bites and ones and zeroes that just do not move us forward in a meaningful way. I congratulate you on this effort, David.

In terms of embracing conflict, it's often the case that there's tension around ideas that are presented that may not necessarily align with an author's vision, that may not necessarily align with an author's understanding of their market, of their networks, of the intent of the book. That I think was the heart of our discussion in Calgary two years ago. The idea was there but it had not, in the book page that you presented, it had not been articulated in the context of intent, which is the core idea of your book.

Coming around to continuing our discussion around intent, we can't realize that the book needed to be a living, breathing example of collaboration. It needed to invite other points of view -- views that may not necessarily agree with other views or indeed your own but that's part of a collaboration process. It's authentic. You do convince, convince may not be quite that word but you do lead people to the sense that there is something called authentic collaboration.

While all collaborations may not result in a happy ending for everyone, the fact that the process is honored is a very solid foundation for meaningful work with people that have diverse ideas, maybe even polar opposites yet collaboration gives people permission to work in that space together and see what can come out of it.

David Savage: I want to just say that those polar opposites are my teachers, those are the ones that challenge me and wake me up. I think that if you see one aspect, just one aspect, Don in the remainder of this very brief interview that you'd really like to challenge authors, subject matter experts to really hone their skills on, what one thing in this moment would you challenge our listeners to do?

Don: I would challenge them to think more deeply. I would challenge them to be more creative. I would challenge them to be leaders. Followers are very important but I think that we need more commanding vision from our thought leaders. There is so much content published because we have the technologies to publish.

We have the technologies to publish without proper editorial guidance or a critical eye on material. I think that dilutes our sense of reliability and trust in our authors and what we read. I would really encourage authors to be self-critical, to be self-aware, and to think about what their originating intent is, how they're going to articulate that, and in that context, think very carefully about their market.

David Savage: Thank you so much, Don. This is Don Loney, President, Loney Publishing Group in Toronto. I would highly recommend anybody that can connect and be challenged by Don. Thanks again, Don.

Don: Thank you so much, David. Best of luck.

David Savage: Before the break, we talked with Don Loney, Loney Publishing Group out of Toronto about his experience in collaboration and how he honors his intention to find challenge and help authors to be great, to be successful. Don challenged me to clarify my intent for my book, "Break Through To Yes." Two and a half years later, we are evolving with authentic collaboration.

Now let's talk more about our theme for today Setting Intention. Here is an excerpt in setting intention, one of the Essential Ten Steps, "Far too often we rush into things without stopping to ask, 'What is my purpose? What is my intention? Even worse, often we think we know the answer before we start'." Yes. Doesn't it annoy you when your boss does that or your spouse does that?

An oft-repeated dictum from an executive is, "Don't bring me a problem unless you are willing to bring me the answer." What if the problem would be better understood, accepted, answered, and celebrated if it was solved together? What if we acknowledged that lone rangers often create danger? Lone rangers often create danger.

Most every morning over the past 30 years, when I awake in the morning before I rise, I set my intention for the coming day. "This is what I hope for today." Do you do that? Set your intention first thing. What are a couple of things that you want to do? More importantly, how do you want to be today?

Think about how you think. How you think creates how you perceive. How you perceive creates your judgments. Your judgments create your actions. Your actions create your life. Your life creates how you think. It is a circle. Intention, thinking, perceptions, judgments, actions, life. Intention and it goes on and on. Even before I set my intention, I must open my heart and my mind.

As an example, a family example, my parents Gordon and May Savage built a beautiful family cabin in the Mountain Valley in Southern British Columbia with the name Tulameen. It's a beautiful name, Tulameen, British Columbia. Incredible place. As a family, we spent many happy times at Tulameen with our cousins, aunts, uncles, and fast friends. Tulameen has been our family touchstone. When Mom and Dad died in 2001, they willed their cabin to the five of us adult children. While experts and friends and lawyers warned us, "Family cabins never work."

We wanted to welcome current and future generations to Mom and Dad's family gathering place. This place is sacred to our family. Tulameen has adventure, nature, love, and family and campfires and fishing and huckleberries. Sacred can be difficult though.

Each spring, the five of us siblings would enjoy the May long-weekend in Canada, Victoria's Day it's called, at the cabin doing our spring maintenance and reconnecting from our busy lives. Each fall, we met at Tulameen again to conduct our business meeting for the year. Yes, our business of the cabin. All sisters and brothers with families and lives of their own have many interests, challenges, and opportunities and hopes.

At times, these clash over what to do with Tulameen, assumptions are made, judgments follow and pre-conceived solutions are not far behind. To be clear, the conversation each year, we began our annual general meeting by setting our intention, "We are here by the grace of Mom and Dad. Let their intentions for this place guide us today."

It sounds a little religious preamble. It might be. This saves us from ourselves each year. We let the intention of our parents come through. The solutions we come up in those business meetings with our shoes left on the front porch outside, the outcomes are greater than we expect.

Now we have a good friend of mine, Patricia Morgan, Solutions for Resilience. Patricia is, well, she thinks she's not an expert in collaboration but she collaborates in most everything she does.

My association with Patricia Morgan is she's a past President of the Calgary chapter of the Canadian Association of Professional Speakers. She's Founder and Chair of the Fast Track Program where she and we have been lucky enough to learn from her and support her in Fast Track in teaching professional speakers the business of professional speaking. A lot of the work that she does is from woe to wow.

Patricia, welcome. What might you add to your introduction and how people can find out more about you?

Patricia: www.solutionsforreselience.com is my place on cyberspace where you can learn about more of my work in mentoring emerging professional speakers and particularly my work in helping strengthen everyday resilience at work and home.

David Savage: Yes. There's a connection there between collaboration and resilience. One of our earlier interviewees talked about thinking that he needs to tough it out and do it all by himself. Yet, resilience often calls for others. Can you talk about that a little bit?

Patricia: Right. In my book, "From Woe to WOW: How Resilient Women Succeed in Work," I discovered that women in particular thrive in the workplace and at home in their community when they have a social network. That's also true for males when they become aware that being a lone ranger doesn't work particularly well.

We know the work of Daniel Goleman's Social Intelligence. From his work we know that when we have a social network, we have a kind of support and energy that helps us thrive with energy, with thoughts, and with everyday living.

David Savage: How have you found the power of working together or reaching out when we need help? Can you share us some personal background? How do you come to that wisdom, Patricia?

Patricia: Well, many of us including women, even though women thrive on connection, find it difficult to ask for help. It feels like a one down to ask for help. Yet, in many ways we know how good it feels, how satisfying it feels to be using our strength to help other people. I'm really interested in this whole arena around using our strength. I think when we collaborate with one another, the best collaborations I've seen is when we acknowledge our own strengths and bring them forward to offer them to other people.

When we see the strengths of other people and celebrate them and ask for them to use their strengths either for pay or in service and definitely I saw that when I asked you to join the Fast Track committee last year. What you have is a wonderful way of collaborating and celebrating that I wanted to have more of that in the program and it came to fruition. Thank you, David.

David Savage: Well, thank you, Patricia. It was just a great experience. The Fast Track Program for the Canadian Association of Professional Speakers was a great opportunity as I've written a testimonial when I went through that four or five years ago is "Best value for time and money."

I think that's what I have really found with your work is I've had a long and varied career but I still don't know much of much. Therefore, your encouragement to reach out and work as a team where we complement was just a great learning opportunity for me.

Patricia: Well, we're not marbles. There's a reason there's billions of people on the planet. When we work together, much more is accomplished. It even takes a village to raise a child. Well, it takes a village to make most significant human endeavors come to fruition.

Of course, I'm in such dismay about a lot of the wars that are going on in the world. That's when we're going backwards. Those same countries could be cooperating, collaborating. ISIS is just crazy, cut off from any kind of connection to sanity. I think we can go crazy. I actually believe this strongly that if for most of us, if we don't have some kind of connection, some kind of cooperation with one another, we can go crazy.

I just finished watching with my husband a series called "Alone." Most of the people had the ability to survive out in the wilderness. The show put 12 survivor experts out in the wilderness and the last person to stay without calling in and saying, "I give up," won the $500,000. People did not leave because they couldn't find food or they were too cold. All those things were happening. One guy was eating mice.

What happened was the psychological. "I miss my grandmother. I miss my wife. I feel so alone here." We need one another for psychological wellness as well as emotional wellness, physical wellness, and of course there's a whole area of social wellness. Your collaboration takes it to a whole another level, your whole study of it and the pitfalls and the success formulas take that whole piece around socialization to a whole another level.

David Savage: Yes. It's like a form of maturity when we realize this. One last comment, Patricia before we close this interview?

Patricia: Collaborate in your back gardens. Collaborate with your neighbors. Collaborate with your friends. Collaborate wherever you are in the world and you have no idea even in an incidental connection with somebody what potential or possibility may arise for you.

David Savage: Thank you so much, Patricia Morgan, solutionsforreselience.com. Thank you.

Patricia: You are most welcome.

David Savage: Thanks to Patricia Morgan, that leader for women, from Woe to WoW and a leader in the Canadian Association of Professional Speakers. Thank you for that interview. We now have past President of CAPS and somebody that mentors me and we've had some laughs together, David Gouthro.

David is from Vancouver. What he wants me to share with you, audience is he's a seasoned but not too spicy speaker. He has a lot of fun. He is very connected to his audiences. He's got over 30 years experience and he's best known for his creative presentations, playful demeanor, and relentless focus on delivering value to his clients, colleagues, and community. Get that? David is focused on you and the audience participants, the people that he shows up for.

David's experience comes from working with clients on four continents in organizations that range from mining, energy, healthcare and financial services to high tech, biotech, government and the not-for-profit sector.

David Gouthro is the father of a precocious 15-year old daughter, Anna. He's been forced to embrace the qualities of humility, patience, good humor, and acceptance of his own parental inadequacies. David Gouthro's words, not mine.

The main focus of his current business involves working with individuals and groups who have no one else to point to as excuses for their own inaction. This has led him to spend the majority of his time helping executive teams and boards make the tough decisions required to grow their businesses in an increasingly complex and unpredictable economic environment.

David, welcome. Tell us more about you, your work, and some thoughts about collaboration.

David Gouthro: Well, I had my first effort in collaboration today when I was going to get up. It's quite early here in Vancouver, as you know. As I was going up to the living room, I figured that keeping your family happy is part of collaboration. I discovered that my daughter was actually sleeping on the couch so quick change of plans.

Most of the work that I do is helping people having higher quality of conversations than they would. In that sense it's really getting people to talk amongst each other when I'm working with them. I'm very clear that it's about me drawing the expertise out of others taught me, provided my own.

First of all, it keeps my liability insurance because I'm not giving anyone advice. Secondly, it's just a lot more enjoyable to see people help each other get through on what's going on. As you mentioned, it's a wide range of clients that I've worked with, most of them only once, which is probably why it's such a wide range.

You mentioned that I was with CAPS. One of the things that I have been trying to persuade others about is that when you're in front of an audience, it's a shame to waste the potential in the audience by having one person talk and 500 people listen. I just don't think there's transfer of value that way. That sort of premise that the value comes from the people really informs all the work the work that I do.

David Savage: Tell me about that collaboration with your audiences, collaboration, bringing them in so you're not simply the expert on the subject talking at people. How do you that? What's it like and what's the experience?

David Gouthro: I've changed the title on my card from Facilitator, which is pretty neutral to Facilitator/Provocateur. The way that plays itself out is let's say I recently was working with a group of about 600 people. Normal wisdom is that all you do with a group of

600 people is talk at them. With myself and a co-facilitator, we basically designed a process by which we could pose a question and actually have 600 people engaged in that conversation. Then the trick of course is how do you collect their input, how do you collect that wisdom.

This was possibly sneaky but I like to think of it as a fact of facilitation is people had a question that was posed at their table. These were diverse groups at the tables. These were board chairs, senior managers from companies across the country. They had to talk about the issue and not drift off as often happens in a group of 600 because each table had a table number.

What we said is, "At the end of this conversation period, we're going to call at a random number," and had a legit number generator on our iPad, "And when your number is called, you're going to have to come up to the microphone and just offer an observation on some of the nature of the conversation you had at your table."

No one knew what table was going to be called and because no one wants to be embarrassed, it's sort of in a subtle way encouraged them to have the conversation. Your table number is called and did come up to the microphone. It was really evident that you hadn't been participating. The structure itself encouraged people to have those conversations and to share them with others.

The interesting thing was by the time we got to the third conversation and we realized people realized that they wouldn't be judged by what they said, that it was all contributing to the greater whole, people were just chomping at the bit to get up to the microphones. Instead of having to call a random number, we said, "When we count to three, the first eight people up to the microphones get to offer their input."

People were racing to get up because it was about contributing to an issue that the entire 600 people were dealing with. Things like that. It's then talking amongst themselves there's going to be a much better transfer of the knowledge and learning than just listening to one person and they don't have a chance to talk about it.

David Savage: Another bonus of the way you handled your audience is I'm sure you learned a lot from that.

David Gouthro: Oh, absolutely. We had them record all of their information so that even those that didn't get to speak, in a group of 600 people, you might get six or seven tables that speak. All of the information that was captured, we had recorders, got pooled together and filtered back. All 600-people got the results of that.

David Savage: Fantastic. That's very honoring of their participation and their ongoing learning.

David Gouthro: Yes, absolutely, absolutely.

David Savage: David, I'm sure that you've triggered our audiences to say, "How do I find out more about David Gouthro?"

David Gouthro: On my LinkedIn profile, which is just David Gouthro. I don't think there's too many of me. Can I offer one other comment? Something was just...I woke up and it was really bugging me about collaboration.

David Savage: You bet.

David Gouthro: I think with collaboration to be effective, there also has to be commitment. I have worked with one particular industry where collaboration is allegedly in their DNA. They will talk about collaboration but as soon as something of higher priority comes out, they bail. They're getting better at this but in the past, someone would bail out.

We're collaborating to do something together, to save money, to develop a stronger brand. Once interest of that organization supersedes that there's less willingness to give up something individually for the collaboration.

I think collaboration to be really effective and true collaboration and true community and things like Patricia was talking about, there has to be an unwavering commitment to make that collaboration work in spite of the fact that you might not get everything that you want.

David Savage: Yes. Building up that respect and trust, that "It's not mine." It may turn out different and sometimes we will fail but working together is more important than being right in this particular instance.

David Gouthro: Yes. I think that's a hard pill for some organizations to swallow but if you truly want to have collaboration, you have to build and not have people spending a lot of time and energy putting systems in place to give an early warning if someone is going to start to bail out early. There's just so much potential when that trust as you say is there but so much goes into worrying and anxiety, "Are they really going to come through when I need them?"

David Savage: Yes, yes. Do I trust this or is it just a thing? Actually, it's a good segue to the whole focus of my book is building a culture of collaboration. Collaboration is a culture, how we do our business together. It's not a thing or an event or a project.

David Gouthro: Well, when I was president of CAPS, I didn't' do anything that really is structurally different with the organization mostly because I'm not smart enough. I don't like doing those kinds of things but the theme of the year was Better Together.

Every chance I had, whether speaking to the chapters or my own board, it was always that at the back of my mind that we're better together and to have people start using that language and have that as a culture, not just a one-word overlay on a piece of paper that said, "Yes, collaboration is one of our values."

David Savage: Yes, that's so important. Of course, you made great strides. As President, you hosted a national and international professional speakers' conference in Vancouver. Let's go the opposite direction. What are some of the most difficult challenges you found when trying to help groups to collaborate?

David Gouthro: Well, ego does come in to play now and again. Especially when you're working with professionals whose body of expertise is really important to them and others that it's sometimes more important to be right.

Finding some people...because people who had ever been in a relationship will recognize this where you're having a conversation with your spouse or your significant other or your child. Half a second into it you realize that they're right and you're wrong. Yet, you proceed to argue your case as if your life depends upon it.

I think one of the most difficult things is a need to be right or to win. The challenge and the opportunity is how you have the energy of a competitive spirit but with a collaborative framework or collaborative behavior. Those two don't often play well together.

David Savage: There's a lot of pressure on politicians to never flip-flop. I'd pressure politicians to listen and collaborate first before they have that firm position.

David Gouthro: We don't allow politicians. If they get into office and find out that the information they have in office is different from what they had that coming in, do we as citizens value more that they stick to what they said they were going to do in spite of evidence that says, "No, it's not such a good idea" or do we value someone says, "Given this listing, given this new information, I think there's actually a better decision that we could make?"

David Savage: Yes. Listeners, this is David Gouthro on LinkedIn. Canadian Association of Professional Speakers is the Canadian version of the

National Speakers Association is Americans and canadianspeakers.org for Canadians to learn more information. As we close this interview, David, what is one thing that you would challenge and encourage our listeners to do around collaboration?

David Gouthro: I think the big thing, David is to be more mindful of any interaction that you're having with someone. Is it about doing something better together or is it about being right and being better than someone else? I think the key to a lot of this is just to be mindful and make sure that the way you're interacting is really what you think as a better way to be in the world.

David Savage: Thank you so much, provocateur, inciter, insightful, mindful, David Gouthro, my friend, mentor, and somebody that actually dramatically increases the engagement and learning with his audiences and his corporate clients. Thanks again, David.

David Gouthro: My pleasure, David. Thanks for having me.

David Savage: Before the break, we listened to my mentor, champion, David Gouthro. He's also a self-described facilitator/provocateur and somebody that's learning to listen to his daughter, Anna. Thanks, David for that.

In my work with the organizations, oftentimes large oil and gas companies in Calgary, I've been told I incite insurgency. I want people to speak up what they care about, what their concerns are, what their visions are, what their dreams are. Speak up and be an insurgent in your organization and around that boardroom table.

Now it's time for our weekly feature, Outrage of the Week. Outrage of the Week. When I wrote this in my book, it was of the week, this week, this time, this month, this day. Increasingly, I'm seeing it as Outrage of the

Weak. This is the amygdala-based reptilian-based outrage or people, mediots as I call them go crazy without really investigating and destroy whatever intention or at least divert from their apparent intention.

This week, there's an article by Ben Hubbard from Beirut, Lebanon published in the New York Times, September 25th. It's titled Hajj Tragedy Inflames Schisms During a Pilgrimage Designed for Unity. I quote, "For the two million Muslims from across the world performing the hajj in Saudi Arabia this year, the annual pilgrimage is a time to forget differences in race, sect, wealth and even nationality that divide believers and focus instead on their equality before God.

But when tragedy strikes, as with the massive human crush that killed more than 700 pilgrims near the holy site, those differences come rushing back to the surface. A Saudi official blamed the tragedy on African pilgrims, prompting accusations of racism. Iran fired up its state apparatus to lambast Saudi Arabia," and then it goes on and on and on in the article. Everybody pointing fingers and blaming. It's a blame fest.

It is so sad. 700 people died. A massive tragedy and a massive blame fest. Where is the love? Where is the learning? Where is the intention? I just wonder at things like this, how will we learn and break through to yes? Well, we be curious. We reach out. We integrate. We form a new and your own perspective. Be in the world curious. David Gouthro spoke about that.

Use the ten steps. Think about how you collaborate. Consider using these as your guide, your guide to the vision, not to division and through collaboration. By working together better, you will have success.

Today, we've explored the wisdom of Don Loney, Patricia Morgan, David Gouthro and the leadership with the Canadian Association of Professional Speakers. This week key messages were:

1) the very first step when you collaborate is to set and declare your honest and authentic intention,
2) when you work together you may create something that is far better than you can do yourself, and
3) participate in organizations. Don't be alone. Don't even be an alone in that organization. Be part of, work together. Collaborate. The Canadian Association of Professional Speakers, the National Speakers Association are excellent if you're professional speakers. We're all part of many organizations.

Where do we go from here? Next week's show I'm also very excited. The theme is Be Aware, the second of my Ten Steps. Future shows will go through each one of the Ten Steps.

Next week, the featured guests are Ken Cloke, Santa Monica, California; Cheryl Cardinal, Calgary, Alberta; and Ryan Robb, Calgary, Alberta.

My call to action this week; think about your honest intention before you do anything else. Be honest. Be clear. Be authentic. Be in integrity.

The music of Break Through To Yes, I've compiled a list of music that aligns to each one of my Ten Steps. For Set Intention, the songs may include;
a) "The Prayer of St. Francis." Listen to the one by the Burns sisters or by Sarah McLachlan.
b) "Up Against the World" by Chris Martin.
c) My friends, intentional, spiritual friends, Deva Premal, Miten and Manose "No Goal But This"

Think about the outrages in the world, think about the silos in your political system, think about how as leaders we must find different tools and systems to break through.

d) My friend, Chuck Rose has created another beautiful song to set our intention. This song is called "We Are One." Thank you so much for your time today in setting your collaborative intention. Here is Chuck Rose in the world premiere of "We Are One."

Chapter 5 Be Aware Plus Aboriginal Collaboration featuring Ken Cloke, Cheryl Cardinal and Ryan Robb

David: Now is our time. Yes, it is our time now to lead more powerfully, consciously, and collaboratively in ways that make our world and our organizations better today and for our future. By listening to this broadcast, I know you are making this essential shift right now.

Welcome, listeners. Welcome, Romania. Welcome, France. Welcome, California. Today's show is titled Be Aware. Form my book, "Break Through to Yes" I set out ten steps that are essential to successful collaboration. Last week, we talked about Set Intention. During the next shows, we will continue to work through these ten steps, one episode per step plus some extras in the 15-week series.

Be aware. This show also features a world leader in conflict resolution and organizational development and two leaders in business and aboriginal development. I'm so honored and gratified that the three have chosen to be with us today.

Just a note, I've got over 40guests in the 15 shows in the fall program. They are also my friends. An example I bring forward is tremendous collaborative leadership for organizations, for you, and for our future.

Our featured guests today are Ken Cloke, Santa Monica, California. Amongst the many things that Ken's achieved and done for us is he's a founder of Mediators Beyond Borders. We also have Cheryl Cardinal, Calgary, Indigenous Energy and Ryan Robb of Calgary is the former Chief Executive Officer of the Treaty 7 Corporation which is a corporation that brings together all of the First Nations in Southern Alberta for business development and collaboration amongst those nations.

Key messages for today:

1) engage with others with an open heart.
2) learn about other cultures and how to best collaborate with them. It's not all about me. Connect with them.
3) decisions you make as a leader can have outcomes that you'd never dream of or had nightmares about.

In our first show about a month ago, our Outrage of the Week focused on the little Syrian boy, Alan, his death and that of his brother and mother. Last night, I attended the University of Alberta President's Dinner with Alberta Heart and Stroke Foundation's CEO Donna Hastings. I want to give a shout out to all the leaders who find positive ways to respond to tragedy.

David Turpin, the new president of the University of Alberta woke up early September and read about Alan. He realized we must be part of the solution, not a judgment, not a "Oh, it's too bad for him. How can this happen?" Within two days the University of Alberta approved and announced the program to fund and support Syrian refugees that attend the university. Now that is agile, responsive, and inspiring.

Thank you, David Turpin and the University of Alberta. That's a great show of collaborative leadership, agility. You had it done within two days and it was over a weekend.

See how we may respond to outrages? See what leaders do and choose. Leaders like Ken Cloke, our featured guest this week see and then do. They do positive, respectful, and collaborative acts. They believe in organizational freedom, integrity, and agility.

Here's an excerpt from Ken Cloke's fine book, "The Dance of Opposites: Explorations in Mediation, Dialogue and Conflict Resolution Systems Design."
"Fundamentally, the role of leaders in an organizational democracy is to expand the number of degrees of organizational freedom and orchestrate these elements to

create learning relationships that link people across artificial boundaries.

Organizational separations and divisions that are not integrated produce role confusions, feelings of irresponsibility, misunderstanding, stereotypes, conflicts, and internal dissension, which can be used to justify and rationalize bureaucratic divisions and hierarchical control.

Every organizational division is simply a different way of understanding, processing, and solving common problems. The task of democratic leaders is to reveal the whole to each of its parts and to integrate the concerns of all into a single, synergistic, strategically-integrated whole."

Did you understand that? "The task of democratic leaders is to reveal the whole and each of its parts and to integrate the concerns of all into a single, synergistic, strategically-integrated whole." That just makes so much sense to me. Ken Cloke makes so much sense to me. He's a passionate man. "The Dance of Opposites," "The Conflict Revolution," he is doing great work.

Ken is Director of the Center for Dispute Resolution. He's a founder of Mediators Beyond Borders. He's a mediator, an arbitrator, a facilitator, a coach, a consultant, and a trainer. He specializes in communication, resolving complex multi-party disputes of all sorts.

The most recent book of Ken's is the "Dance of Opposites." If you go to Ken's website or Google him, you will find this is a very wise and great spirit for our world. Enough of me trying to tell you how much I love you, Ken. Can you introduce yourself to our listeners?

Ken: Thank you very much, David. It was very kind and generous. I have been working in the fields of collaboration and conflict resolution for I think nearly all my life but professionally, certainly for the last 35 years.

I think what's most interesting about it is that it has a variety of different forms that activity assumes but beneath that activity, there's a lot that's in common between all the different things that you mentioned; between mediation, facilitation, coaching, dialogue, and various of what I think of as the collaborative arts and sciences. That's my passion and my work.

David: Yes. Wonderful. What is about what people call collaboration that is so often misleading?

Ken: I think the first thing that's misleading is that there is a single thing that is known as collaboration. We can certainly think of it as singular but we can also think of it as having a kind of infinite number of manifestations. There are small-scale collaborations, which we engage in every time we have a conversation. There are larger collaborations that we engage in in communities and families.

What we have a hard time I think imagining is how far exactly this can go. What is the deepest level of our collaboration? What's the highest achievement that we can make in this field? I think when we begin to think in those terms, we begin to see all of life completely differently. What we then, I think see is that the collaborative project, if we can call it that is one that is been building over the course of human history and had yet to realize complete fruition.

David: Do you see this, Ken as a building, evolutionary, positive progression then towards collaborative leadership and a collaborative culture?

Ken: I do. However, we have to talk a little bit for a moment about what progress means in this context. The reality is that there are two fundamental forces that drive us. It's the conflict between those forces that end up creating a kind of two steps forward, one step back outcome when it comes to collaboration.

The first of those forces is the force that unites us, that brings us together, that touches us in our hearts, that allows us to connect in a deep fundamental level. We can think of this as the force of love, the force of spirituality, the force of heart. There are a number of different ways that we can describe it but they are all essentially the same. They are the things that bring us together but when we come together, we don't just come together in a single unit.

We have unity and we have diversity. The most wonderful thing about diversity is not just that it's a nice thing to have, but that it allows us to achieve higher orders of unity. Diversity on the one hand creates the basis for conflict and unity creates the basis for resolution.

That's why it's a dance. It's always been a dance. It will always be a dance. What we want to do is to learn how to dance and to do it with the greatest style that we possibly can be, to bring to it, to become, if you will the Fred Astaire's for our conflicts.

David: Wonderful and so well stated in the Dance of Opposites. We've talked about the progress and the big dream of collaborative culture and leadership and spirit. Let's get a little more tangible. What's the value of collaboration? Why do it?

Ken: I think if we imagine collaboration on a large scale, it becomes a little difficult to manage. Whereas, if we think of it on the smallest possible scale and ask the questions slightly differently, what do we get, each individual one of us, what do I get from the collaborations that I engage in. The answer is I get myself. The self isn't just a thing that stands alone. As philosophers have said, "The smallest human unit isn't one; it's two."

In South Africa they have a concept called "Ubuntu." "Ubuntu" means I am who I am because you are who you are; that you create me just as I create you and together we create each other. That's what collaboration is.

It's actually a road to the self. It's not a denial of the self. It's not an elimination of the self. It's actually the highest road to the self just as the self is the highest road to collaboration. It doesn't mean denying who you are or not having desires or wishes. It means adding your desires and wishes to other people's desires and wishes in a way that's constructive and produces a higher order of outcome.

David: The sum is truly greater than all the parts or collaboration is not compromise. It's actually creation is part of what I'm hearing.

Ken: Beautifully said.

David: Ken, as we close this interview, how can people find out more about your work, how to connect with you, how do they connect in to your network?

Ken: Check out any of the books that I've written. The one that you mentioned, "The Dance of Opposites" is a good one to start. Those would all be very nice.

David: I hear an airplane in the background. That must be collaboration is taking off.

Ken: Must be.

David: Any last comments, Ken?

Ken: The last comment is really kind of an aphorism. The aphorism is this: it doesn't matter whose end of the boat is sinking. We're all in this together. We must realize that we have to take responsibility for it and start working on our problems together. It doesn't mean it's easy. It just means it's the truth.

David: Thank you so much, Ken Cloke. Thank you for your wisdom.

Ken: Thank you very much, David.

David: Before the break, we talked with Ken Cloke about collaboration as the highest road to self. It constructs a higher order of creation. Ken directed us to understand the range of collaboration -- not thinking it's one simple thing. It isn't. It's a whole range.

To quote, "We have a hard time imagining the highest achievement we may make." As you heard, Ken is a brilliant visionary with a large heart. He also shows us so much about our own awareness that comes through conflict, diversity, and unity.

Now, we've got the pleasure of a discussion with Cheryl Cardinal. Cheryl Cardinal is a dynamic First Nations leader who works to ensure indigenous voices are all at the tables, are at all the tables as well. Cheryl is currently President/CEO of the Indigenous Center of Energy. Through her work at the Indigenous Center, Cheryl supports and fosters mutually beneficial relationships for indigenous communities and the energy sector.

She is a trusted source who has facilitated multi-stakeholder sessions with government, First Nations, local community members, and the energy industry. Cheryl's got over 20 years doing this work. She's one of the most respected First Nations leaders, facilitators, I would say not only in Alberta, Canada but increasingly around the world. Cheryl, introduce yourself a little more. Blow your own horn a little bit. Who are you and how can our listeners learn more about you?

Cheryl: I Thank you very much for having me on your show. guess the best introduction I can give is what got me into this work. I've been thinking about what would the listeners want to know about me or from me that I could contribute to other people.

I think the biggest thing for me is that it's been a life-long learning process. Granted, I don't have the age that a lot of people do, I have great life experiences that I can treasure. My father was a great First Nations leader who took collaborative approaches. My grandfather was also a great First Nations leader. My grandfather in the 1940's fought for First Nations peoples for their rights to remove some of the most racist pieces of the Indian Act.

David: Cheryl for our listeners abroad, can you name them? Tell us a little more about what in fact that they did because they were very important leaders and collaborators.

Cheryl: Yes. My grandfather was Frank Cardinal from the Sucker Creek First Nation. He was chief at the time in the 1940's when he helped remove some of the most racist pieces of legislation.

As for his mentorship and guidance, he helped my father, Dr. Harold Cardinal who I guess is best known for being the author of "The Unjust Society" and "The Red Paper" as responses to the Canadian government's "White Paper" and Prime Minister Trudeau's "Just Society". When they tried to extinguish treaty aboriginal rights in Canada. He stood with many First Nations leaders to get that act repealed before it became legislation.

My uncle in British Columbia, Philip Paul helped start the Union of BC Indian Chiefs. I am fortunate to have such great role models in my life and examples that have led me down the path that I'm now on.

David: Yes, very, very honoring heritage that you have and you have much more than that, Cheryl. You've shared with me stories about your initiatives not only within Western Canada but also internationally. Please tell our listeners a little more about that work that important work that you've been doing.

Cheryl: I've always been a type of person who looks at what areas are indigenous people face and how can we fix those. My daily mantra, we've had this discussion, the reason I get up in the morning is to leave the world a better place than I received it. I have got kids. I think about their kids. I think about many indigenous people. I think about the future generations and I want to leave it better than I received it.

My brother was Chief of Sucker Creek First Nation at the time and he wanted to do an indigenous economic summit, an international indigenous economic summit. He had the vision to bring in numerous leaders who have signed the United League of Indigenous Nations Treaty that looked at international trade amongst indigenous people at an international level from trade between nation to nation.

He had brought me in to get me to help plan an event that would host these people. We've hosted an Australian community at our treaty days. That led me to my work in energy and naturally the progression was you could look across this country and see the diverse news that we have as indigenous people in relation to the different energy programs.

We've got some Nations that are for it. They're trying to figure out how can they get involved with the projects helping how they can benefit economically from it. When you've got other Nations, who are greatly opposed to your development, they want to be what the way it is and they worry about the environment. They worry about the common issues and they worry about those issues.

Having all of those viewpoints in mind, I wanted to come together and see how we could talk about energy.

One of the things that I had done was I put together an energy summit. I had people from New Zealand, Australia, from Iceland, from Finland, United States, Canada. I had some people come from the Middle East come and talk about some of the things that are going on in their areas.

When I started this whole process, I just thought, "Oh, we could come together, and it would be great." When I went and talked to the Maori and it's just something that we have discussed, when I talked to the Maori, they said that they wanted...their greatest vision was to look at sustainable development, look at how we could look at climate change, at renewable energies. Their comment to me was, "Sure, we'll come if you can get people from Iceland come."

I, of course, I sold it. I said, "Absolutely. Yes, I can get people from Iceland." I didn't know at that time anyone from Iceland. I was sitting there. I said, "Yes, absolutely. I'll do my best." They said, "Okay. When you get that confirmation, send it to us." I hung up my Skype thing and I went, "Oh no. How am I going to make this happen?"

I think what it came back to is just the looking at why. Why are we doing this? Why was it so important to come together and to share these views? I'd actually ran into the Iceland Ambassador to Canada. He's now the Iceland Ambassador to Great Britain, an amazing ambassador for their country. I had done all my reading and review and everything you could think of related to Iceland and some of the things, the technologies that they're looking at and trying to understand why.

It's a good thing I did that because when I ran into the Ambassador, I said to him, "Great. This is fantastic. I need you up my event. I need someone from Iceland so you need to come." He said, "What do you know about Iceland?" For me I just stopped and I went, "Great. This is my time to share everything I've learned and see if there's something that I missed or that wasn't proper." Maybe there were some things that he could share about what made this country great.

I made the comparison in talking to them that this is what indigenous people in the world strive for. They strive to find something that helps identify them as a community that allows them to come together. I said to him, "This is one of the things that we as indigenous people look for. We look for it. It's amazing that 80 to 85, you're almost at a hundred percent self-sufficient on geo-thermal technologies."

He smiled and his backward stare, he said, "We're not at a hundred percent yet." I said, "That's the exact attitude that we need to see when we're sitting here and we're looking at possibilities energy-wise, whether it be through renewable, or oil or mining opportunities that we made for our communities to strive for."

David: Yes, we're going to that 100% inclusion, diversity, honor, respect, and the leadership. Cheryl Cardinal, as we close this interview, I would ask you to challenge our listeners who are in many nations around the world one thing that you'd like them to become more aware of or actually act on. I would ask you to do it in both of your language, your native language and in English just to honor a little bit more and allow your native tongue to be heard.

Cheryl: I think I'd like to...that's a fantastic question. Those are questions I often get asked by different people that I meet in different countries. Understanding. I think it all brings back to Mr. Thórdur Ægir Óskarsson, the Iceland Ambassador. He had looked at me after the summit was going on here on our second day and we had done our cultural exchange meet.

David: We've got about 15 seconds left.

Cheryl: Okay. He'd come together. I'll be quick. I promise. He had looked at me and he said, "You have brought together some of the most successful people across this country and it's beautiful to see our cultures and how you present yourself."

My challenge to your listeners is to open up and see the beauty that we have amongst our nations. I say thorough because we are not all the same. You're different. You're beautiful. You're humane people. I challenge you to see the beauty in our people and to come together to common terms to find resolutions that we will put together.

David: I just also want to give a shout out and my gratitude to Chuck Rose. He wrote, performed, and recorded "We Are One" and "Win, Win, Win, or Walk Away." He's granted me the opportunity to use those beautiful songs for this radio program and podcast.

Before the break, we talked with Cheryl Cardinal. "See the beauty in our people" is one of the challenges, the opportunity she gave us. Aboriginal people have such a gift for us. They have so much of what we need and we have so much of what they need.

Cheryl reached out to the Maori people in Australia who in turn wanted to ensure that people in Iceland participated in her summit. True enough her courage was rewarded with a great summit where indigenous people from across the globe came together.

On our theme of be aware this week, often we must talk straight with others. Straight talk can lead to strong bond or real conflict. Straight is honesty. In 2012 at the invitation of Scott Manjak, former mayor of Cranbrook and former COO of the ?aq'am St. Mary's Indian Band, I facilitated a three-day strategic planning session for the ?aq'am St. Mary's Indian band of the Ktunaxa First Nation of the Kootenay Rockies of British Columbia.

That's my home. We worked thorough their strategic plan and what the leadership chose to make their priorities. This is a great model whereby the hierarchy of the aq'am band is the inverse of most European organizational structures. ?aq'am and many First Nations see the community at the top and the chief and counsel at the bottom of the pyramid.

The "Nasukin" or Chief and the other counselors do not put their name forward for election. Instead, their community put forward names and elects the ones they feel will be best.

I have a profound respect for the leadership for the ?aq'am band and the Ktunaxa First Nation. I was also delighted to experience three days of planning and impact assessment without a single PowerPoint. Instead, I heard their stories.

At the end of the three days, Nasukin Jim Whitehead told me, "David, this worked well. I want to tell you that I generally dislike white men." Well, that's not unexpected after the residential school process that he went through. Process is such an incomplete word. I replied to Nasukin, "Honestly, in my long career in oil and gas, I generally tried my very best never to deal with Indians." Nasukin Whitehead laughed and said, "We will get along just fine."

After more than three years of working as a volunteer for economic development for the band, we've had successes and failures. We look at joint ventures, partnerships, and innovative ideas to create positive outcomes for the people and the partner. The people and the partner. Economic. Have you connected with a First Nation aboriginal economic development group in your area? How might you collaborate? See the beauty, see the gift, see the challenges.

Ryan Robb is our next guest. Ryan received his Bachelor's Degree in Economics from Queen's University in Kingston, Ontario. Upon completion, he accepted a position in Calgary with a supply company working in the Oil & Gas Sector to manage and grow their division. Ryan was most recently the Chief Executive Officer for both Treaty 7 Management Corporation and the Treaty 7 First Nations Chiefs' Association.

This is really important. I'm really honored to have Ryan as our guest today. I'll ask Ryan to tell us more about that work and what Treaty 7 is because many of our listeners around the world will have no idea but I think once they hear this will give them a brand-new perspective and an opening.

In a number of different capacities, Ryan served as Director of Business Development and Information Technology. He completed his work with Treaty 7 as CEO. Currently he's Regional Manager of Government and Aboriginal Affairs for Opus Stewart Weir, where his skills are being utilized to increase business through a balanced approach between contemporary business practices and respecting traditional values of all parties.

I'm just so interested in delving into that comment. What I want to do, rather than me continuing on, I want Ryan to expand a little bit on Treaty 7 and what he means by contemporary business practices respecting traditional values. Ryan, welcome.

Ryan: Thank you very much for having me, David. Yes, sure. I can certainly expand on Treaty 7 without going too far into history. When Canada was settled, specifically in the West, treaties were signed between the Crown and the indigenous populations. In Eastern Canada, we might have pre-Confederation treaties. What we had was post-Confederation and we actually ended up numbering treaties as we came from East to West.

Some of that of course went along with the rail line coming through to bring BC into confederation. It ended up with 11 numbered treaties. They just happen to coincide with days they were signed. Treaty 7 is for the most part, the bottom third, the bottom third of Alberta and was signed in 1877 between the tribes and depending on how they're accounted, there's either five or seven, sometimes they're only identified as three.

The tribes in this part of the world are large. Amongst those seven tribes you have about 30,000 people that it represents amongst those tribes. That's what Treaty 7 is, and how Treaty 7 was arrived at in a nutshell.

Do you want me to explain a bit about sort of what we did, what manner and courses?

David: Yes. Yes, please do.

Ryan: We had two organizations. One was called the Chiefs' Association and one is called Management Corp. That was the decision that was made about a decade ago, a little over a decade ago. What it was it used to be known as Treaty 7 Travel Council which people are probably more familiar with. The thought was we needed to separate business from politics as best as we could. They tend to get in the way of one another.

We ended up with the Chiefs' Association, which was the political arm that really took on the level of tribal council function. We also developed Management Corp, which then became its business entity. Of course, what we can do is you're never going to be funded to be a political advocacy group that is difficult or may call into question some government decisions. That's why we wanted to make sure that we had a spread base of dollars to the Management Corp that could feed our political interests if they were required to do.

With that, we ended up growing our business side so much so it's probably ten or 12 times the size of the political arm. We decided to diversify. Even though we are in Alberta, we tend in our self, we don't have the luxury of living on top of vast oil fields or other types of minerals that other parts of this province have.

We ended up in non-traditional businesses. We are into things like insurance brokerages, high security data centers, and a lot of more of the intellectual work, if you will rather than the physical work. That was done very much on purpose to do that. It was grown out of relationship building.

I'm proud to say that when I've taken over, about 80% of our revenue came from government and that was core funding. This year we're probably closer to 4%. It comes from core funding. We might do projects for the government but actual core funding it's now only about 4% for us. Some of that because of government cuts but obviously the vast majority is from growth in other industries.

David: Ryan, how is collaboration served as a value add? Because there is a real challenge there between the political, the cultural, social, and the economic. How have you figured that out and what can you share with our listeners as to a direction that you'd encourage them to take?

Ryan: I'm thinking this is a difficult question and those of you with the written book I think probably have found that it is difficult and it's generated the need. I'm a big believer in people sort of understanding a bigger picture of where an organization is going.

Internally, we had to develop our collaboration amongst the Nation, which quite often would have different directions and different desires. Our board is composed of the seven chiefs that are elected. Us having elected officials can be difficult because they have their own Nations still to deal with.

The next group we have would be the employees. The same thing, I would have people in charge of health, their education, their business or what have you. They can have different desires. Third group you have will be the government groups or stakeholders. The fourth would be industry.

I think it's important for these groups to know, have a common view of where we're going and why we're going there. That's something I think comes from a manager's perspective of helping people understand that because that then breeds ownership in the direction. I'm not saying every specific piece of information goes to every specific person involved in that continuum but I think a general overview of that is really helpful to have buy in from all those involved.

For the chiefs, knowing that the interests of their Nation will be taken into account is important. Same with employees. Same with government or other stakeholders. Same with industry partners.

David: There's a whole management structure there. I volunteer with the aq'am Economic Development Board of their Ktunaxa Nation of Southeastern BC. It's so important to realize that while I'm asking you questions about your involvement in collaboration with aboriginal leadership and success, really, it's no different isn't it, Ryan? It's we are one and let's have a vision first, figure it out.

Ryan: Right. The analogy I use quite often...in a Western business school, a Western business, we tend to be, I personally think, too rigid in how we do business and maybe it's from being born in the 1970's and started the rat race in the 1990's. Everything was hurry up. Everything was get it done.

I would set meetings. When I first came in the business world, you sort of do that traditional thing where you set a half-hour block for a meeting and you have 25 minutes of meeting and five minutes for notes and coffee and washroom break and then you're off to the next meeting. I think some of that's lost.

An analogy I like to use with how to do business with indigenous groups is somewhere to how we do business with Asian cultures. What I mean by that is, Asian cultures cannot do as indigenous companies. We don't like to jump into business immediately. What we'd like to do is learn a little about each other first. That might be breaking bread. That might be having social time.

We'd like to have discussions. What you find when you sit, we'll try to find common ground with each other first. Who do we know from this project? What families do we know? Do you know this person or that person?

I think some of that sort of foreplay, if you will really, helps you consummate the business relationship. I think it's much better understood when put in the context of observation of Asian businesses and aboriginal businesses rather than just purely how we do it in the Western world.

David: We're out of time, Ryan. I want to ask you if you can give one challenge to our listeners about collaboration, what might it be?

Ryan: One challenge of collaboration?

David: Yes, one thing that you'd put in front of people to say think about this or do this. This is what I would encourage you.

Ryan: Because I've done a lot of negotiations in my life, I think one of the biggest tools I can use is trying to understand it from the person that you're trying to collaborate or negotiate with. Try to understand it from their view.

What are they bringing in to it, their preconceived notions? What is it that they're able to do or not able to do?

Don't force someone to try to do something that they aren't able to do because you're going to end up not being able to have that collaboration and that discussion point. You're going to end up building walls instead of taking them down.

David: All right. Ryan Robb, while I've put you into a very brief time slot like what white guys tend to do, thank you so much for your wisdom. Thanks, Ryan Robb.

Ryan: My pleasure, David. Anytime.

David: What is collaboration? We've heard today from Ken, Cheryl, and Ryan. It's unity. It's time. It's not an event. It's a continuum. It's diversity. It's awareness. Collaboration is agile. I'm learning this. That's why with you, our listeners around the world, I'm bringing forward 40 guests over this 15-weeks series, I write the book, I do the radio show, I do my work to learn. It's so important to me and I believe to you.

Before the break, we were talking with Ryan Robb about how we tend to act in our Western business world as we're always in a hurry with overloaded to-do lists. Rather, Ryan talked about building relationship first. Business relationships with First Nations people take time and they are earned. Try to understand rather than force our way.

In my book, "Break Through to Yes" I use sex as a metaphor for a collaboration. I want to make an important point about being aware. Sex usually gets people attention. When you are present, take your time. Pay special attention to the other, to your partner. Explore and enjoy.

Like sex, collaboration is fantastic. When you rush in with only your own needs and desires in mind, not considering the impact on others, very often you finish not very satisfied, wishing there was more to it or worse. Collaboration is a way, a discovery, a journey, and an experience. "If you want to go fast, go alone. If you want to go far, go together," according to an African proverb.

The Outrage of the Week is Volkswagen. We've been hearing so much in the last few weeks about Volkswagen. CNN Money, October 2nd says, "Volkswagen's emissions scandal could be far more painful for investors than BP's disastrous 2010 oil spill in the Gulf of Mexico. Credit Suisse estimates the total cost to the company could hit 78 billion euros or $87 billion in a worst-case scenario. That's about 60% more than the cost of the Deepwater Horizon spill to BP."

Designated Chairman, Hans Dieter Poetsch warned managers that the diesel-emissions scandal could pose "an existence-threatening crisis for the company," as it pleaded for public trust with full-page ads.

Now be clear. We don't know the whole story. Think about the conversation and assuming they did know for now that the leaders within Volkswagen had. In hindsight, it's easy to say, "That was effing stupid. Why risk your entire corporation for something that's as ridiculous as this?"

Who stood up? Who failed to stand up? Who didn't speak up? They broke our trust. Who's responsible? It's a culture of responsibility. More people know than what we'll know. The managers, the nations, the public, and their buyers, the loyal buyers have been screwed.

Thank you today for Ryan, Cheryl, and Ken. Our key messages were engage with others with an open heart. Learn about other cultures and how to best collaborate with them in their way. Third, decisions you make as a leader can have outcomes that you never dreamed of or had nightmares about.

Next week's theme is Embrace Conflict. That's another one of my essential ten steps to collaboration. Yes, conflict is a gift. As my oldest sister, Carol advised me about 25 years ago, those that you're in conflict with bring you a gift. It's your choice how you receive it.

Next week's featured guests in Break Through to Yes are Esther Bleuel of California and Jeff Cohen of New York, both good friends, both wise people.

My call to action this week on Be Aware, I want to share something Ken Cloke told us today. "It doesn't matter whose end of the boat is sinking. We are all in this together. Start working on our problems together. It doesn't mean it's easy. It means it's truth." It's not easy but it's true.

Just think about that. Think about the outrage. Think about in your company and you're not for profit and your political system. Are you really aware or you're looking the other way? Are you allowing things that you find cross boundaries or unethical, that are lies? Who's speaking up? How will we learn from Break Through To Yes? Be curious. Reach out. Learn. Stand up. Form your own perspective. Participate where you are.

Next week, Embrace Conflict with Esther and Jeff. Be aware. Thank you so much for your time and collaborative awareness today.

Chapter 6 Embrace Conflict featuring Esther Bleuel and Jeff Cohen

David: Welcome, listeners across the planet. Today is a special day. Today is International Conflict Resolution Day. Thank you to Justin, Nick, Camille with the Voice America. Thanks for making this so easy.

Today I'm thinking about collaboration in sports. Pretty much every sport requires some or a lot of collaboration between players, coaches, owners, marketing, finance, operations. Take a moment to think about the collaboration in football, world football, volleyball, hockey, lacrosse, even tennis. No one plays well alone. No one wins without collaboration.

I've loved sports and been reasonably active in my life. As I move through my middle age, I know I must get more active, not less and keep moving. I love to hike, bike, kayak, walk, ski, cross-country ski, snowshoe, and more.

This summer I backpacked part of Canada's wild Great Divide Trail, mountain climbed Via Ferrata near Banff, and rode in two Gran Fondo road biking events. "Move it or lose it," says the Heart and Stroke Foundation. Nature gives me energy.

In the Banff Gran Fondo, riding the beautiful Bow Valley Parkway. That is such a beautiful parkway between Lake Louise and Banff, Alberta, I'm not a fast and competitive rider but I am determined and I love the endorphins that come with the action.

During the Banff ride, the experienced fast riders and teams would cut in front of me and it would scare me a bit. I like riding alone at my own pace and I am slow. There would be a conflict between the fast teams and the slow riders. Think of the peloton where riders tightly group together at high speeds.

According to Wikipedia, "the peloton," that's the peloton, "travels as an integrated unit similar in some respects to birds flying in formation. With each rider making slight adjustments in response to their adjacent riders particularly the one in front of each," and the one in front of each can be inches apart and going 30, 40, 50 miles an hour. It's a little strange for those of us that are not use to the peloton.

"When developed, the riders at the front are exposed to higher loads and will tend to slip off the front in order to rejoin the pack farther back. With sufficient room to maneuver, this may develop into a fluid situation where the center of the peloton appears to be pushing through its own leading edge."

Speed, like drafting in race car driving, like you see on semi-trailers on the highway, in the Gran Fondo, several riders pass me and I decided to keep up instead of getting nervous or shaky or pissed off. I decided I'm going to keep up. Guess what? The peloton pulled me along. It was so much less work.

See how a peloton is a collaboration that makes the long road race much less work for those in it? Think of the Tour de France. Visualize the peloton in collaboration. A peloton felt like conflict to me then I learned how it would make my work easier. If I could keep up for more than a short distance, yes, I couldn't.

This summer I also rode in the great Kootenay Rockies Gran Fondo near Cranbrook, British Columbia, my home. By the way, thanks so much for the Sunrise Rotary in Cranbrook, Kimberly Rotary, the Wasa Lions Club, the Canadian Rockies International Airport, especially the hundreds of volunteers that make the Kootenay Rockies Gran Fondo one of the best anywhere and I'd say anywhere.

That weekend in early September, my grandkids Sara, who's six, and Quinn, who's eight, rode in their very first Kids' Fondo. We all had a great time.

Here's a potential conflict. After riding 90 kilometers or 55 miles, I crossed the Fort Steele Bridge riding towards the long hill, the Fort Steele hill that goes up for, I think it's about four kilometers and about an 8% grade. I was about 30 meters or 100 feet behind the group.

Suddenly, a large male grizzly bear came out of the highway ditch behind the group in front of me. He was a beautiful large, cinnamon-colored brown bear. The Kootenay Rockies have been called the Serengeti of North America by National Geographic. We live in an incredible, natural rocky mountain environment. Bears are common but I did not expect to have one run 30 meters in front of me and rise up on his back legs.

He was surprised to see me and I was surprised to see him. I stopped riding immediately. No bear mace. If you're backpacking or hiking, you got to have bear mace around here but not on a road bike on the blacktop. Nothing to protect me. I stopped and waited to see what he would do. After a 90-kilometer ride so far that day, I wasn't going to turn around. It isn't a very good idea to run away from bears anyway.

Looking at each other, we noticed something. We noticed that there was a truck coming down the hill from the opposite direction. My friend, Roger, was driving the truck. He saw what was happening and scared the bear back into the ditch. That grizzly ran away for a distance. Luckily, Roger stopped to look. While that truck was between me and the grizzly, I pedaled my ass up that hill. It was motivating.

Road bike races have shown me conflict with the peloton. I learned to use their energy and ride with less resistance. Road bike races gave me a grizzly bear. By stopping and not reacting, I found a way to where I needed to be. Embrace conflict. Don't fear it.

By the way another bear was on the road when my grandkids completed their Kids Fondo the next day. And as a volunteer guide rider, I did have my bear spray where I usually have my water bottle.

Today's show is Embrace Conflict. In my book "Break Through to Yes," I set out ten essential steps to collaboration. Last week, we talked about Be Aware. This week, we talk Embrace Conflict. Next week, Seek Diversity. Today's show, also, features two respected international leaders in conflict resolution and difficult conversations -- divorce and tough talk.

I'm grateful that over my 40 plus year career in agreement and relationship building and business development, I've met and become friends with so many amazing souls. Two more join us today. Our featured guests today are Esther Bleuel of California and Jeff Cohen of New York.

Key messages:

1) dialogue allows us to create meaning together, shared meaning;
2) conflict, if positively responded to, can generate possibilities and strong relationships;
3) ethics and standards provide integrity to any process that builds understanding, trust and, ultimately, agreement.

Let's look at the personal dynamics within your company. I'd been a leader in organizations for decades. I've, also, been a professional executive coach for the past eight years.

It seems the following challenges arise almost every coaching conversation I've had in the last number of months. How do I deal with a command control or bully boss? Does that resonate with you? Another question that I hear very often is; how do I deal with the team that's so negative and finds fault but rarely looks for resolution? The "Negative Nellies" that sit back and watch others are not productive.

When does the boss cross the line between assertiveness and being a bully? What self-awareness might grow when we increase our internal radar for when we may be crossing that line? What part of the negative team energy have you contributed to?

When are you ready for tough talk? How will you make the changes you need? These are profound questions. Profound questions that a coach can help you with and you can reflect on in this moment or today and tonight.

What about accountability? There is a line. If a team isn't accountable, then they do whatever they want. Where's the transition point from support to firing or letting them go? Send me your ideas, thoughts and share your solutions. I'll share them in future broadcasts.

Think about this. What about your accountability? What can you change that makes a difference, a positive difference when you're in a situation with a bully boss or you're leading a team that just seems immovable and negative?

Before we talk to Esther Bleuel, we're going to listen to my friend, Chuck Rose's song "Win or Walk Away."

David: We have Esther Bleuel from West Lake Village, California with us right now. Esther has agreed to talk to me. I've met Esther in Los Angeles about two years ago and she very much impressed me for her ability to do the tough talk.

Esther Bleuel, Master of Arts, provides training to empower employees to resolve conflicts successfully and with confidence and to deal with challenging people effectively.

Esther, thank you so much for giving your wisdom. One of the things that I am delighted is that so many great people like you have stepped up to collaborate with me on this radio show. Hello and just maybe provide a little more information on the work that you do, Esther.

Esther: It's very exciting to talk with you, David, because I so much respect your commitment to collaboration. I've been thinking about talking to you a little bit. It seems to me that, my background is in business and teaching and doing conflict and it seems to me that trust is the cornerstone of many things, certainly relationships.

With regard to you, collaboration, because true collaboration requires risk taking and when people don't feel safe and comfortable, they don't really open up and show up with their entire integrated self. When you come from a place of integrity and you can be clear about what you actually mean and you have the confidence to kind of know what you know, then you are available to listen deeply to other people.

I like the word "dialogue" more than the word "conversation" with regard to collaboration because dialogue really is to create meaning together and we have this experience when we we're together that I would say something that would spark an idea and you would add to it. Then I would think of something I hadn't thought of before based on what you said.

It's a true dialogue, which really began to be a collaboration, which is bigger than just one interaction. That ability to trust and when people come from a place of integrity then you're able to be compassionate and really not judgmental and really able to see different perspectives and hear different voices and then take risks.

That idea of even doing improv where you can connect things that you might not have thought of based on what's happening with other people in the process.

David: That sounds like incredibly rewarding work. Thank you for your friendship and your collaboration. Isn't that easier just for me to play small and hold my cards really tight and not trust you and let you do all the work?

Esther: Sure, it is but then we don't get too far and it's not very fun. I know you. You like to have fun.

David: Yes. It's just like wow. That was a fantastic response. I was expecting that from you, Esther. Play big and what I hear you say constantly in what you do with your clients has actually helped them to open up, express their needs.

Esther: I think the way that we learned is you would learn a skill and then you would practice it and try it. As you begin to internalize a learning or a lesson or a skill, you then have confidence with it. As you do that and start to share those things with other people, it's really exciting.

Sometimes you can prevent problems. Sometimes you have to fix them. Sometimes you get to create new ideas and solutions which is what you're doing -- really different new ways to look at things and to solve problems and imagine. It's exciting.

David: If you were to challenge our listeners to just one thing that they might be more aware of today, what might that be, Esther?

Esther: I think the thing that I see the most is that people, individuals, myself included have a hard time staying in their own chair and understanding that the power that you have when you are really in alignment with your words and actions and all that and you're in a place of integrity and then you can truly be available to hear somebody else and not be triggered, not react to them but should be able to be present with another person.

I think so often we get anxious, we get scared, aggravated, annoyed, worried, whatever and then we try to fix a problem. We try to make it be different and then we kind of start causing trouble, if you will when we are reaching out or getting out of our chair, so to speak.

The more you can stay grounded in your own self and be available to interact with somebody else, I think managing yourself, Goldman's emotional intelligence and social intelligence, when you can really, really live that, it's so powerful.

David: Yes. Now, together we're bringing collaborative intelligence. Esther Bleuel, toughtalkcoach.com. Thank you so much, Esther for your words of wisdom.

Esther: Thank you. Thank you, David. It was great talking to you.

David: Now, here's an excerpt from "Break Through to Yes". "Too often, leaders avoid conflict, give in, get reactionary or waste resources focusing on being right, punishing or paying off those who oppose." Yes, those who oppose are trouble.

"Such leaders provide an incentive to be a dysfunctional team. They create teams that are just like them -- homogeneous, groupthink, yes men. Yes women. Around the world, the best performing teams have one thing in common, they embrace conflict, hate 'groupthink' and seek out those who disagree and or challenge the team." Even better, challenge within the team.

"Avoiding conflict is a major mistake. Conflict is positive in many ways. It indicates that the organization employs and supports people who speak up for what is most important -- their values and those of the community's and stakeholders'. A high functioning team or organization finds their wisdom through adversarial perspectives. A high performing organization also embraces all personalities, strength, and styles."

"The different perspectives allow the organization to experience the responses and outcomes internally before the proposal or plan goes out the door. Leaders who embrace diverse perspectives and challengers from within will find their culture dynamic, inclusive, agile, and successful."

Consider this from my friend, Pierre Alvarez. Pierre is the former President to the Canadian Association of Petroleum Producers. "In a world where technologies such as smart phones, e-mail, and the cloud making working alone, isolated by both distance and time, the need for collaboration has never been greater." Yes, the need for collaboration has never been better but never been greater or better.

The business world, and in oil and gas in particular, must resist the temptation to use these tools as ways to avoid collaboration -- Emails, meetings, clouds, phones. Just talk face-to-face. Don't avoid conflict.

Pierre continues on, "Saying, 'I sent an e-mail' is just not good enough. Rather, business should use these tools to generate more effort and enthusiasm to work together with all stakeholders to resolve issues before they reach confrontation. If one believes the old adage that 'two heads are better than one', imagine the possibilities of harnessing the creativity and wisdom of thousands enabled by even faster and more inclusive technology." Thank you for that, Pierre.

In Canada, in small towns, small cities and around the world, the trend is to live and work in mega cities. Most youth want to live in large metropolises. Those of us who prefer to live in smaller cities and towns, for example in the Kootenay Rockies of British Columbia, are looking for ways for greater economic development.

Laura Hummelle, Becky Pelkonen and I have invested months and months, probably about a year now, working on economic development from a multi-stakeholder perspective to create a Center of Excellence where we build collaborative leadership skills amongst those regional leaders and their organizations.

We dream of creating a place where we can learn where the resources (money, assets, people, intelligence...) are; whether they're in Kimberly, BC, whether they're in Timbuktu, whether they're in Languedoc, France or Romania. Once we identify the network of resources then we seek out the resources that are most appropriate to any given opportunity. Then we take the highest priorities for economic development and move them forward together.

This is a slow process. Admittedly, even in my own backyard, I get frustrated because people think that means calling a meeting every three months and brainstorming. That's a start. That's just not good enough. More meetings with more of the same people in control do not make a peloton. They do not make that shift easier. It takes time to build that culture of collaboration.

We're going to take a break now. After the break, my good friend, Jeff Cohen will join us. Thank you.

David: On this International Conflict Resolution Day, I'm just so delighted to have my good friend, Jeff Cohen join us. Jeff has been mediator and facilitator in private practice since 1991, concentrating in the resolution of disputes involving business, commercial, organizational, workplace, labor, and domestic relations issues.

He is presently on a national mediation roster serving the United States Department of the Interior, a New York State roster mediating labor contracts for the Public Employee Relations Board, and is a mediator for the City of Albany, New York. Jeff also served on the Board of Directors because he just recently stepped off, of the Association for Conflict Resolution (ACR) from 2008 until 2014 and acted as Chairman of the ACR Ethics Committee.

Since completing his term on the ACR Board, Jeff continues as co-chair of the ACR Ethics Committee. Ethics are fundamental to Jeff. Nature is fundamental to Jeff Cohen. Action is a great friend. Jeff, I'll just stop talking. Tell me more about you and the work that you do.

Jeff: Oh boy. Well, the work that I do is mediation primarily. I do some facilitation work for larger groups as well, but my job is to help in most cases small groups and individuals collaborate because in fact that's what mediation really is. It's about helping folks eliminate or lessen fear. Some of the things Esther said earlier, I could just sit here and say, "Ditto." She was very articulate about these things.

Ethics are a very important part of my life, a very important part of how I practice. We can have that discussion now about what that is.

David: Yes. I think it's really important. For example, with my local Rotary Club yesterday, I did a presentation on values and ethics to our high school students. Rotarians are pretty giving, altruistic, strong, and trustworthy people generally. Every time we are lost or in conflict, we need to revisit this situation about what are ethics and how does that guide me. Tell us how you help guide us, Jeff.

Jeff: Okay. Let's start with the underlying framework. The ethics that I abide by are the standards of practice, model standards, if you will that were adopted by or approved by the American Bar Association in conjunction with the Association for Conflict Resolution, the organization that I'm involved with and the American Arbitration Association back in 2005.

On top of that, I abide by the ethical principles that I helped to create. I co-authored them about seven years ago, eight years ago. These are the ACR Ethical Principles, which are the lens through which we see, our organization sees and interprets the ethical standards.

From my standpoint, whether I'm working with a small group, a large group, just two individuals in a divorcing situation, I want to make sure they understand that there is integrity to the process. There are six areas where we talk about integrity.

Number one, the idea that mediation is about un-coerced self-determination of all issues by the participants, that it's not my job nor is it my in any way my thought that I am going to be making decisions for them. It's not a directive process by the person sitting in front of them. It is in fact their job and their choice to make their own decisions.

Secondly, I talk about that fact that I am impartial at all times. I'm on both of their sides and no sides, as I like to say. My job is to use the various interventions and techniques that I'm trained in to help them have, as Esther talked about, the dialogue, not a debate.

My job essentially is to change the culture of their conflict by creating a specific structure around their discussions so that they can perhaps see things differently. I like Albert Einstein's view of this where he says that, "No problem can be solved by the consciousness that created it. We must see the world anew." I see my role as the impartial facilitator, if you will or mediator has to help people see their conflict anew.

Number three, I have to talk to them about what a conflict of interest is and under what circumstances I may or may not be able to continue with the case or how we can avoid those things moving forward.

Appearance of impropriety we talk about. We talk about my competence. I'm not going to take a case if I'm not competent to do the work. It's important that they understand my training and my background. We talk about confidentiality, which is a very important concept.

Finally, we talk about quality of process. I find that when live folks come in to talk to me for an initial interview, they walk out feeling very safe and very comfortable because they understand the process. They understand that there is a set of standards, by the way which I give out to everybody that walks through the door so they can take them home with them.

David: Let me just ask, Jeff for our listeners, our audience today who are getting very interested in what you're saying, how can they access that information?

Jeff: Go to the Association for Conflict Resolution website. They will be able to download those ethical principles, even both the principles and the practice standards. They're all there.

There are also other ethics that relate to every single section at ACR. For example, there's a family section that has their own set of ethics. There's a workplace section, on and on and on. They all have similar practice standards that dovetail with these greater standards.

David: Thank you. I think that's a great resource and a reference. I'm hearing you say ethics is the foundation. You create a different structure and a big part of that is trust and openness. What else?

Jeff: Safety. Again, Esther talked about that. I see my role as a mediator is in creating shift, the shift from fear, trepidation, misunderstanding, too understanding. I see this as one of my initial interventions, if you will with groups is that I am going to, in the very beginning, make them feel safe and comfortable to the process.

In a way, it's a buy in to the process. If everybody's willing to drink my Kool-Aid, guess what? We're going to get something accomplished. Part of that is understanding my role and what it is that I do.

David: Yes. What's coming up for me, Jeff, is it's almost like a conundrum. "Well, Jeff and David are saying embrace conflict but then the first thing you want me to do is feel comfortable."

Jeff: Absolutely. There's a thread that...I can't remember. I would like to give credit where credit is due. Probably 30 years ago, I remember reading an article that stayed with me on mediation.

The thread is: number one, you create a safe space for people to come in to, whether in a large group, it's a U-shaped room or working within circles or whether it's in an open seating arrangement in a comfortable place for folks that are going through divorce; number one, you create a safe space.

Number two, you create the safe dialogue within that safe space. Again, it's my job to help them have the dialogue, not the debate. My job is to change the culture of how they conflict one another and to get them beyond their own automatic behaviors.

Again, whether it's an individual or an organization, we all have automatic behaviors and lenses through which we see a conflict. It's my job to take people 180 degrees or organizations 180 degrees from themselves so they can again, as Albert Einstein said, see their conflict anew.

Safe space, safe dialogue, what does that do? It creates understandings. For me, that's where the shifts tend to occur. It's, "Aha! I've never heard that before. Gee, I didn't understand that that's what you were trying to do in that circumstance."

Those types of things, those are those "aha" moments, the Holy Grail for a mediator. Those understandings, the dialogue and the understandings create the key word, "trust." Understandings and trust get to the agreement. It's that process.

David: Let's go a little bit back to that when the shift happens. It's fascinating to me that when that shift happens, it doesn't mean you agree with me. It's you understand me at that point.

Jeff: Absolutely.

David: Tell us a little more about the magic of that moment. To me, that is magic.

Jeff: It is magic because in all of the years that I've been doing mediation and facilitation work, I don't think we've been able to capture exactly when and in what circumstances that shift occurs. It's our job essentially to plow the fertile ground, plant the seed, and allow these shifts to happen. Sometimes it occurs as a result of following this general thread.

Of course, for everybody listening, there are hundreds of psychologically based interventions and techniques that are used throughout this thread to help folks to gain their understandings. There are times...I had a case that I like to talk about and I'll make it as brief as possible.

A very powerful, very wealthy couple, both of them used to getting their way, for four, five sessions I was getting nowhere with them. I came back to my office. I scratched my head. I pulled out Ken Cloke's book "Mediating Dangerously." I talked to a colleague. I came up with a whole set of questions to help these folks perhaps open their heart space.

I came back to the table with them the following day. I started asking them these questions. All of a sudden, he started to cry. It was the first time there was any chink in the armor at all. He started to cry. She put her hand on his knee. She stood up. She went over and hugged him at 6'4", 230 pounds.

I just disappeared in the room and let them have their cry and their discussion. They came back to the table and literally within the next two or three hours they resolved everything.

When I asked them later what happened, what was it about those questions? I was humbled in that moment because he said, "I had no idea where you were going with those questions. They didn't speak to me but what did speak to me was the fact that you were dedicated to our needs. You were dedicated to try to help us and I felt comfortable enough for the first time in my life to cry in the presence of a man."

Just being there and caring can create the shift as well. As I tell you this story in its very shortened fashion, I'm getting the hair going up on the back of my neck because that is magic. It wasn't what I intended but the process, going through the process it was something that came from it. It was unintentional on my part except for the fact that obviously I do care about my clients and I'm passionate about them.

David: Thank you, Jeff. You and I and many others are building the Collaborative Global Initiative. We don't have any time left to talk about CGI but I will mention that Duncan Autrey, Kathy Porter, Sarah Daitch, Charalee Graydon, and many others are creating this international network of mediators, facilitators, and system design professionals that provide assessment, training, facilitation, mediation, and process designs. This is to help multi-stakeholders work together to achieve common goals.

As we close this segment, Jeff, in this moment, what's one thing that you choose to invite our audience to do or become more aware of when it comes to collaboration?

Jeff: We all have automatic behaviors. If all of us are honest with ourselves, we know that when we conflict with others, it's always in the same way or has similar characteristics. I would invite everybody to be thinking about their own automatic behaviors and what you bring to the conflict.

I think this is a thread, I think Esther said something similar or you did. I think that that is incredibly important. Conflict is a matter of choice. The more aware we are of our own underlying natures, the less conflict we will have and the more understandings we can gain.

David: Thank you so much, my good friend, Jeff Cohen from Albany. Thanks, Jeff.

Jeff: Thank you. Be well.

David: Before the break, we were talking with Jeff Cohen. During the break, Jeff and I were saying, "Let's write a book called 'Shift Happens'." Shift does happen. Trust it. Trust the other that's standing up to me. Before that, we talked with Esther Bleuel about tough talk and seeing what's real but not necessarily easy.

I just want to take a moment. Tomorrow, I'll be going to this celebration of life, in Calgary, for another good friend, Dale Fisher. Dale and I wrote articles, spoke, created not-for-profits around conflict resolution and negotiation best practices. Condolences to Dale's family especially to Kyla who's doing this great work in Colorado now. Our listener, my listener, you, think about your legacy. Think what you can create from conflict.

Other friends, Doug Stone, and Shiela Heen along with Bruce Patton wrote an excellent book, some of you may be aware of, "Difficult Conversations: How to Discuss What Matters Most."

From that book, I want to give you a quote. "In difficult conversations, too often we trade only conclusions back and forth without stepping down to where most of the real action is -- the information and interpretations that lead each of us to see the world as we do." Yes. Step down. Find that shift.

Each week, I do an Outrage of the week because one of the things that we're doing with this Break Through To Yes and our collaboration is identifying those things that outrages on social media, by politicians, by corporate leaders, by environmental leaders. We're working so hard to, in this digital age, this connected age to circumvent those negative influences, those negative Nellies.

The Outrage of the Week, I want to talk about CO2 emissions and climate change. Jeff and Kathy Porter and others around the world and I in the Collaborative Global Initiative are planning Climate Adaptation Summits. Forget about the argument whether climate change is real or not and who caused it. Go to "what do we need to do when extreme weather happens?" and "How do we plan our infrastructure for greater resilience?"

Are fossil fuels bringing the death of mankind? Or is this a predictable weather trend that we've seen over the past ten thousand years? The fingers start pointing at each other. Then the money rolls in for environmentalist organizations and the government and industry...

Significant money rolls in to environmental organizations that are against the Canadian Oil Sands. I'm told that a significant part of the money that comes from billionaire American oilmen. Hm, interesting. Why would that be? A little bit of a conflict there. Integrity? Ethics? Fixing your own marketplace?

Fossil fuel energy producers are condemned. Renewable energy is seen as the only way to save ourselves. Then the learning pretty much disappears from all of that division and accusation and shaming, that outrage. What if we were looking at all of this conflict with "why"-ness? What if there is another perspective that has taken a back seat to this debate? What if the real inconvenient truth has little to do with where Al Gore pointed?

"Cowspiracy" on Netflix. Take a look. It's very well done, very interesting. A number of my friends and associates were talking about it so a couple of nights ago I watched it. As a Western Canadian who cares about the environment, business, and community, mention the name Leonardo di Caprio and our eyes may roll. We tire of multi-millionaire movie stars, rock stars, politicians who fly in their private jets to dump on Canadians about our Oil Sands and environmental stewardship then fly home without much dialogue and reality. Yes, I am proud of the Canadian industry and its environmental and social standards. We can compete on most every standard with any other nation and oil.

Leonardo, if you want to make a difference, take a look at Hollywood and California. If you want to talk about aboriginal rights and entitlements, opportunities, economic development, look at the carbon emissions from your own backyard. Look at what you've done with those who are not like you.

To Leonardo's credit, he's the Executive Producer of "Cowspiracy." "Cowspiracy" became so interesting that people like Leonardo jumped on and helped it. Thank you for that.

Here's a reading from the Cowspiracy that's conspiracy but with cows. "Cowspiracy may be the most important film made to inspire saving the planet." Another quote, "A documentary that will rock and inspire the environmental movement."

According to Wikipedia, "'Cowspiracy: The Sustainability Secret' is a 2014 documentary film produced and directed by Kip Andersen and Keegan Kuhn. The film explores the devastating impact of animal agriculture on the environment, and investigates the policies of environmental organizations on this issue. Environmental organizations investigated in the film include Greenpeace, Sierra Club, Surfrider, Rainforest Action Network, and many more."

While the Canadian Oil Sands and perceived inaction by oil companies, the Provincial and Federal governments of Canada are the target of most every activist communications coming from Washington, from London, from all over the world. "Damn you, Canadians and your Oil Sands." Guess what? They Oil Sands are responsible for the less than 1% of global carbon emissions.

What is responsible? According to "Cowspiracy," ranching and agriculture are responsible for a huge part of the greenhouse gas emissions. Why target oil sands and not cows? Why are the environmental activists decided to deceive?

Watch "Cowspiracy" for some insights. It's very interesting. It's engaging, well done. It makes me think of becoming vegan. Truly. They've got a 30-day challenge, vegetarian or vegan challenge and I'm going to do that.

Watching any of this, whether it's an Oil Sands executive or whether it's Leonardo di Caprio or Neil Young or President Obama or Hillary or the Donald, where's the balance?

For decades, we've known that methane from the animals and the clearing of the Amazon is hugely destructive. What changed now? According to the United States Environmental Protection Agency, "Agriculture is responsible for 14% of 2004 greenhouse gases." 14% compared to far less than 1%.

The producers of "Cowspiracy" tried many times to get the reality, get the environmental groups to own up. Guess what? It didn't work. They didn't want to talk. I'm running out of time but what I want to say is find out. Talk to ranchers, the environmentalists, the oil people in your network and get your truth. And, let's reduce the arguments and shaming Let's fix the problems and learn together how to change our future.

Today, we explored the wisdom of Esther Bleuel and Jeff Cohen. Thank you for your insights, Jeff and Esther. This week's key messages are: dialogue helps us create meaning together; conflict can generate possibilities and strong relationships; and ethics and standards provide integrity to any process that builds understanding, trust and, ultimately, agreement.

Next week's show is Seek Diversity. We have Joan Goldsmith and Amy Elizabeth Fox, internationally respected women in leadership in organizational development.

Thank you very much for your time today. Embrace conflict. Look forward and see how you can turn it positive. Thank you.

Chapter 7 Seek Diversity featuring Joan Goldsmith and Amy Fox

David: Is there anybody out there? Is there anybody out there? Is there anybody out there? Sounds kind of lonely, almost like "The Wall," 1979 from Pink Floyd. Is there anybody out there? Sometimes we broadcast, we talk, we get on the phone, we send e-mails, we send press releases, we send memos to our divisions, and we wonder whether anybody is out there.

This is the seventh episode of our Voice America Break Through to Yes with Collaboration show. In this channel, through this channel, I've got the potential, I'm a long way from it but I've got the potential of reaching 3.6 million listeners in 160 countries. That's pretty damn good.

No one may be listening. Is there anybody out there? Are my friends in Kerrobert, Saskatchewan out there? Are my Languedoc, France friends out there? Is my friend, Esther Bleuel in California out there? Give me an answer. Send me an e-mail with the heading "I'm here". Let's start a chain. Let's start a collaboration. I'd like to hear your thoughts, hear that you're out there then whatever you want to talk about.

A big reason for my coaching and consulting, my books, and this radio show is to circumvent the increasingly perverse collaborations evidenced in organizations, media, social media, and politics. Yes, perverse. If you've listened to prior shows, I coined the term about three years ago, four years ago, mediots. Those are the ones that act to trigger our reptilian brains into judgment, separation, and anger or joy or fun.

I watch John Oliver on Last Week Tonight. He triggers my reptilian brain and it's in the positive. Oftentimes in America, in the Netherlands and everywhere we hear things, we read things and we just get enraged.

Let's come together here through this radio show, through my book, and through your "I'm here" e-mail. Join me in circumventing these toxic relationship patterns with the internet. With telephones and with travel today, we make connects with an estimated four billion, that's a billion, people in the world.

When bad things are happening, when great things are happening, and when we simply want to reach out to people with diverse backgrounds, expertise and perspectives, go beyond the established systems and processes and organizations and media to connect and learn together, to collaborate.

Yes, collaborate. Don't get spoon-fed what they want us to know -- their truth, their interests. I believe we're only separated to anyone in the world by two degrees of separation today, not six degrees, two. As I dream of incredible collaboration, that dream includes reaching out to people that are very different from me.

Turn off your stupid TV shows or if you have to watch TV, watch Al Jazeera, watch the BBC, watch the Chinese news. Get a sense of what the world is thinking. We in North America tend to think we're at the center of the universe. We're not. We are one. Now is our time to lead more powerfully. Leaders in companies will make this essential shift now.

Listeners, today's show is titled Seek Diversity. In my book "Break Through to Yes" I set out ten steps that are essential to successful collaboration. Last week, we talked about Set Intention.

During these shows, I'll walk you through every one of the essential ten steps. Each step is a theme in this radio show. Next week, it's Design the Collaboration.

This show features two world leaders in leadership in organizational development. Our featured guests are Joan Goldsmith of Santa Monica, California, organizational development expert and coach to many great leaders. I'm delighted to introduce you to both women.

The other guest is another organizational development and leadership expert, Amy Elizabeth Fox of Mobius Leadership in Boston and around the world. Both Amy and Joan have world influence and certainly my respect.

Key messages for today:

1) bring in many perspectives to make your collaboration more successful,
2) the answer to "Is there anybody out there?" is yes, of course. I'm getting the analytics on this show and I'm just delighted. We've got a lot of people listening and people are starting to pay attention and talk back, and
3) we need to look for ways of caring for our mothers and grandmothers. They are our wisdom. They provide us diverse perspectives. Their life is very different than ours and our grandchildren.

Here's an excerpt from "Break Through To Yes". "Diversity and experience, expertise, personality traits and types, and knowledge are all cited as critical aspects of successful collaboration."

My friend, David Milia of the Haskayne School of Business at the University of Calgary gave me this quote "Ask yourself, does collaboration mean that everyone must agree with everyone else? Can we collaborate when our selfish polarized views are in conflict with those we should be collaborating with?"

In business, we have a name for a group of folks who all get along and all have the same opinion on something. It's called groupthink. It is not good for business. I would put forward that true collaboration is a willingness to have a set of people with diverse competencies, worldviews, and experiences.

With the added ingredient of wanting to pursue a clear and concise objective: come together in a safe space to talk about their position and how they would hope to add value to reach that objective even if they're not in alignment together. Thanks, David Milia for that.

Let's look at the primary information source for most of us today, the internet. In addition to mediots, I also invented a word or at least I believed I invented "Googlization" about three years ago. Googlization is our information flow severely limits the nature of the data we're provided and diversity of perspectives we see.

We have been warned by Eli Pariser in "Filter Bubbles" that our internet searches only give us information that is consistent with our previous searches and the content of our online communications.

If you don't believe that, seek out two people in our network in different nations and have different networks and different perspectives and type different words in your e-mails. Then at a precise pre-arranged time, each of you, whether it's two or ten of you, ask the same question. See what happens.

Here's one that I did a couple of years ago: Will America ever collaborate with Russia again? When I searched this, I got 323 million results. I expect a contact in Russia will get 323 million results as well. I expect others searching will see very different results than mine. Here's your opportunity to learn and get away from the "Googlization effect".

Seek different people, different political affiliations, religions, education, nationality, career, and other differentiators to help reveal your truth, your considerate truth, your informed truth.

There's a great book "The Formula: How Algorithms Solve All Our Problems and Create More" by Luke Dormehl. I read that about six months ago. Excellent book. How algorithms solve all our problems and create more. We learned that most of us trust the objective and non-judgmental results scientific based algorithm provides us as compared to perceptions and judgments of humans.

Dormehl, however, warns us that algorithms are constructed by humans and therefore have shown to be subject to human prejudices, beliefs, and judgments. They limit our vision. Algorithms are so powerful and we're being spoon-fed what the algorithm thinks we need to know or will sell us the best thing or will track us, whatever.

Think about the diversity in your organization. Think about the diversity in your network. Where are the gaps? What's missing? Where are your blind spots? What source of information or conversation or relationship may save you from making decisions based on incomplete information?

Think of something that's very simple. Think about a process, even a perception. Think about considering communication. Today for most of us in the world, texting by cellphone is a primary communication tool. Think about what happens when you e-mail. You get more information out there but often not easily understood, the tone, the message, the emotion. Think about the telephone and then think about meeting.

Isn't that interesting that we've preferred, we've gone down the route of typing with two thumbs very brief, staccato messages. Humanity started with meeting in person. Alexander Graham Bell showed us the telephone. Then we found e-mail about 30 years ago and then texting about ten. We're going the wrong way.

After the break, we'll talk with Amy Elizabeth Fox of Boston and later Joan Goldsmith of Santa Monica. These are two great women who encourage, challenge, and inspire me. I hope they inspire you, too.

David: Listeners, we have Amy Fox, an international entrepreneur, leadership and change agent specialist. Amy is the co-founder and leader at Mobius Leadership. Amy, there is just so much to say about you, the consulting group that you have and your heart and spirit that you have for leaders and senior leaders around our globe. Tell us a little more about yourself and Mobius.

Amy: Let me just say I'm absolutely delighted, David to join you and your listeners and have a chance to talk about the work that we're doing. As you mentioned, Mobius was co-founded by my sister, Erica Ariel Fox and myself. Erica is a longtime lecturer at the Program on Negotiation at Harvard Law School.

She and I together have been teaching the body of work that has emerged from PON over the last 20 years as a real international think tank but also cross-disciplinary consortium that's been looking at best practices for mediating disputes, resolving conflict, and peacemaking efforts around the world.

In particular, we've been very focused on skills for leaders in both the public and the private sector for managing difficult conversations, for building high-performing teams, for creating organizational cultures that really thrive on qualities such as authenticity, transparency, giving and receiving really candid feedback, developing people.

Perhaps underneath all of that, David I would describe it as how do you build an organizational frame or sense of inspiration and engagement with the mission and purpose of the organization in a way that everyone regardless of where they sit in that organization can feel a part of that, a sense of connection to that in a really meaningful sense of being tied to something greater than themselves.

Mobius was founded in 2005 and is built on a network model. We have about 250 facilitators, trainers, coaches, mediators who work with us serving clients. That gives us just this rich tapestry of expertise and methodology and also sense of community honestly for those of us that are practicing within Mobius that I think is part of the aliveness that clients find when they work with us.

David: Wow. I'm hearing inner emotional intelligence. I'm hearing a corporate culture. Big important work. Amy, why is it so important for a leader to focus on their inner life or emotional intelligence?

Amy: I think that because most business climates and I think this is true whether you're operating in the social sector or in a big corporation or experiencing in this moment in time such a sense of volatility and ambiguity about the future that we're all facing that executives are under disproportionate or a unique sense of pressure and emotional volatility.

In that context, if you want to be able to lead others, create followership, and keep the organization having an aligned execution focus, you really have to be able to help people manage that stress and manage their energy.

Many, many of our clients are spending a lot more time thinking about not just developing people and their technical expertise, whether it's legal expertise in a law firm or strategy expertise in a strategy firm or technical expertise in a high-tech company or medical expertise in a pharmaceutical.

Of course, you need to do that but all of those different industries are starting to realize that there's what's now called kind of a vertical development that has to happen in tandem with that which is really about emotional accountability and emotional self-management, energy management, and how to create high performing dynamics among the people.

Exactly as you said, it's both an intrapersonal skill -- how do I manage myself as well as interpersonal sophistication -- how do I influence and coach others.

David: Complimentary to that work and your work in everything that you and I have communicated together within the last probably eight years now, Amy.

Amy: Yes.

David: Your sister and my friend, Erica Ariel Fox published the New York Times bestseller, "Winning From Within." Tell us a little more about that work.

Amy: I'd love to. Erica, as I mentioned, is a longtime lecturer at PON and had the privilege of being a direct protégé and student of Roger Fisher, its founder and Bill Ury and Bruce Patton, some of its greatest thinkers and was involved for many, many years teaching this seminal work that came out of PON introducing into the culture the concept of win-win or value creation principle of negotiation.

One of the key ideas in that book, Getting to Yes, was separate the people from the problem by which Roger sensibly meant, rather than seeing the other party as your adversary, what if you were both able to sidle up to each other on the same side of the table and see the issues that you're negotiating as your joint problem.

That was a really powerful, powerful set of technology that's being used still today as best practice. What Erica and other colleagues found as they were starting to mediate real disputes and dealing with pretty intractable global conflict was in many cases that methodology was a Break Through and pivotal but in some cases really insufficient because there was such long-held enmity that sometimes the people really are the problem.

Everyone listening I'm sure can think of situations in which they're negotiating with somebody informally or formally in their personal or professional life where they're thinking to themselves, "This would just be so easy if the other person wasn't so darn difficult."

The second body of work that Program on Negotiation (PON) undertook was to really look at the human dynamics or the people dynamics in the negotiation or problem solving or collaboration. That research was summarized in a book by our friends Bruce Patton and Doug Stone and Sheila Heen a little over ten years ago called "Difficult Conversations: How To Discuss What Matters Most."

It's a wonderfully rich resource for people particularly when they're dealing with interpersonal conflict. Erica and I thought that worked for a long time and Mobius does continue to offer a Masterful Conversations course based on Doug and Sheila and Bruce's book.

What we found there was as we started to use that set of technology, we were still seeing what Erica coined as "a really fascinating performance gap," where even in the most senior most, very skillful, very mature executive, there was a gap between their intrinsic skills, what they knew to do in theory, what they have learned from courses or years of experience and what they actually did in the heat of the moment.

That gap between their potential and their actual behavior was causing them significant downsides in business-critical conversations. Erica started researching what, if any additional advice could we give people for managing themselves so that they can actually bring their best self to the key interaction particularly when the stakes were very high for the business.

In a sense, Erica started asking a different question, not what if the people are the problem but what if you're the problem? What if you're getting in your own way in such a way that is causing collateral damage all around you?

Her book "Winning From Within" is I think a brilliant, wonderful synthesis of that research. Very, very practical advice for people about how to close that performance gap.

David: Yes. I'm not sure what to say because that strikes me as so true and I just love the work that you and Erica are doing and Mobius Consultants.

Amy: Thank you. The other thing that is interesting about Erica's book, David, that would be of interest to your listeners is that she's really captured the inner negotiations that we all face every day. Introducing the notion that it's not really the case that we're singular in our thinking or approach but to quote Whitman, "We're sort of made up of multitudes."

How can you focus on what perhaps is the most important negotiation of all which is the negotiation with those different voices inside your head? She's used sort of the metaphor of the inner C-suite to codify or sort of capture, encapsulate these various inner negotiators.

On the one hand, you have the CEO or the dreamer aspect of you who innovates and thinks about the future and can intuit and sense possibility and imagine worlds that don't currently exist. Often, the part of the organization that is really holding the vision that everyone is aligning around.

Then you have the inner COO, the part of you that's in execution mode or warrior from an archetypal perspective who's not only leading in to action and taking steps but also setting boundaries and saying no.

The inner VP of HR, you might say or lover dimension of you whose building trust and rapport and goodwill, building the strong relationship, cause these relationships that many clients for example want from their financial planners or their legal consultants or their strategy consultants. Many, many professional services firms, for example put a very strong focus on cultivating that trusted advisor or lover dimension.

The final one, of course, is the inner thinker, the aspect or dimension of you that's thinking about risk, doing problem solving, doing analytics. You could think of that as the sort of CFO function.

How many of us have really cultivated or paid attention to one or two of those dimensions of our inner C-suite unless aside or in shadow? Other dimensions or important leadership capabilities which we're able to bring them back online and have a wider range or move more fluidly between those four energetics or voices or action moves would have such more amplified impact in every dimension of our business life and our personal life, frankly.

It's not unusual for clients to come to our programs and have their family members send us thank you notes afterwards. Often, that's so touching to know that these programs, these immersive programs that we offer help people not just in their organizational life but in their family life.

David: The programs do really change lives and dynamics. In collaboration, Amy, oftentimes, we think we need to pair ourselves up, getting in a circle of complementary skills. With your work and Erica's work, it's, also, from those dimensions, from those different C-suites and places it's learning how to relate to those people and it's also developing those skills so we're not out of balance.

Amy: Absolutely. Erica's bias I think is to say that everybody is intrinsically capable of bringing any of those capacities forward. Every leader has each of those dimensions available to them. It's often the case they just have been probably disproportionately dependent on certain capabilities and not placed attention on really ensuring that they have that full range at their disposal.

You're absolutely right. At one level you could say, "Am I bringing all those voices in response to another person?" Another interesting question to ask is "Am I capable of hearing, receiving, and discerning each of those voices when I'm on the receiving end of someone else's communication or comments?" Or, "What voices do I tune out because I undervalue them?" "What's the cost of all that miscommunication?" I think is another really interesting question.

David: Thank you so much. Amy Fox, co-founder of Mobius Leadership. Thank you, Amy.

Amy: My pleasure, David. Take care.

David: Now we've Joan Goldsmith. Yes, we have Joan Goldsmith. For our global listeners, Joan is a friend of mine and somebody that I truly, truly look up to as a leader in organizational development, education, and leadership.

Joan has been an organizational consultant coach and educator for the past 45 years. She specializes in conflict resolution, leadership development, and team building. She's been a family therapist, a coach to women leaders, and co-author with Warren Bennis of the bestselling "Learning to Lead: A Workbook On Becoming a Leader." She has co-authored three books with Ken Cloke on a variety of related topics.

Joan, welcome. I could just talk for the whole show about the accomplishments that you've done in the role of leadership development, leadership development for women, and conflict resolution. What would you prefer to say in your own words about your background and the work that you do?

Joan: David, I'm very happy to be with you. I think probably what I want to say most of all is that I am so inspired by people like yourself who have taken the field of conflict resolution and leadership development to many new places that I never dreamed of when I first became involved in the early 1960's.

I would like very much to support any efforts that are taking place now in supporting grassroots people especially women but all grassroots families in being leaders in their own lives and in their own communities.

My initial work in community was in Chicago when in 1964 when I walked through Robert Taylor Homes, a 15-story housing project for poor families to talk with women about would they like to have an early childhood education program for their children, would they like to create a school together.

They invited me in to their kitchen. These were mostly African-American families and I'm Caucasian. There was great trust. There was no hesitation. These women committed themselves to creating a school, which we did and they taught their own children to read and write in preschools.

Those preschools continue to grow and develop. President Obama worked in the same housing project probably ten years after I was there. He continued the community organizing there and has continued it as our President.

David: Wonderful, meaningful work. In your book "Learning to Lead," that's attracted a lot of worldwide attention, what are some of the key messages there, Joan?

Joan: The most important message I think was stated so beautifully by my colleague, Warren Bennis who passed to the other side, died when he was 89 a year ago. He said, "Becoming a leader is becoming an authentic person, becoming your own person."

My work in leadership has been, especially with women, to encourage women to listen to their own voice, to make choices that are best for them, their families, their communities, and to hold leadership roles in simple, small ways at work and at home and in the community.

For example, there's a block party where Ken Cloke and I live tomorrow. It's been organized by women volunteers. Little signs on the trees, little notes in mailboxes, women are organizing this block party to create a safe and welcoming community in a working-class neighborhood that's quite diverse and quite grassroots. We're very excited about it. I'm so proud of the women who organized it.

David: Wow. Very powerful stuff and very personal stuff coming home. Our listeners and I am listening to your voice and thinking, "Joan really slows it down and holds us." Even in the way you speak, Joan, you speak so that we can really slow ourselves down.

Joan: I'm glad to hear that. My focus began in 2000 in working with women because I've learned internationally from a woman whose name is Graça Machel. She's the second wife to Nelson Mandela. She was his wife when he died. She had been the wife of Samora Machel who had led the independence of Mozambique from the colonial power of Portugal.

Graça Machel told me personally that she was committed to working on rehabilitating child soldiers. They young boys especially who were taken into the army and made killers in Africa.

The way she was rehabilitating them was bringing them home to their mothers and grandmothers because she said that the women in the family understand that violence is not a solution. They're the peacekeepers. They are the women who hold the communities together.

Wangari Maathai, who was named the Nobel Peace Laureate about five years ago, won the Nobel Prize because she was finding many women joining her in ending the dead encroaching desert in their land in Kenya.

The way she did it was she just very simply planted a tree, planted a tree in her yard. Other women saw that that tree was holding the soil so they planted a tree. She created a peaceful network. It's not just about planting trees. It's about joining hands with women to end violence and create peace.

David: Wonderful. Joan, you reminded me of one of the most respected Canadian First Nations Chiefs, Chief Clarence Louie of the Osoyoos band. I had the opportunity to meet with Clarence a few years ago. He has been so successful in making his band an economic powerhouse and respected from all nations.

When I asked him, "What's your inuksuk? What's your talisman? Where do you go to get your wisdom?" He said something very similar to what you just shared with us. "I asked myself what would my grandmothers tell me?"

Joan: Ah, yes. As a grandmother, what I would like to tell you and our listeners is that we have a crisis in the US. The largest population of homeless people in the United States is elderly women and in part because women are the first to be fired, they're paid less.

I don't know if you saw the figures from the Senate Budget Committee, the US Senate. The median weekly earnings for full-time workers in 2015 was $801 but for female full-time workers it was $726. Women are earning less in the US.

Worldwide, the UN has let us know that in the last census they did which is 2010, professional women -- doctors, lawyers, managers, professors were on the whole earning 76 cents on the dollar compared to men worldwide. As women we need to unite and we need to speak up and we need to ask what we deserve for our good work.

David: As people, we need to do all those things.

Joan: Yes, that's true. That's true.

David: In the spirit, Joan of collaboration, as we close this interview, one of the questions I want to ask you is how would you challenge our listeners to make those changes for your audience, for women and particularly elderly women? What can we ask of our listeners in either awareness or action?

Joan: I think we need to teach our daughters, the younger generation to value themselves and ask for what they need and want. We need to look for ways of caring for our mothers and grandmothers, having them live with us, having them be cared for.

In every organization where we work or we interface, we need to ask, "Are women being treated with the same level of respect and are they being valued with the same income and the same job opportunities as their male colleagues?

David: Thank you. Joan Goldsmith, how do people find you online? How do they connect with you? This is such a powerful piece that you've given us.

Joan: Thank you, David. It's been wonderful being with you. Bye-bye.

David: Welcome back, listeners. During this show we've heard the wisdom of Amy Fox and Joan Goldsmith. Amy talked about the importance of personal mastery and her sister's and my friend's, Erica Ariel Fox, author of bestselling book "Winning from Within." Yes, it's a great book. Read it. It's about personal mastery and archetypes.

Joan talked about elderly women. She brought elderly women in to the conversation and the sadness of seeing elderly women in Santa Monica on the street. Our culture in North America is very different from many cultures.

In so many cultures, elderly women are considered the crone, the matriarch, the wise woman, and are seen as central to the current and future health of our communities and the communities that they've served, they've nurtured, and they've grown up in.

In North America not so much. Consider what you might learn from elderly women in your life, in your community. Let's bring them back with grace, with love, and in collaboration. They're a gift. Let's collaborate. Let's respect. Let's not send them away.

At this point, we have a little bit of fun each week. This is time for Outrage of the Week. Still not sure whether I should change that from W-E-E-K to W-E-A-K because I think it is the outrage of the weak. That's where we get in to reptilian brain reactions.

I have been thinking about Outrage of the Week and I've been doing some posting on social media for the last year about outrage of the week. There's just so many outrages to choose from. I will try to pick ones that are generally understood and sensed from where you are, my listener.

Recently, Planned Parenthood in the United States has been a big deal for the extreme right of the United States politicians and leaders in communities. Another one for Canadians is Montreal, pumping billions of liters of raw sewage into Saint Lawrence River. Another one is Russia actively bombing in Syria.

Outrage. Outrage. Outrage. Of course, when you look into what's true and what's your true, what your global community can teach you, you find very interesting insights and rationale and interests and perspectives. In this broadcast, we're taking about inclusion, respect, and collective learning.

We go another direction for this week's weekly Outrage. This is kind of fun. It is global because it's two women that live in the city that I spent most of my life in, Calgary, Alberta, Canada developing an app. They've been in the world media. They've been on Last Week Tonight with John Oliver. They've been all over the place.

The Times of India reported on October 3rd, "Peeple," this is the Peeple app, perhaps you've heard of it, "is an app," this is a quote from The Times of India. "Peeple is an app for rating and commenting about those who one interacts with in daily life personally, professionally or romantically."

"According to forthepeople.com website, 'Founders and close friends, Julia Cordray and Nicole McCullough,' yes, they're from Calgary, defended their creation 'as an online venue for praise and constructive feedback.' A firestorm of criticism at Twitter, Facebook, and other online venues countered that the creators of Peeple were either naively or intentionally downplaying how nasty commentary can get on the internet."

That's the quote from The Times of India. What were they thinking? What were they thinking? This is the internet. The internet, social media has not become the place of conscious communications. It's the place of mediots. Peeple still plans to launch in November. We'll see what happens with that.

We can easily understand why the Peeple app may be offensive. What gives me, David Savage, permission to publicly rate you? What is the value to me being rated by others? Yelp rates restaurants fairly or unfairly. Peeple, yes, yes Peeple; I'm going to think about that. Isn't Peeple more destructive? It's intrusive at least, at least if not abusive.

So much of our discussions today about leadership generally focused on the value of curiosity. Yes, curiosity, inclusion, what is that? Why would we have something that rates people? That separates. If you seek diversity, be curious, restrain judgment, and come together for the greater good. I think you'll have a greater good. Peeple appears to appeal to the exact opposite.

What are the conversations that are going on between Julia and Nicole at Peeple? How have they understood this outrage? How will they adapt and revise the app? How will they learn and break through to their yes?

Think about the early years of Facebook. Initially, Facebook was a rating system for peers and dates and women and professors at Harvard but they started stealing information and ideas from MySpace and another group at Harvard and they built something very unique and very progressive and then it changed. Nicole and Julia, think about breaking through to your yes.

Today we've heard the collaborative wisdom of Amy Elizabeth Fox of Mobius and Joan Goldsmith. Thank you, Joan and Amy.

This week's key messages again: bring in many perspectives to make your collaboration more successful, seek diversity; secondly, the answer to "Is anybody out there?" is yes. According to my analytics, I have over a thousand listeners around the world. Hello, USA, Canada, France, India, Philippines, China, Romania, Netherlands, and Saskatchewan. I think Saskatchewan is a country, isn't it? Third key message, we need to look for more ways of caring for ourselves, for our communities, and especially as Joan points, our mothers and our grandmothers. They are our wisdom.

Next week's show and guests are, the theme being Design the Collaboration, Richard Schultz of Wisdom Ways, Laura Hummelle, Ahead of the Curve, and Colin Campbell, Guidance Planning.

My call to action for you as we close this show: seek diversity in every team, meeting, project, and organization. Bringing people together that don't think like you will protect you from your own blind spots. With higher awareness and respect for others, more and more of us are seeing the manipulations and intellectual dishonesty too often represented in the media and social media.

Thank you for your time, your diversity, your collective and collaborative awareness. Thank you. Please seek diversity.

Chapter 8 Design the Collaboration, featuring Richard Schultz, Laura Hummelle, Colin Campbell

David: *Who are you? One. I was raised to do one thing. Today the force awakens.* Now, that's a pretty lame imitation but you know the commercial, the trailer. This is not in a universe far, far away. This is around our planet with people like you, we move from command and control leadership—that's kind of like Darth Vader—to collaborate leadership.

Luke, we are your father! We have everything to fight for. I have my life-saber charged and ready. Let's move forward! This week, in Calgary, Alberta, my collaborative global initiative meets for strategy sessions. We Are Duncan Autry of Oakland, California, Kathy Porter of Vancouver, British Columbia, Jeff Cohen of Albany, New York, Sara Daitch of The Netherlands, Doreen Liberto Blancke of San Luis Obispo, California, and me, David B. Savage of Cranbrook, British Columbia.

Our Collaborative Global Initiative is an international network of mediators, facilitators, system design professionals and coaches that provide assessment training, facilitation, mediation and process design services to help multiple stakeholders work together to achieve common goals. We focus on projects where organizations and individuals with differing interests require effective communication and learning across perspectives, cultures, and sectors to help all parties to achieve sustainable, cost-efficient solutions. We work with any scale or complexity of conflicts and will work anywhere, but only for select clients—those that are ready to make the change.

So today, our show is titled, *Design the Collaboration.* In this *Design the Collaboration* with our CGI team, it's more than meetings, more than getting together. We live in various locales around the world. But when we designed our collaborative meeting in Calgary this week, we ensured we included not only vision and inclusion and strategy and maybe the odd PowerPoint and flip chart and virtual meeting technology to bring in our representatives from Spain, but in our gathering, we also designed our time with hiking to Stanley Glacier in Kootenay National Park and hiking the old Growth Forest Trail at Island Lake near Fernie, British Columbia. We enjoyed food together at the River Café on Princes' Island in Calgary and at St. Eugene Mission near Cranbrook.

We met with Laura Hummelle and Becky Pelkonen of Kimberley, British Columbia, with whom I'm building the Center of Excellence in Collaborative Leadership, and introducing my CGI co-founders to my wife, Lise, and members of my family—my daughter, Alissa and her family. My point is that we combined two days of strategy sessions in Calgary and two days of fun, hiking and family in Cranbrook. How do you design your collaboration? By including activity and nature, meetings are far healthier, fun and innovative and our brains open up beyond their common pathways. Yes, thinking about the force awakens. Duncan, Jeff, and I will be Jedi Knights this Halloween with my young grandkids, Quinn and Sara Amos. I love Halloween with my grandkids—it's just so much fun. We get to play. And now, they get to play with my friends from Oakland and Albany.

So, we will work to clear the Darth Vaders from our planet from their future. The next generation of leaders will be collaborative leaders.

The world heard nine days ago that the people of Canada elected a new government and will soon have a new Prime Minister. I salute everyone in every nation for serving their people in democratic processes'. I salute those who put their name on the ballot for political position. I salute democracy. Remember Winston Churchill's advice? Democracy is the worst form of government except for all the others. Now, more than ever before, I salute the indigenous peoples and the 18-35-year olds for getting out and voting. Now, what happened in Canada's elections, I hope is a signal. Leaders in the Republican Party in America and the Conservative Party in Canada are seen too often—they're not really this way but they brand themselves this way—to be all about creating fear, separation, and disrespect of others. Separation, be afraid, vote for me. Unless you vote for me, your family will be exposed to terrorists, and your bank account will be plundered by those other folks.

To be clear, I am fiscally conservative and socially liberal. I haven't voted anything but Conservative federally since my late '20s. I'm a serial entrepreneur and a businessman. I love business and I seek Conscious Capitalism. That's capitalism with a heart and with a look into the future and the shared future; conscious capitalism. This election, I did not vote Conservative. I'm repelled by ignorance, fearmongering and separation. Almost 70% of eligible Canadian voters marked their ballots. Fantastic! Justin Trudeau's Liberal Party won a majority of 184 seats. That's 148 more than they had four years earlier. Four years earlier—two years earlier—they were near death and they got a majority government.

Justin Trudeau talks about inclusion, respect, vision, leadership and possibility. In his 2014 book, *Common Ground*, Trudeau stated, "I have a strong sense of this country—where it has been, how it became great and how it can be even better in the future. We have problems to tackle but they are no larger than the ones we have solved in our shared past. And solve them, we will, the way we always have, by building on common ground". Yeah, he talks about common ground. That is collaboration. That is inclusion, diversity, resolution, listening, commitment, dedication, so that we—Trudeau always talks about 'we'. So, we Canadians are hopeful for our new government. And yeah, the problems are going to be difficult. The expectations may be too high.

But thinking about my 10 Essential Steps for Collaboration, the new government and the people of Canada have set a new intention, and we intend to seek common ground with vision and awareness, not separation and fear. The government of Canada is at this very moment, designing their collaboration. Now is our time to lead more consciously and collaboratively, to make our world a better place and the future a better place. In my book, Design the Collaboration is step 5 of my 10 steps. Take a look at my website for more information.

This show features three respected leaders who are also my friends, people I greatly respect. Richard Schultz of WisdomWays, Calgary, Alberta, Laura Hummelle, Ahead of the Curve Consulting of Kimberley, British Columbia, and Colin Campbell, Guidance Financial Planning of Cranbrook, BC. The key messages that we're bringing to you in this episode of *Break Through to Yes* are;

1) In are true co-creative space, we are enriched individually and collectively. Yeah, individually and collectively

2) Where firms used to employ a sales team years ago, we now work collaboratively with our clients, customers, employees and communities—and that creates greater business. Yeah, it's not sales. It's service. It's collaboration. It's working together.

3) By learning more about the necessary pre-conditions and best practices of collaborative leadership, you will become more successful. Take the time. Learn. Do. Act.

At the top of the show, we contrasted our collaborative expertise to that of the command and control like Darth Vader of Star Wars. I agree that the force is awakening but rather than buying tickets to Hollywood blockbusters that separate ourselves from our own courage and power and wisdom, I encourage you everywhere to turn towards your community and your own network when you design your collaboration. Imagine circles and spirals. Spend far less time in top-down hierarchies and minimize meeting around rectangular boardroom tables.

The great indigenous Canadian artist, Buffy St. Marie, has released a new and critically-acclaimed album, *Power in the Blood*. Buy it. It's really good. Here's a song I particularly like: *We Are Circling*. While I don't have the rights yet to broadcast Buffy's music, here are her notes and the words to *We Are Circling*. "Growing and changing is the key to survival. I wrote new verses to this hippy old campfire song. Here is the chorus: *We are circling, we are circling. We are spinning, singing our heart's song. This is family. This is unity. This is celebration. This is sacred. We are spiraling, spiraling together. Babies, elders, bozos, and angels. This is how we grow. This is how we know.*" Thanks, Buffy, for that. And now I want to play again some beautiful music by my good friend, Chuck Rose, *We Are One*.

Do you know who you are? Do you care? There's so much we have to share. And the light in our soul keeps on shining like the sun. I am you, you are me, we are one. We are all one spirit, we are all one heart. We are all one together, we are even one apart. We are one in our soul and together we are whole. I am you, you are me, we are one. Who are you on your own? Do you know? What's still there when you let everything go? If you find who you are when it's all been said and done, I am you, you are me, we are one. We are all one spirit, we are all one heart. We are all one together, we are even one apart. We are one in our soul and together we are whole. I am you, you are me, we are one. We are one with the seas and the flowers and the trees. We are one with the future and the past. We are one everywhere and in everything we share and the most important question we can ask is who am I? Am I cold? Who are you? Are we more than just the things we say and do?

The answer's been around forever and it's only just begun. I am you, you are me, we are one. We are all one spirit, we are all one heart. We are all one together, we are even one apart. We are one in our soul and together we are whole. I am you, you are me, we are one. I am you, you are me, we are one.

David: Greetings, Richard Schultz. He's a good friend of mine in Calgary, Alberta, Canada. Richard Schultz of WisdomWays. Richard loves to play on the leading edge of human potential. He facilitates processes that shift people and cultures to new paradigms of thinking, believing and collaborating with others. He's an expert in shifting or limiting subconscious patterns that hold individuals and organizations back from reaching our goals. He's an international facilitator, trainer, and he's worked with hundreds of people. In his prior life, he worked for about 15 years for large companies like Big Blue (IBM) and others, and he's taken a different path to seek his vision and purpose towards making leadership more successful and wiser. Here's a quote that my good friend Richard has given: "The wisdom is always in the room and it's within us". So, the wisdom is always in the room and within us. Beautiful.

Richard, what else would you like to share about yourself and the work that you do?

Richard: Thanks, David. It's great to be here. My expertise is really about working with the unconscious and bringing what's unconscious into awareness and then to change it from that place. It's about working with limiting beliefs and assumptions about the subconscious emotional drivers that hold us back or propel us forward and the underlying values and purposes that we work with or don't work with us. So, I really like to work with those deeper layers and leading from the inside out and that's my passion.

David: Every time Richard Schultz and I have a conversation, it goes deep very quick and I walk away thinking, wow, I want more conversations like this. This is a very intelligent and connected man who can teach me many things. So, Richard, let me not go too deep very quickly—

Richard: We only have eight minutes.

David: I'm sure you can. I'm not sure I can keep up. So, why collaborate? What's the value?

Richard: Well, with the value for me, if I look at my own background is, myself, I have a huge independence streak within me and I figure I can do it all myself and I've got this perfectionism and operate from that place a lot within my life and I've realized over time that that really limits me. We can learn so much more in the reflection of others if we come into others. We can learn more about ourselves and this interoperability with others and we can get a whole lot more done in terms of understanding who we are in those spaces and actually understanding about groups and increasing our own authenticity. We can get a whole bunch more done than we can individually.

David: You often use language such as taking the opportunity to open this space instead of closing it, like leaders often do, because it's uncomfortable. Tell us more about why leaders shut themselves down and the teams down or what's the value of opening the space.

Richard: I learn again and again and again that we—and I've done it myself again and again and again—is we get attached to the outcome, we get attached to the agenda, and what we would think we want to accomplish in a meeting and we forget to notice the things that are happening in the background. What's arising within ourselves? What's arising from others? And some off questions or grief or anger, and those moments are priceless. If we dig into those and we dive deep into those experiences of when there's a charge in the room, either a positive or a limiting charge in the room, often, what's holding us back or keeping us stuck is right in those moments.

But instead, we try to shut those down because we're uncomfortable with anger or whatever. And we try to push on with our agenda. But sometimes when we slow down, we can go much faster and we can get more accomplished in the end. So, kind of slow down to go fast.

David: Yeah, it's like what's coming up for me, Richard, is acknowledging each other. Opening the space for emotions, the spirit, for business, for spreadsheets, whatever that is, and learning to trust. Learning to have a sense of our team, our company, our organization—holds this space, not just opens it. It holds it. I know in one of my organizational development programs in a very large Canadian oil and gas company, the leaders get very comfortable very quick. By the second session, they're dancing in their seats and, "I don't like this; I don't know what's going to come". But what happens when it comes?

Richard: Yeah. And it is a dance, isn't it? It is a real dance with all the things that are brought into the room and there's so much richness and wisdom there that can really, in this co-creative space, can really enhance everybody individually and collectively. More creativity there.

David: I've had the experience where I sense that if something is going on for somebody, it's going on for the entire group. Tell us about that.

Richard: Well, that's absolutely true from my own experience, too, is there's these indicators happening in the room. There's this question that comes out of right field that seems totally off topic where this emotion and what we'll tend to do is try to ignore that, shut it down, because it's uncomfortable, but often what's happening is those conversations in the hallways, those things that are unconscious—if we can allow them to come into the open, have a discussion or live in the question rather than the conclusion, we so much live in the question. That's what's happening. That's what that person is versus what's happening over there? I wonder what's in this space right now. What is this coming in? And when we live in that question and investigate, often, it's much wider spread than that individual or they have the clues to what is limiting you.

David: Yeah, living in the question. Fantastic. So, I'm going to ask you a couple more questions. One is, what's your dream for WisdomWays and collaboration? Is there an end? Is there a visual? Is there a dream that Richard Schultz holds as to where you'd really like to help us get to?

Richard: Wow, I wasn't expecting that question. Came right out of right field.

David: It did.

Richard: For me, it's just an avenue, a platform, for me to continue my own personal growth and contribute to the world, to serve in the world. There's so much being polarized in the world. We're living on two ends of the spectrum, in opposition, in so many ways in this world and noticing more and more and more. if I can help people find that center, find that balance within themselves, or organizations find that sweet spot in the middle versus the polarization that happens and the fight back and forth, that something wrong—then, my dream would become true if we can come to that place of peace in the center versus experiencing this very polarized world, which I'm noticing right now.

David: Yeah, it seems to be what I call the mediots, or mediot control of the message. The people that want to bring in separation and dysfunction and disinformation as opposed to what's really going on for me and you and us.

Richard: Yeah, there's a lot of fear being propagated in the world, and that closes the space. That closes the creativity down. It closes the collaboration around. It drives us into more older patterns of consciousness of control.

David: Richard Schultz is a teacher of mine. He's helping to guide my self-awareness and my techniques in group. Richard, as we close this interview, what's one thing that you wish to challenge or encourage our audience to do as they collaborate?

Richard: Just to take 100% responsibility to create the experience you're having is—turn it back inwards. If you have a charge against something in the space of working with others, if you get a personal charge, then live in the question. What's happening here—what's happening inside of myself versus blaming others for it. So, take 100% responsibility for the experience, and if it's someone else in the room where this charge or this event that's happening, then live in the question there. What could be happening over there? What are the beliefs and assumptions versus labelling them or judging them as being this or that or lazy or incompetent? Live in the question—what's happening over there? What's happening with you? Living in the question and taking 100% responsibility for what's happening in the space.

David: Thank you so much, Richard Schultz.

Richard: Thanks, David. It was great to be here.

David: Think about Richard's comment. There's so much polarization and separation in the world. He helps us find that sweet spot in the middle. And that's where he says our dreams come true. Since there's a lot of fear in the world that closes this space, ponder this and consider how you open your collaborative, your medians, and your networks. Do you want a narrow, tight space? Or do you want open? Social media has served us in many ways to separate us, divide us, enrage us, provoke us, connect us and we are moving away from Facebook to Instagram. We're moving away from Twitter to Periscope. Video engages audience like text rarely does. We are tired of social media outrage, yes. The outrage, the viral videos—we want something very different.

As we go to break, think about how you communicate. Want to send an interesting e-mail? Send a video e-mail through services like iJot. Want your message to be read? Send an old-fashioned, personal letter. Want to move from misunderstanding to possibility? Well, have a face-to-face conversation. I even trip over those words. Competition is not a conversation. Let's talk. And now, we'll take a break.

David: We've got Colin Campbell, a good friend of mine, who lives in my city, Cranbrook, British Columbia. Colin and I have done many things together. We've been working on collaborative leadership together. We've been trying to develop a leadership group called Kootenay Leadership to mentor, coach, challenge, and provide support for young people in the Kootaney so that they can build their businesses, lives, and happiness in southeastern British Columbia.

Colin is a real gift to this area. GuidancePlanningStrategies.com is Colin's website. Colin has been in the financial businesses for over 40 years. Guidance Planning Strategies is an independent insurance wealth management firm with four advisors, serving business and families in the area of wealth and communication, retention and risk management. And I think he's the unofficial mayor of Cranbrook, I believe. Colin's been a Rotarian for 37 years, past president, charter and member and founder of the Cranbrook Sunrise Rotary Club. He's very active in the Masonic Lodge and his wife, Jane Campbell, is the same in Eastern Star.

In 2010, Colin was named Cranbrook Newsmaker of the Year because he almost won Kraft Hockeyville contest on CBC. He got us a million votes on that and he also brought the Canada Cup Curling Championship to Cranbrook in 2012. Colin, thank you so much for your collaboration and your collaboration with my book, *Break Through to Yes*, and for your insights today.

Can you start off with anything you have on your mind and will share with our listeners on what you know and what you want them to know about collaboration?

Colin: Well, thank you, David, it's a pleasure to be here. I'm impressed with the bio. I'd forgotten all of the things that I've done, especially those but I really do enjoy the volunteer stuff and the community, so that was a special event, both the Hockeyville and the Canada Cup, the memorable events that I won't forget for the rest of my life. I find it interesting that we're talking about collaboration.

After being in this financial services business for as long as I have and watching the business develop. We just celebrated, on September the 2nd , our 20th anniversary since we opened our doors in Cranbrook and it's been a really rewarding 20 years. But how the changes have happened and where we might have been salespeople 15 or 20 years ago, today it's really about collaboration with our clients and with our suppliers. And the one thing that one of my associates made a comment about two or three weeks ago—she said, we have the nicest clients. And I thought, isn't that a wonderful comment to make because it is all about the fact that we collaborate. We no longer come to logger heads about costs or what we're going to do. It's an ultimate result of conversation and meeting to find solutions to problems.

So that has become the way that we've done business and I think it's the way that business is being conducted in a number of areas these days and I hope it is. As you know, I'm a very avid proponent of reform in the school system and I think that one of the things that we should be doing is giving the school teachers more opportunity to collaborate with their students instead of having to try to make them follow a lesson plan that's going to allow them to pass a standardized exam. And that's a real key.

David: Teach them to collaborate. Teach them to build and co-create what is in that classroom and in that heart?

Colin: Exactly, yeah. I'm concerned about it because I think that the way our system is now, that we've got children who are very good at passing exams but are they competent to be professionals or carpenters or accountants or lawyers or anything? And that's a concern.

David: Why does a successful businessman need to work well with others? We're often graded in school about "gets along well with others". Why is that important with business people? Men and women?

Colin: You know, I have to look at history and say that it's rather interesting that the greatest mind of the 20th century, Albert Einstein, spent very little time in school. He was registered at the University of Zurich but he hardly ever attended class and he had a terrible time convincing the mandarins of the university to allow him to do his PhD thesis, and similarly, Ben Franklin only spent three years in school. He said that it was a blessing that his father couldn't afford to send him to Harvard because he figured they'd probably beat all of his creativity out of him, the four years that he would have been there.

So, there's a testament to the fact that collaboration, getting back to the subject of collaboration, I think that that's what allows creativity, is when you have a situation where you're facing a problem and coming to a solution instead of having the people at the table arguing about who's right and who's wrong. They're so right after it. There's a meeting of the minds and that's what it's all about.

David: You reminded me of another metaphor of collaboration is, Canadians, Americans, Russians, everyone loves hockey, loves soccer, football—and there is a sense to your point. Because we're so organized as we developed these young athletes, they lose their creativity. They lose their Einstein.

Colin: That's right. We have. It's forty years ago, you didn't make it to the NHL because you played in minor hockey. You made it because you learned how to play on the pond. And similarly, with baseball. You learned how to play on the sandlot and maybe you got to go play in some bush league like in southern Alberta or Saskatchewan or Northern Montana or Wyoming where you played in tournaments on a regular basis for the summer and somebody discovered you. A scout found you.

Today, it's a whole different world. Somebody told me the other day that their costs to have their son in minor hockey, because he's on a rep team and he's pretty good, was $25,000. That's pretty high. That's a steep price to pay. And I think it's because we have taken out that creativity which comes from collaboration. If you think back about it, when you played baseball in the sandlot, the first collaborative event was, who's going to be the pitcher and who is going to be on first and who is going to be up to bat first?

David: Yeah. Organizational development. There's really no hierarchy. Everybody has to do their part.

Colin: Exactly. Yeah.

David: Colin, that's the end of our time. Is there one last thing that you'd like to challenge our listeners to think about, be aware of, or do as we close this interview?

Colin: I truly hope that everybody will examine themselves and their position on education. And go and talk to the people who matter and start the discussion about how can we fix this problem? Adam Smith said 200 years ago that they had to create an education system to create, to produce literate workers for the industrial age. We haven't done anything to change the way we approach education. And I think it's tragic. In fact, I think the problem is going to become more acute because of course, the young people, young children can learn so much on the computer, by the time they get to grade one, they might be smarter than the school teacher. It's not a question of being smarter than a sixth grader. It's, can you be smarter than a six-year-old?

David: Thank you so much, my friend, Colin Campbell of Guidance Planning Strategies. Thanks, Colin.

Colin: Thanks, David. Bye.

David: Now, think about Colin's hope that we change the way we approach education. When we're talking about Design the Collaboration, the theme for today's show, Step 5 of my 10 Essential Steps to Collaboration, what is the right design that will spark young hearts, minds, and spirits? What is the best design for engagement to enhance learning? We can't continue to put people in boxes or treat them with less respect than they deserve. Less accountability than they deserve. We tend to want to put everything in cookie cutters. Like so many neighborhoods in North America, box after box after box. That's not life. That's not natural.

You know, another similar call for reform is through Ken Robinson. I would expect many of you have watched his TedTalk, *Changing Education Paradigms*, on TedTalks. Ken Robinson. Think about fitting our education to suit the learning styles of the student. Think about getting out of our limiting boxes. Be very purposeful when you design your collaboration. It's not, okay, let's get together in a couple of hours in the meeting room, and we've got to have a conversation. How you design that collaboration, that space, the energies, the windows, the artwork—who's with you—all of that affects how creative and how successful you will be. Or do you just want it to be another bloody meeting? And now, we'll take a break.

David: Today, we've got my good friend, Laura Hummel, from Kimberley, British Columbia. Laura is an organizational development specialist. She's done work across western Canada with some major corporations and provincial governments. She and I are developing leadership skills and collaborative leadership, not only in British Columbia, but around the world. Laura's company is Ahead of the Curve Consulting and she lives in Kimberley, British Columbia. We're going to talk a little bit about Laura's dream of a Center of Excellence.

But Laura, before I start asking you those questions, what might you add to our listeners today so that they can learn a little bit more about you? How do they get in touch with you and what are your thoughts leading off this interview?

Laura: Yeah, well, thank you so much for having me as your guest, David. It's a real pleasure assisting you and getting your program off the ground and I've certainly enjoyed working with you over the past couple of years. As you mentioned, my company is Ahead of the Curve. Yeah, I came back to Kimberley a couple of years ago after being in the big cities and as you mentioned, working at mostly government organizations and a few corporations lately. And when I came back here, I was really enthralled by the opportunities I saw in the area for collaboration and yet, I did a bit of an environmental scan and I saw that there was little evidence of a structured approach to change and realized that working from a collaborative approach would be quite a different approach to doing business in this area.

So, I wanted to see what the receptivity was to working collaboratively and just to see how people were going about doing so. So, it was quite an interesting little journey to find out that there wasn't a lot of best practices out there and people weren't putting their best foot forward to try and collaborate, to come up with more innovative approaches and incorporated multiple perspectives. But they were really struggling. And that's about the time I actually reached out and tried to connect with you, David. And we had some very interesting conversations right from the get-go.

David: Yeah, I just want to read some—listeners, what I want to share with you is Laura and 99 other people from five countries have added their wisdom on collaboration to my book *Break Through to Yes*, and here's some of the words that really resonated that Laura has shared with me. "Collaboration is often stated by leaders as a key solution to the very real economic challenges that we face. Yet, no organization has taken the lead in support of this form of leadership. Nor is there any organization that has appeared on its own to be agile, innovative, and designed to work across the silos that currently exist".

Now, Laura, you've done a lot of research with respect to, what is excellence? What are best practices? And I know from us, from our work in the Kootenays and in British Columbia, often times, people will use the word collaboration but not actually collaborate. So what else can you share?

Laura: Yeah, so true. It gets sort of bantered about quite a bit, that word 'collaboration' to the extent that people are tired of hearing about it and they're getting exhausted from their efforts to collaborate. And that's often an indication that they're not working from a best practice point of view where it's really about, from a leadership perspective, creating a participatory decision-making process.

So, you're getting multiple perspectives that are incorporated into those decisions and you know, in order to get to that point, it requires a lot of trust and giving up your power. It must feel like that for a lot of leaders at the beginning and at least giving up control. But really, what they're doing is just distributing it and leaders still have a role to play in that leadership. But they're stepping back quite a bit and they're really bringing out the diversity of participants and helping them to recognize their value as well. Yeah, so I would say really the #1 thing is really trust. And it takes the leader really checking their ego at the door and that takes a leap of faith for a lot of people these days but I think as they work through it and they get some experience in doing so, they begin to see that the benefits and the outcomes are much, much greater than they can achieve on their own.

And in today's society, it's really difficult for those leaders at the top to have a wide enough and a deep enough view of all that is going on in their business or their organization as well as in that environment of which they are a part. So, it's really about recognizing that they can't do this all on their own. They need that collective wisdom to guide their organization and their business, so those are a few of the things that I think are required as far as the mindset and the best practice approach.

David: Yeah, the business world, the organization business world is full of people that believe they need rock star leaders and then there's many who just don't lead. They put it to a committee and this doesn't work. So, the work that you're doing is really trying to get that new collaborative intelligence. In the last 15 seconds, Laura, what's one thing that you challenge or a vision that you have for your Center of Excellence? One remaining comment that you want to share with our listeners.

Laura: Well, David, I think it really is a paradigm shift that's taking place around the globe and this isn't just the nice or the right thing to do. It is really a need out there and I see every day and all levels of our society the need for collaboration. The competitive model, the command and control model, it is no longer serving us and a much different approach is needed and I truly believe in collaboration and that we can all really benefit from it and experience new outcomes, ones that have yet to be seen and realized. So, I'm really excited about this and I can't wait for us to bring this together to a fuller state.

David: Well, thank you so much. This is Laura Hummelle working together with me and others—Becky Pelkonen included, to create a Center of Excellence and collaborative leadership and change management to help leaders and organizations move into and create their new paradigm. Ahead of the Curve Consulting, Laura Hummelle, thank you so much.

Laura: Thank you so much, David. Great to be here.

David: Today has been really interesting. Thank you, Laura. Thank you, Colin. Thank you, Richard. Very different perspectives and the same perspective. Design the collaboration. We've also noted *Star Wars,* the collaborative global initiative, mountain hiking and music. Incorporate movement, music, poetry, nature and outsiders in your meetings. Not just PowerPoints and economics and to-do lists. You will change that energy.

Key messages for today have been

1) in a true co-creative space, we are enriched individually and collectively,

2) where firms used to employ a sales team years ago, we now work collaboratively with our clients, customers, employees, and communities for a greater business,

3) by learning more about the necessary preconditions and best practices of collaborative leadership, you will become more successful. I'm really

also excited about next week's show, Step 6: Come Together.

Our guests are the Heart and Stroke Foundation of Canada, executives Donna Hastings, Art Korpatch, Rod McKay. Fantastic people, fantastic philanthropists, fantastic leaders. I just can't say fantastic more than three times but I will. Fantastic. Heart and Stroke is a great organization doing great things for heart and brain health. They have also gone through a challenging and successful national unification. We'll talk about that next week.

My call to action today, for you, as we close this show, this episode: Design your next collaboration with the end in mind and create the container for co-creation. Design the next collaboration with the end in mind and create the container for co-creation. Do it consciously. Thank you for your time, creativity, and collaborative awareness.

Chapter 9 Come Together featuring Donna Hastings, Rob McKay, Art Korpach

David: Now is our time to lead more powerfully, consciously, and collaboratively in ways that make our world and our nation and our communities a better place today and in the future. Leaders are making this essential shift now. Welcome, everybody. This is our show called Come Together. Yes, come together. Think about that great Beatles' song "Come Together." "Here come old flattop, he comes moving up slowly. Come together right now." I'm not even going to try to sing it.

In "Break Through to Yes," I set out ten steps that are essential to collaboration. See my website for the download of all the episodes. Too often, leaders think about collaborating, the first thing they do is call a meeting. In my ten steps, come together actually doesn't happen till the sixth step.

Before meeting, we enhance our probability of success by first setting intention then becoming more aware of the circumstances -- the people, the players, the interest, then looking for where the conflict is. We talked about that, there's real gift in conflict, making sure that we have diversity in our group so we avoid groupthink. Design it carefully. We'll talk a little bit more about that. Today, we talked a little bit more about...last week.

Today, we're talking about step six, Come Together. I'm really delighted that this show features three of my more respected leaders in Canadian Business and Philanthropy. They're also key leaders in the Heart and Stroke Foundation in Canada. These three are quality people and my friends, Donna Hastings, Rod McKay, and Art Korpach.

The Heart and Stroke Foundation serves as an important part in the research in heart disease and stroke prevention. This organization of which I'm part of the

Provincial Advisory Board has progressed through a complete reorganization that has been very challenging, necessary, and successful.

For those of you that don't know, those of you that are in France, Malaysia, China, you've got similar organizations, I hope. The vision of the Heart and Stroke Foundation is "Healthy lives free of heart disease and stroke. Together, we will make it happen."

What does collaboration mean inside a national not-for-profit organization?

Key messages for today are:

1) do far more to create the container when you come together to achieve more than your objectives; take care; think about it; be prepared.
2) by committing yourself to the Heart and Stroke Foundation, you will build your network, learn much more about leadership, and serve the greater good.
3) Every organization must continually adapt to change and find even better ways to serve its clients and market.

Here's an excerpt from my book "Break Through to Yes: Unlocking the Possible within a Culture of Collaboration." Notice it's culture. It's not an event or a project or a meeting. "Take your time going through the first five steps before you come together. Rushing to meet too soon is equivalent of a quickie with your lover." Yes, I said that. "At times, it's just right but most often you're missing an amazing experience. Take the time it takes to make it the best it can be."

Assuming you all hope for a healthy family, economic, environmental, and social future together then how would we design that? How would we come together?

Here's some characteristics of great collaborations. For your organization, can you say that "Our intention is authentic?" Can you say that "We build relationship and trust first?" Can you say that "We invite and respect diversity of opinion? We listen. We seek new ideas from the collective wisdom?"

At our Heart and Stroke Provincial Advisory Board, we have a tremendous cross section of volunteers, wise women and men who come from life in very different backgrounds, different business expertise and it works. In your organization, can you also say that you commit to action and hold accountability? I hope so.

According to Mark Leslie, "Putting the "we" in leadership, stewardship is about what we can do together to build something great that we can be then proud of." The best-run organizations create the environments that attract the best and the brightest. Those people can then use their judgment and autonomously make decisions consistent with mission and vision of the company.

What do you need to move this from just a meeting or a project to a culture in your organization? Oftentimes, it's changing how you do it, shifting your brain, getting outside. I'm proud to say that our Heart and Stroke Foundation of Alberta, Nunavut, and the Northwest Territories, our provincial advisory boards, our meetings always include walk-in portion. We walk while we meet. Get outside.

Other room designers, architects, et cetera, they look for ways of changing the meeting space. They have different rooms for different types of meetings. Ritual is important but it's been much ignored over the past 50 years.

Ritual beginnings and endings to collaborative groups serve as an important marker to our brain, hearts, spirit, and body that something different is happening and we need to be open and aware of, just realize that collaboration, coaching, dispute resolution, and most transformative processes are step changes. If they're one-time events, they'll be abandoned and learnings lost.

Who likes Dilbert? I love Dilbert. Dilbert's amazing. Scott Adams says, "Few things in life are less efficient than a group of people trying to write a sentence." The advantage of this method is that you end up with something for which you will not be personally blamed. Is that what collaboration is for you?

After the break, we're going to talk to the key executives of the Heart and Stroke Foundation of Canada. Go to heartandstroke.ca to find out more. Also, look for opportunities to get involved -- your time, your resources, and your expertise. Upcoming is our 40th anniversary, Ski for Heart. If you're in Western Canada or wherever you are, join us at Lake Louise.

David: It's my real pleasure to introduce you to our featured guest. What I'll do is I'll introduce them separately, ask them for their insights, and then before our day is finished, we'll have all three of them have an open discussion with you.

Let's start with Donna Hastings. She is the Chief Executive Officer for the Heart and Stroke Foundation, Alberta, Northwest Territories and Nunavut or HSF Alberta. She's an experienced and dedicated leader of both employees and volunteers and she's served for five years as Alberta's Vice-President, Health and Research.

She's a paramedic, an adult educator, a not-for-profit leader, and leadership coach. She's coached me. Donna received the 2011 Heart and Stroke Foundation of Canada Chair Award in recognition of her leadership, commitment and outstanding contributions.

Hi, Donna. What else would you like to tell our listeners about you and your work?

Donna: Thank you so much, David for featuring the Heart and Stroke Foundation and our learnings. In my role, I have lots of variety and lots of opportunities to collaborate within the Heart and Stroke Foundation and with other organizations that I volunteer with.

The classic definition of collaborate that I learned was two or more people co-laboring together to achieve an outcome greater than the individuals could. I used a picture in the olden days, a group of people doing physical labor together building a retaining wall or a railway.

Today, the purpose of collaboration is more likely to be innovation, solutions or building better organizations. Where I see collaboration living is in teams and partnerships, in associations and alliances as each person brings all their abilities and includes their networks and all of those resources that they can tap in to.

I've created my own current definition for collaborate. I've broken it down into three-word parts.

The first one is "co." Who needs to be collected? Sometimes it's colored and coerced to come together to co-create something or to contribute to a cause. There has to be a draw there.

Secondly is "labor." I have found initially that there can be more labor upfront involved. As we've all experienced, the forming, storming, norming that a collaborative collective can have. However, it's been my experience that the outputs and the outcomes are almost always superior by doing it this way.

Third is "ate." In my opinion, ideally, the collaborators should meet face-to-face and be fueled by food especially in the forming phase. Just the simple act of eating or sharing a beverage together really facilitates trust. From the initial intention to implementation, collaboration is really about quality of the relationship.

The best example that I've experienced in recent years is with the Heart and Stroke Foundation. Just a piece of context for everyone listening, for 60 years, the Heart and Stroke Foundation had existed in a federated model organized by province across Canada. In 2011, the CEOs, the national board members, and the provincial board chairs teamed together in a collaborative to find a better way to serve Canadians.

Face-to-face, we resolved to unify into one foundation. Many organizations looked on and told us that they've tried that and it just couldn't be done. It didn't work. In less than a year, we legally unified and then began the exciting work of creating a coast-to-coast strategic plan, maximizing our mission, and being the best stewards of our resources.

One of the keys as I was reflecting back in preparation for this was to have a senior statesman whom everyone knew and trusted to be our what I'm going to call, collaboration broker. That person was Rod McKay from Calgary. He was the former Board Chair for Alberta, Northwest Territories and Nunavut, our region and a member and leader within the national board.

I watched and listened as he brought provinces together, the leaders from the provinces, as he would follow-up with one-on-one calls to address insecurities or needs or hopes of an individual or groups of individuals. I don't know what his cellphone bill was like during that year but he was continually connecting with people and just facilitating that collaboration to happen.

It's thanks in large part to Rod and many others, all the right people in the right place at the right time willing to do the right thing.

David: Thanks, Donna. I guess what I'm hearing underneath that is yes, it's teamwork. It's together. It's a national unification. Rod was your quarterback, the go-to guy that made things happen. Good collaboration is a combination of individual champions, quarterbacks, and a healthy team that has the same vision.

Donna: I think that's a very good metaphor.

David: Let me introduce Rod now, if I might, Donna and we'll come back to you. Rod McKay is Chair of the Board of the Heart and Stroke Foundation of Canada. He's also Chair of the Board of Tourism Calgary and member of the board of the Calgary Sports Tourism Authority. He's a busy guy. He's a Fellow of the Chartered Accountants of Alberta and has been a member for six years ending 2013 of the Alberta Securities Commission and Lead Independent Member.

He serves in a whole bunch of boards including the Board of the Institute of Corporate Directors–Calgary and Art who you'll be introduced to later is the Chair of the ICD-Calgary. Prior to Rod's retirement in 20016, he was a partner in KPMG, the international audit, tax, and advisory firm.

Rod, tell us more about your perspective of collaboration and unification as a National Chair.

Rod: Again thanks, David. One of the things that is key from Donna's comments that one of the things that what happened at the Heart and Stroke Foundation through collaboration, working together, it was a team effort.

It was many folks coming together, each of them adding their skills and their interests together to achieve what we achieved through unification and that continues now through what unification was the first step.

It was a big step but then the next thing becomes one of how do you work effectively through what you've created? You cited, David at the beginning, when you're introducing Heart and Stroke Foundation even our vision.

Our vision is clearly set out based on...one of the phrases in it is together, "together we will make it happen." That's critical to how we approach unification and how we are continuing to deal with the challenges that we face.

One of the things that I think we were fortunate in many respects of a number of people with common interests coming together at a particular time and a particular time in our history. If we wanted to make a difference and we wanted to make a difference across the country, we really had to sort of set aside some of the boundaries, to take down some boundaries and create a new organization with a new vision and a broader vision.

In those conversations that happened, there's a couple of things that would highlight one of the things that you mentioned. I think you talked about this coming together was step six. That I think reflects our experience. A lot of stuff has to happen, a lot of things have to happen before individuals and before people can come together to collaborate.

One of the aspects is you don't have to like the folks that come together, but you must respect them. The respect that happens and the respect that's gained through the things that Donna talked a bit about was whether it was eating, whether it's drinking, whether or not it's playing games and it is actually doing things...even meeting and taking breaks actually helped very, very effectively in coming together in developing both respect for the individuals and understanding of their particular perspectives.

Our experience in what we believe we created and are continuing to build on wasn't around compromise. It wasn't to say, "We'll meet in the middle ground." It was actually to figure out what individuals wanted to achieve and then what it meant. Some folks might have been...and I know one of the things we wanted to do was to bring more funds and more of the money that we raised towards our mission.

There has to be a conversation around what the mission is. There has to be a conversation about what that means and how do you deliver it. There you have a number of bringing experts together and bringing lay people together. The lay people are the ones that might go door-to-door, the people that are actually looking for the funds to put in to research and brought together with the researchers and what they wanted to do and what they want to achieve.

What we found was that there was a wide array of interests and stakeholders that needed to be connected and consulted through the process, but also trying to work to ensure that we didn't...individuals didn't compromise their particular points of view and so that they'll say, "Oh yes, sure. We'll go ahead with that," but fundamentally they didn't want to do that.

That comes out during the course of social events and also in the form of meetings. I think what has happened and what happened with us was very much interactive, different people meeting different times and getting together in different ways. We had a series of meetings across the country and brought together a whole host of interested individuals with their perspectives and also respectfully debated those in public form where people could express their particular views.

David: You've said so much there, Rod about not compromising and understanding people's interests, understanding, being aware of the different factors that are influencing people.

Before we got to break here, I really want to underline what Rod McKay has shared with us today. It's not about compromise. It's using the metaphor of the orange. It's not about cutting the orange halfway down the middle. It's actually finding, "Okay. Who wants to use the pulp and who wants to use the rind?" There is so much more through excellent collaboration.

We'll be right back after the break.

David: Thanks, Donna and Rod for your insight on collaboration in the Heart and Stroke Foundation-Canada and Alberta, in unification and challenges and what's required. Let me now introduce Art who's the newest to the Heart and Stroke Foundation with his Alberta perspective. Art again, just like Rod and Donna is somebody I have the deepest respect for.

Art Korpach is ICD-D. Chair of the Institute of Corporate Directors, Calgary Chapter. By the way, any of you that want to really enhance your skills, your awareness, your capabilities, and your network with respect to current or future director positions, get involved with the ICD. It's excellent.

Art is a corporate Director serving on the boards including Canadian Oil Sands. He's a little busy this week because of unsolicited offer from Suncor. He's on the board of Cenovus Corporation, Freehold Royalties, and HPC Energy Services.

Art is also Chair of the Alberta Heart & Stroke Foundation Board and past Chair of United Way Calgary. Art is past Vice-Chair of the CIBC World Markets where he managed the firm's global energy investment banking business.

I could go on and on about all three of my guests. Art, tell us more about you and your perspective on the Heart and Stroke Foundation and collaboration.

Art: David, thank you. Thank you for having us on the show and thank you for the notes on ICD as well. I guess my view is that collaboration is absolutely critical to achieving value creation and success. I think collaboration is especially critical when you have a complex situation or challenge that you're trying to manage or you have a complex organization in which you're working or interacting with.

If I look back at my 27-year career in the financial service sector, collaboration was absolutely critical as we brought together experts in derivatives, fixed income, credit all to work together to provide the best advice and service to our corporate clients. I think of those corporate clients who were primarily in the energy sector and they are collaborating as well every day.

In fact, 14 companies in the Western Canadian energy sector have entered a collaboration called COSIA where they shared over one billion dollars of research that they've undertaken in an effort to try to have the best technology and processes to manage their environmental compliance programs and to minimize impact on our environment and to minimize and help solve the climate change problems.

When I look at Heart and Stroke Foundation Alberta and I certainly have to thank Donna and Rod for getting me involved in this organization. It's an absolutely wonderful organization. I see collaboration being core to everything we do.

We collaborate with multiple levels of government, with the federal government on trying to place ADs in our community centers and hockey rings throughout our province, working with the provincial government as well as the federal government on advocacy initiatives where we're trying to get better health programs, reducing the sugar intake of our population

We're doing a couple of things that are really key to my heart, David. One of them is with the school system. We are reaching out and we focused on grade 10 students but there are many different levels of students where we have different activities. For the grade 10 students, we've been focusing on some heart health education and training on automated external defibrillator (AED) use and on CPR (Cardio Pulmonary Resuscitation) training.

Those kinds of initiatives are huge collaborations where we're bringing together survivors, who can tell the story and the need for this kind of programs, our bringing together our trained professionals who deliver the services and the information. We're bringing together teachers, students, and government and educational system representatives.

It is a broad group of individuals working to try to effectively make a change in the education of the next generation. I think that's exciting, but it is a huge collaborative effort.

Another area that's very near and dear to my background being the corporate business world is the wellness of employees. I think many corporations recognize that healthy employees lead to strong performances and good business outcomes. It's that relationship and success that I think we need to communicate broadly through the corporate sector.

Heart and Stroke Foundation is trying to provide our professionals who are trained our information and bring that to the corporate world so that on a collaborative basis their employees can be offered better programs and better information to their own well-being and obviously a great contribution, we believe ultimately to our society.

David, when I think of collaboration I think of a number of elements. Probably top of my list is passion. There has to be an area and I think others have referred to it as a quarterback or a leader or a driver. In the group of entities and individuals, there needs to be passion to get to a particular goal.

Along the way, I think it's important that there be lots of information and lots of understanding and a definition on where you want to get to and then measurement of whether you're actually achieving it or not. I think many collaborative efforts may start out fine but may need to be adjusted along the way. I think continuously, you have to look at the dynamics of the people and you have to measure how you're moving so that you can make the adjustments that will be required.

Those are some of the thoughts that I have. I certainly see it being key to some of the successes that we've had at Heart and Stroke Alberta and what we need to be successful going forward.

David: Tell me a little more, Art about measurements, that saying what gets measured gets accomplished. What kind of measures do you have in my mind with respect to Heart and Stroke and how we're collaborating, how successful we are in our mission?

Art: Thank you, David. I think the key is and you start at a number of different levels. You can measure both outputs and outcomes. Let's start with outputs, which I think are building blocks.

How many grade ten students did we reach in the province this year in terms of educating them about heart health? How many people did we get through our training for CPR and AED? How many AEDs did we place in the communities? How many communities are yet to receive them? Those are I think measures of building blocks or outputs. We need to accomplish that to get to the end results.

The end results, the outcomes would be ultimately have we changed people's lives? Are they behaving and living a healthier life that will cause to have and contribute to a lower incidence of heart disease and stroke? Those are the outcomes that we ultimately want to achieve and measure and our goals and objectives. Along the way we have these building blocks, I would say, David.

David: Thank you so much. Before we close this interview with the executives of the Heart and Stroke Foundation of Canada and Alberta, Northwest Territories and Nunavut, I want to ask Art and Rod and Donna what is one thing you would challenge our listeners to do or to be more aware of to make their collaborations more successful? Art?

Art: I would challenge your listeners to recognize that they have many collaborations to look and see the best elements of the ones that are working well and try to transfer those to the others. Every day we collaborate to others at our family level, at our work level or at our not-for-profit level. I think identifying of those best elements whether they're passion measurement or other items and seeing how you bring that to all elements of your life.

David: Yes. Learn from what's working well. Rod, what's your challenge?

Rod: I think the key is to listen. Each of us probably knows it. We think the issue. What we think is the solution. I think the key is to listen in anything you're trying to do with others. I think you'll find that the solution is not likely what it appears to be for the issue. It's not frequently what it appears to be at first glance. Only by listening and listening to the other stakeholders both and what their issues are and their concerns are but also with their ideas are. If you do that, I think workable solutions can be found.

David: Thank you. Donna?

Donna: I came across a quote recently and have searched. The author seems to be unknown and it seems to sum it up. "We may not have it all together but together we have it all." I really agree with Rod about listening being the catalyst. I cannot resist playing off Dr. Frasier Crane and saying, "Hello. We're listening. Let's collaborate."

David: Wonderful. Before we complete, any last words from each of you? Donna, you first.

Donna: I'm looking forward to your book release.

David: Thank you. Rod?

Rod: Collaboration is not easy. It's hard work.

David: Thank you. Art, you do get the last words.

Art: I want to make it a thank you to you for all of your efforts with Heart and Stroke Foundation and for having us on the show today. David, it's been fabulous and we look forward to more discussions on collaboration going forward.

David: Thank you. To my listeners, wherever you are, I'm delighted that we've actually heard now and I believe 12 nations around the world, think about Art, Rod, and Donna and who the Arts, Rods, and Donnas are in your country, your community serves?

Now we'll go to break.

David: During this show, you've heard the wisdom of Art Korpach, Rod McKay, and Donna Hastings. We talked about mission, unification, collaboration, and more. We talked about listening. We talked about vision. We talked about having each other's back, taking care of each other in service.

If you want to build your network, your sense of worth, your service then volunteer, donate, and support organizations that align with your interests and community. These three leaders, Rod, Donna, and Art have made huge contributions to our well-being and our communities. Of course, Dr. Michael Hill with his E.S.C.A.P.E. Project, that's a research collaboration across the globe on stroke recovery.

Maybe you're in France hearing this, you are touched by the work of the Heart and Stroke Foundation research that our researchers are doing and we're touched by yours. There is only one world. Thank you for the Heart and Stroke Foundations around the world, cancer, whatever cause you see.

Normally at this time, I focus on Outrage of the Week. Past outrages have been Syrian refugees, Volkswagen, Peeple app, Uber... When we're talking about heart and stroke and health and caring, I don't want to talk about outrage this week. That just feels toxic to me right now. I want to go to vision and caring for others. Let's focus on how we do that? How will you do that?

Think about and use the Break Through to Yes system. When you think about what not-for-profit research, environmental, political or other organizations suits you best, use my ten steps. This is a process. This will work. Don't run out because you know somebody, or your daughter came down with something that scared the heck out of you.

All of those things are good things. Slow down. What is the intention? What do you need to be aware of? Where are the uncomfortable things that you need to learn from? Is this a group, a not-for-profit health angle whatever that is unusual to me? Can I learn from diversity? Does their design, how they come together, does it meet my needs?

Today we've really heard a lot from the Heart and Stroke Foundation in Canada and Alberta, the Northwest Territories and Nunavut. Thank you for doing that. Our key messages are: do far more to create the container when you come together to achieve more than your objectives. As Rod said, "It's not about compromise." It's about getting more, getting bigger, making the pie bigger and not cutting up that pie.

Number two, by committing yourselves to organizations like the Heart and Stroke Foundation, you will build your network, learn much more about leadership, and serve the greater good. Here's one of the things that we know is true. If our life is difficult, if we're under a ton of stress, if we feel separate, one of the healthiest things we can do is volunteer. Help others and therefore, build self.

Third key message is every organization must continually adapt to change and find even better ways to serve their clients and their market and their purpose. Thinking about your organization, your company, your not-for-profit, how do you assess the state of your organization's collaborative ecosystem?

Yes. What is your organization's collaborative ecosystem? How would you assess your organization? How would you assess the challenges and opportunities, your connection to other networks, your strengths and weaknesses? This is an evolutionary assessment. This will be a success indicator, a first in and a continual assessment you can do in your organization every month, every year, whatever it is.

Go to my website davidbsavage.com and you'll take a look at the preliminary assessment. Test it for yourself. I offer it to you freely. Here's some great work. Here's some aspects and questions, topics that you can prioritize. Think about the elements of the essential collaboration. Rank your team specific to a project on a scale of one to ten representing one being not very effective, five being very effective. Check this out.

Here's some of the questions on my assessment tool on collaborative ecosystem. There's 40 of them. Here's a sample.

> a) We start with the end in mind and work back to today. Yes. Start with the end in mind and work back to today. How effective are we at that? Are we a one or are we a five?
> b) We have positively experienced the value of collaboration together, have we? Have we celebrated? Have we had that glass of Scotch together or that walk, that hike, that high five, punch it? Do we celebrate what our collaborations have been? Have we

experienced the value that the bonuses could be, "Wow, we impacted that family because they had a stroke and they were able to respond quickly with the fast technique?"

c) do we understand our clients' needs? If you want to be collaborative, you need to really listen to those clients.

d) our clients or communities actively collaborate with us. In other words, they come to your organization for your guidance, your expertise. They seek you out.

e) do we seek those that we disagree with, that we're in conflict with? If you do, that's a great thing. Give yourself a four or a five. If you like groupthink and being blind, give yourself a one.

f) do you have a clearly stated principle for working together that respects the ethical values of all the members?

g) are you clear on your intention for each collaboration? The intention will be different.

h) do you make sure a variety of perspectives are represented?

i) thinking about Rod again, do you listen, listen, and listen, listen for what's underneath, really listen for this?

Before we go, I want to really thank the Heart and Stroke Foundation, all of the Cancer Foundations, and all of the people that are seeking to give us healthier and happier lives.

Next week's show and guests are Linda Matthie, business development consultant, joint venture consultant from Cabo San Lucas, Mexico; Tara Russell, Tara is President and Global Impact Lead at Fathom Cruise Ship Lines. Tara lives in Boise, Idaho. A third guest is Steve Smith. He is Senior Advisor, National and International Stakeholder and Government Relations at the Alberta Energy Regulator in Calgary, Alberta. Viki Winterton, also, joins us. Viki is the creator of the international best seller, a collaborative book that I co-authored, Ready Aim Excel.

The show theme for next week's show is the seventh of my essential ten steps to collaboration. It's Listen Deeply.

Thanks again for joining us. Let us know how we can be of service to you.

My call to action now, as we get ready to close, is long before you come together as a team or as a project group, create the conditions that will make your collaboration more successful than you hope. The investment of your time and resources and your people and your network will pay you back.

It may not happen in this moment. It may not happen next year. Build your collaborative ecosystem, your culture of collaboration in your organization. Really come together powerfully.

I want to thank you for your time and your collaborative awareness. I'll talk to you next week.

Chapter 10 Listen Deeply featuring Tara Russell, Linda Matthie, Viki Winterton, Stephen Smith

David: You are a leader who has great vision and yet feels constrained. Go from challenge and complexity to innovation and success with collaboration. We're at a time in human history where we are educated and connected and have the resources available like never before. Now. leaders and companies are making this essential shift now.

Welcome, listeners across the planet. I believe I now have listeners in about 12 countries. I'm so thankful for you. In my book "Break Through to Yes," I set out ten steps that are essential to successful collaboration. This radio show podcast theme is Listen Deeply. That's step seven of ten. We're making great progress going through the ten steps, one each week.

I'm delighted to provide you with the insight and stories of my collaborative network. Step in and step up.

This show features my contacts, people I have a great, long-term respect for: Viki Winterton, Expert Insights Publishing, Alto, New Mexico; Tara Russell, Social Impact Travel, Fathom Cruise Lines, Boise, Idaho; Stephen Smith, Alberta Energy Regulator, Calgary, Alberta; and Linda Matthie, MJM Grand Enterprises, Cabo San Lucas, Mexico.

Key messages today include:

1) learn to listen at several levels to understand what is really going on. Yes, several levels; there's at least three, maybe six levels you can listen at. Learn that. Listen for what isn't said but is meant.

2) create sustainable social impact models by collaborating with people, governments, corporations who align through

social impact. This is a strategic advantage in your human impact journey.

3) collaboration requires a high level of respect and trust. Walk your talk every day. Every day, every moment, be. Be. Not do, be.

Here's a quote from my book on step seven. "Listen deeply. Realize what wants to be heard and is not spoken." My friend, Tina Spiegel of Australia gave me this quote for my book. She's one of the hundred people I quote in my book, "To listen is vital; it means that you take on afresh what a person is saying without interference or judgment." Thanks, Tina.

There's a reason we have two ears, two eyes but only one mouth. Early in my career when I was participating in boardroom discussions, I would spend most of my time thinking about how best to state what I wanted others to understand. This took me out of the discussion and in to my head and away from the discussion at hand, away from my heart.

In doing so, I missed so much opportunity to hear the others and build on that conversation, the one in front of me as opposed to the one in my head. With my experience and confidence, I soon learned that by listening first and talking later, my contributions were far more valued. By having faith that I knew what I wished others to understand after hearing them, I could craft my communications appropriately.

Steven Covey, you know this quote, in Seven Habits of Highly Effective People, "Seek first to understand then to be understood." Seems like that might actually be a religious quote as well.

I'm going to train professional certified coach and I've been trained to listen at level one; listen to my internal voice. Listen at level two; listen with intense focus on the client. Intense focus. Listen at level three;

sense the entire room and its energy. What's really going on? What's the shadow? What's the trigger? Are the people leaning back? Are they leaning in? Are they with me or is there friction? Listen to that and communicate with that.

Try all three levels of listening. Try it with your wife or husband, friends, and colleagues. How well do you really listen? People want to be heard. People want to be witnessed. They deserve your full attention.

If you find that you're becoming distracted or judging or already working on solutions then you are not listening. Let it go and come back in the conversation. Listen for what is said and what is heard but not said.

If you are really listening, what does your internal voice tell you? Are you able to notice tension or confusion or deception? What does your intuition inform you?

What doesn't fit with the words being said? What needs clarification? If there's only one person who does not agree, discover what they may teach us. We tend to minimize the dissidents. Instead, explore together. What is not understood or accepted?

Viki Winterton is a very special guest and somebody that's helped me a lot in my publishing and branding career. She is an exceptional collaborator. You can find out more about Viki at bestsellerlaunchpad.com or getei.com. Viki Winterton is the founder of Expert Insights Publishing, home of the bestselling and award-winning books and magazines, where visionaries and those on the rise come together to create immediate impact.

Expert Insights Publishing is built on the solid foundation of over 25 years of expertise in promotion, publishing, product development, networking, and success. Fortune 100 companies and individuals across the globe know Viki for fostering powerful and loyal relationships and supporting her communities in wildly creative, unique, and wonderful ways.

She is a number one international bestseller and I've got to say that I'm delighted that I am in one of her international bestseller books at "Ready, Aim, Excel!" A few years ago, I think it might have been three to five years ago now, Viki, you put me in with 51 others including Marshall Goldsmith in to the book "Ready, Aim, Excel! A Weekly Guide to Personal and Professional Leadership."

It became an international business bestseller on Amazon. I think that's a perfect example where just like this radio show where over a 15-week, fall 2015 session, I've got 35 guests. Viki has outdone me. She's had some of the most influential wealthy people in the world on her stage and on her pages and some of the rest of us.

Viki, welcome. What else might you want to share with our listeners about you and the work that you do?

Viki: Thank you so much, David. It's just a pleasure to be here. I have to say that our whole thrust and our whole purpose of being for business is to help people get their stories out and many times to help them get their stories out either through broadcast, magazines, books.

By really engaging with those people and in the media, that we've developed, it really helps them to become quite famous very quickly. It gives them a lot of influence.

David: Yes, it's a great tool, a great collaboration. Tell me about your global network.

Viki: I actually was in advertising going way, way back and I developed an ad agency when I was in mid-20's, which was quite a while ago. We hit eight figures in three years, which was a lot of money back then. I realized with that ad agency and with the consulting and coaching I've done and now with all the publishing and broadcast that we're doing, it really revolves around relationship building.

I realized that the one thing that all of these things that I've done with my life have in common is I really look at myself as a collaborator and almost an intermediary between people who need something and people who can supply it. That has been true with everything I've done. Collaboration is just huge for us. It's the basis on which we're built for everything that we do.

David: Yes. You're telling us about how collaboration has impacted your career. Are there some significant things that come to your mind right now about stories or people as a result of the impact that's had on you, Viki but also the impact that you've created in the career of others?

Viki: Oh, yes. It's just amazing. I'd have to say that the most powerful medium that I have ever worked in is publication of books. You know only too well, David, what it can do for your career. We've have people that have opened doors with it for huge client contracts.

We had a women's book and one of our authors took that book and then was able to secure with one interview, one face-to-face interview based on her work with women and her desire to really share with women, a really fantastic management job for one of the biggest non-profits out there.

It just goes on and on. It helps people build their platforms. It helps people be able to get speaking engagements. They get out there and get known. One of the things that I really like to stress is not only is it, "Are you John?" or to be involved in a book especially a bestselling book, but it is also I feel everyone's really, obligation, not just right. They need to get their story out.

I had a very dear friend who passed a year or two ago. Her name was Joan King. She was a coach and neuroscientist. She used to always say that when you do not get your story out, no one else can tell your story the way you do and it leaves a hole in the world. That's how important I think it is for people to be able to tell their story so it resonates with people out there that need your help.

Many times, people don't think they have a strong enough story. There was a time when I thought I didn't have a strong enough story. I'm realizing sometimes day-to-day activities and things that you do that you take for granted can really move people's lives in just a marvelous way. It's a tremendous service to the universe and it's also a tremendous privilege for you to be able to do that and reap the rewards that having a book brings.

David: Yes. I really believe that. I've had a number of people in my peer network around the world saying, "Why did you work with Viki? Why are you working with Camille Nash at Voice America?" I say, "Let's find the audiences and the community that understands our message, our stories, our hopes, our dreams. Let's make it easily accessible to them."

You do that. Camille Nash does that as well. I guess the story that I don't think I've shared with you, Viki is the golden guy on "Ready, Aim, Excel!" that we published a few years ago and became an international business bestseller is Marshall Goldsmith.

A few months after that, I met Marshall Goldsmith at a conference in Calgary, Canada where we had a good conversation. I invited him to provide his wisdom in to my book "Break Through to Yes". Marshall knew me, thought I was worthwhile and he, like you, are now in my book "Break Through to Yes."

I look at that and I say, "This is a global community and we've got like-minded people. Let's take advantage wherever we can with successful collaborators." Viki, I really thank you for that opportunity.

Viki: Again, it's a pleasure. I feel it's really my purpose in life. I had a chance to meet Marshall at a very Mastermind at Maryville Resort face-to-face. We'd always talk by phone and do interviews that way. It was just an extraordinary experience.

I think that Marshall is such a good example of collaboration at the best because if he believes in you, he is so generous with his time. There are a number of people out there. I know. We think they're too busy or they wouldn't consider working with us because they don't know us or whatever.

I think with collaboration if you have something to offer them, so many people will say yes. We've had just extraordinary people because we were willing to ask them if they would like to be showcased. So many people it's like the prettiest girl in a high school that doesn't get asked to the prom because everyone thinks she already has a date.

That's what one of our authors pointed out to me, Jensen Blow. I just slipped it in that it's so true. You really have to step up with a lot of confidence and yes, I get that you might get some no's but the yeses are out there to collaborate in abundance with some people that I never dreamed I'd ever meet. We've gotten to know them really well, partnered with them on a number of different projects.

David: Yes. In today's digital world, there is only one degree of separation. Viki, as we come to a close I'm inviting all of my guests to challenge our listeners what is one thing that you would challenge our listeners to do or become more aware of to make their collaborations more successful?

Viki: I would say in the words of Joseph Campbell there, my favorite words, "Follow your bliss." If you were doing what you love, you are a delight to work with. You will be so in passion by what you do that you will not let anything stop you including maybe that little fearful of asking someone who's really a big name to collaborate. All of that will come very naturally to you if you're doing what you love and just as Campbell says, "Doors will open that you never even knew were there."

David: Wonderful. Thank you so much, Viki Winterton.

Viki: All my pleasure. Always wonderful to spend time with you, David.

David: Listeners, I am just amazed that the quality of interviews that I'm able to do on Break Through to Yes. Today we have just a huge spirit, a huge generous spirit and a leader for the social impact, Tara Russell, president of Fathom. Fathom is a social impact company that offers a new category of travel and global impact led by the Carnival Corporation, the world's largest travel and leisure company.

Tara generated the idea for Fathom in 2013, and led research, design, and development of the brand, business model, and experience from January 2014 to this past June 2015. She now leads the Fathom team as it offers a unique experience to purpose-driven travelers who desire authentic, meaningful social impact opportunities.

Fathom provides the opportunity to immerse in another culture and community, and systematically work alongside that community to make relevant contributions that endure. Prior to joining Carnival and creating Fathom, Tara Russell was founder and CEO of Create Common Good. That's createcommongood.org.

That's a non-profit social enterprise that provides training and employment to refugees in a wide variety of other populations with barriers to employment. Since 2009, CCG, createcommongood.org graduates have earned in excess of $18 million in additional wages. Check out Tara Russell more at fathom.org.

Tara, welcome and thank you so much for being with us today. Tell us more about you and your work.

Tara: Thank you so much for having me today. It's quite an honor. My joy in life has been really trying to figure out what are the unique gifts and talents that I have and how do I use those the best and most significantly impact the world.

My personal passion is really helping other people connect to their passion. I love to leverage the opportunity to use business for social impact. I'm a firm believer in terms of combining real market demand with social needs in communities and pairing those for sustainable impact.

My background is a little bit diverse in that I started in engineering. I'm an engineer-turned-businessperson. I started my first career working the corporate world for General Motors and Intel and Nike. A lot of that time I was living and working overseas especially in Asia. It was really during that time that I was trying to figure out how to combine my love of business and my desire to have a significant humanitarian impact on the world.

At the time I thought it was two very different paths and I really felt during that year that the vision became clear to me that I needed to figure out a way to use business for social impact and really think about this space of purpose-driven business. Those are the adventures that I've been busy on over the last 16 years building a variety of different start-up companies.

I've been fortunate to have lived and worked across the world in different countries and always focused on marginalized community groups -- women living and working in prostitution, families living in slum communities, refugee population, homeless population, and lots of other people who often are falling through the cracks and sometime forgotten about.

It's been my real passion to figure what are market-driven solutions to poverty and to social needs. That's really what Create Common Good is about. Create Common Good is a food production company and we work to empower a lot of these populations through this food production model. At the same time, we're selling saleable food products to lots of different restaurants and food service locations day-to-day, week-to-week.

That helped us just form the model because we all realized that so many social and humanitarian services cost a great deal of money. To me, sale and profit efforts only go so far. Really sustaining a strategic operation requires an earned revenue stream. For me, it has often been best to identify and work to build an earned revenue stream that really sustains that social impact.

That's really what Fathom is about. I have loved living and working and traveling around the world and so many of our friends and community members have often leaned on us to help them find meaningful opportunities to do social impact efforts on the ground when they travel.

Anecdotally, I have just had the experience of helping other people do trips like this. Yet as we begin to really explore the market and the desire out there, we found there's a large and growing audience that wants to engage with travel that also combines with making a difference. That's really what Fathom is about. We say that Fathom is a different kind of cruise for people who want to make a difference.

We're creating an entirely new category of travel and very focused on this systematic, a long-sided opportunity to impact a community and place over time. It isn't about a one-week trip. It isn't about fragments of efforts. It's a very strategic partnership with a country with a community region and an opportunity really amplifies some of the great things that are already happening there.

David: Tara, what are some of the countries? I believe it's mostly the Gulf of Mexico region that you travel to?

Tara: I have been fortunate to live and work in a variety of places globally but our efforts with Fathom are focused on two initial partner countries. Our first partner country is the Dominican Republic and our second partner country is Cuba. Both of those are down in that region. We see this as phase one for Fathom as the tenth brand to the Carnival corporate family, phase one of our social impact efforts.

Our goal is really to build sustainable impact models that we could replicate to any one of the number of places that we go globally. Just corporately we have 10 global brands now including Fathom. We visit 700 plus locations around the world. We have a scale and a platform that allows us the chance to really touch and influence a large number of communities over time.

David: I got to tell you that I'm sure I'm not the only one listening today that says, "I want to go on Fathom. I want to create common good while I travel and incorporate it all." Tara, looking from the other side of the coin, so to speak, there really is no other way to do business is there? This is the way that current and growing businesses align to their customers' interests so that by doing this kind of work we actually create better business.

Tara: We think it's just smart business. I wholeheartedly agree with you. If you think about it, as we do this right, which we're very focused on because our board is authentic and intact. We aren't going to do something that isn't genuinely both needed and making a tremendous difference in the region that we're serving.

Beyond that, the reality is as we work to help these communities flourish, we also create a better atmosphere for all of our travelers to come and visit. It's a win-win here where by investing in the region and in the people and these partner communities, our travelers, again we have ten global brands and nearly 11 million passengers a year. That's 11 million people's experience who was enhanced as they were in that region as we invest in these communities.

When we do this right, it's an opportunity for our travelers to really grow, to be enriched, and our goal is for them to come back different. We really believe every individual has the opportunity to use their different talents to make a difference in the world in a way that nobody else does. Yet we also believe most people still want to figure out what's that path and what's that journey supposed to look like.

What we do is we make it really easy for people to have a human impact journey progress that we help them discover what do they care about? What are they good at? How do they use those things when they get back home? That's really a huge transformative opportunity for us with the travelers.

In the places that we go, by coming alongside these efforts that perhaps couldn't invest as fully in what we're doing. We're radically affecting the education outcomes in the region. We're radically affecting the economic development opportunities in the region. We're making a hugely positive contribution to the environmental efforts in regions.

It's both what the market wants to do, but there's obviously real need in communities globally and it's just what we believe as real sustainable development. It's good for everyone. Everybody wins.

David: Tara Russell, as we close this interview, what is one thing that you wish to challenge or encourage our audience to do as they reset their vision on collaboration?

Tara: I just believe so much in having a very kind of student-minded, humble approach to everything in life. I love to learn and my lifelong commitment is to keep learning. I think collaboration requires a very humble posture and just the kind of student perspective I think.

Recognizing that we all have something to learn in any relationship is one of the most helpful pieces when you're pulling off any collaboration. That's just one thing to perhaps kind of think about as you enter in to new potential partnership opportunities.

David: Thank you so much, Tara Russell, President of Fathom. This has been awesome. Thank you for speaking to our listeners on a very busy day for you.

Tara: It's a treat to be with you. Thanks so much. Take care.

David: Today we've got Stephen Smith. He's a good friend of mine. We've known each other for a long time. He's a 1979 graduate of the Southern Alberta Institute of Technology, Petroleum Tech program and has been with the Regulator in its various forms, EUB, ERCB, and now the Alberta Energy Regulator.

Since his graduation in 1979, Stephen has worked throughout the organization doing Reserves, Applications Audits, and led the Facilities Applications areas. For our listeners around the world, the Alberta Energy Regulator is the entity, the non-government regulatory agency that actually holds court, makes the approvals, sets the processes for energy development in the province of Alberta, Canada.

In 1996, Stephen and I worked many other professionals through the Calgary Chamber of Commerce

Appropriate Dispute Resolution Committee that I chaired. We worked hard as volunteers to create and promote then assist with the development and implementation of the Alberta Energy Regulator's Appropriate Dispute Resolution program . Stephen has been an advocate of ADR ever since.

Here's a piece of how I know Stephen. He and I along with Arden Berg, Bill Remer, David Gould, and Noel Rea, and many others in industry, the AER and the communities in Alberta came together. It's high conflict, high emotions, high engagement, high money and Stephen was an important part of creating that regulatory ADR program and process.

Since that time, Stephen has taken an even easier road in Fort McMurray as Executive Manager of the Oil Sands and then as Executive Manager of Applications Branch at the ERCB. Another one of the places where Stephen and I have worked together is with respect to tailing ponds from oil sands mining.

I know that tailing ponds and that Canadian oil sands is a trigger for some our listeners and many around the globe, both positive and negative. I'm just proud to say that my friend, Stephen Smith, has been adamant that we do better, we do right and we balance all the interests while we move forward.

There was recently an election in Alberta. Since that election, Stephen Smith is now working with the National and International Stakeholder and Government Relations Division to bring the AER's regulatory experience to other energy regulators and jurisdictions around the world.

While the Alberta Energy Regulator is world-class. It has dealt with these challenges in so many ways.

Welcome, Stephen Smith. Enough about talking about your bio. What would you like our listeners to know more about and how do they learn more about you and the Alberta Energy Regulator?

Stephen: Thanks for the very kind introduction, David. It has been a long time that we worked together on a number of very seminal issues particularly important for the public in Alberta, I think in terms of regulatory excellence, one of the things that the regulators strive for many years.

If you want to know more about the Alberta Energy Regulator, certainly our website has some excellent information on all of the different services -- the ways that we engage our applications, processes, our dispute resolution processes.

Certainly, if you're a resident of Alberta, member of the public and you're interested or concerned about oil and gas development in the province, that website's the perfect place to go and learn more about us as an organization.

David: Before we get in to some of the more detailed questions, tell us a little bit more, Stephen about your work with the National and International Stakeholder and Government Relations Division. That's quite the collaboration and quite the title right there.

Stephen: It's been an interesting evolution of work here at the AER and its numerous as you reflected on, numerous iterations and manifestations over the years. We have always though as a provincial regulator and our chief concern and focus is certainly the regulatory framework in Alberta and developing the provinces' resources in the public interest.

We have always been sought out by other jurisdictions. We host 30 to 40 different delegations a year from national and international regulators looking to see how we as an organization do our work to the level that we do. Just as a point of context, Alberta has some of the world's third largest resources of oil and gas globally.

We've been regulating that resource for almost eighty years.

We have a huge responsibility and we have a huge amount of experience in how to manage that particularly when it comes to managing issues such as stakeholder or public concerns related to oil and gas development.

You're right. We're criticized often by people that see our work as promoting development, but in actuality our job is really all about balancing the needs of all the parties in the process. In fact, if we actually do end up pleasing somebody too much, we're probably not doing our job very well.

The national and international component is one that has taken a larger perspective here in the last little while in that we're now I think more actively trying to learn from other jurisdictions and help them and assist them more proactively in learning about how we regulate the oil and gas business here in Alberta.

David: Stephen, tell me specifically a little more about the role of alternate dispute resolution in the regulatory framework.

Stephen: We've always tried to engage with the public with other parties. Sometimes we have industry and industry disputes and we need to work through those. The majority of the ones that are of high profile for us and certainly a specific concern are the ones where the public feel like they're being impacted by oil and gas development and feel like they need to be heard better through the process.

In disputes, the more formal dispute resolutions, as you're familiar because you've helped us and supported us in the development of that process here at the AER, previously the ERCB, was finding some more structured way of giving people support through that process, helping our staff understand that process better so that they will better able to implement the engagement and to do it in ways that are supported by the best education of the time in those concepts doing interest-based negotiation instead of trying to defend positions.

That support and that education really, I think facilitated our ability to manage the disputes, put the issues on the table, have people think about why it was that they had concerns around oil and gas development and get to the core of what it was that they were concerned about in a very practical and pragmatic way.

At times in our organization we process as many as 50,000 or 60,000 applications a year. In those years, the requirement to go to a sort of a more formal arbitration at a formalized hearing process, which is both time-consuming and very costly, has only been required to occur in a dozen or so cases.

When you're processing 50,000 applications and only a dozen of them are actually requiring that level of arbitration then the continuum of dispute resolution that occurs between the application being considered by the company and then their stakeholder engagement being done and getting to a point where you can resolve the matters and it has to be turned over to a panel of folks to do arbitration means that the dispute resolution process that we have in place here organizationally I think works very well.

Does that mean that everybody's always happy with it? No. It does mean that I think everybody gets their opportunity to be heard, to be understood, to feel like they've been heard and understood, and allows us to come to a decision that's essentially in the best interest of the province.

David: Yes, that is just so critical. Getting the parties to get together face-to-face and actually listening to each other is critical. Before we end this interview, Stephen, is there one thing that you could challenge our listeners to become more aware of or do more frequently with respect to collaboration?

Stephen: I think it's really about exercising integrity and communication, making sure that when you're talking about the issues that you have, you're talking about the issues, not your position. Quite often we get companies that get polarized with stakeholders around certain pieces. When they don't think about why it is that they're defending the position that they have, the sense of reason would end the discussion and gets lost.

If people exercise integrity around the issues that are really a concern to them then you can work on the issues and resolving the issues rather than on defending positions. That really for me is the critical piece that people need to get to.

David: Thank you so much, Stephen Smith of the Alberta Energy Regulator for your wisdom and your commitment to the public and to the economy.

Stephen: You're more than welcome, David. Thanks very much for the invitation.

David: You've just heard about the focus and processes of the Alberta Energy Regulator. The AER has been creating its role and system through networks in Alberta and across the world. The AER is seen as a model for others around the world. They have recently worked with Penn State University in developing their regulatory excellence program. Stephen's challenge to you included exercise integrity in your communications and relationships.

Early November 2015, I convened an interactive presentation titled Rethink Stakeholder Engagement in Regulatory Processes. That was at the Synergy Alberta annual conference in Calgary. I poked several bears. Yes, I poked the AER, Synergy Alberta, the National Energy Board in Canada, professional land men, the Canadian Environmental Assessment Agency, and others.

I've been convening stakeholder engagement conflict resolution, conflict engagement, all of these things for a good part of my career bringing people to round tables, circles together to build respect. I think the system is broken. My intention is to rethink the way we relate, engage, and make decisions related to our applications from mining, oil and gas, pipelines, and more.

Here is our learning in the past decade in Canada. If you are a proponent, just because you get approval doesn't mean you can proceed. That's right. Just because you get approval doesn't mean you can succeed. If you're the adversely affected landowner, that doesn't mean you will be heard.

Both business and landowners, too often, find our processes and expecting there are many nations around the world, jurisdictions around the world that have these same problems. Our processes diminish respect, trust, innovation, transparency, interest in collaboration.

You'll be soon able to view the video of my talk via my website and on my You Tube site. Are you ready to rethink your systems and behaviors? What is your social impact and license to operate? The system serves the system. It doesn't serve business or landowners well. Be careful. Rethink it all.

Now we'll go to break.

David: Our next guest is Linda Matthie. I'm just very pleased. Linda has been a good friend of mine for a long time, somebody that I really have mentored by. Linda is a versatile and conscientious professional with over 30 years of experience in the oil and gas industry and 20 years plus as an independent business owner and entrepreneur. Yay, entrepreneurs.

She applies solid technical skills in joint venture operations in multi-tasking, leadership, relationships, mentoring, organization, writing, communication, negotiation, and problem solving. She does develop very effective working relationships. She is well loved, well regarded by...it just seems like the list is ever expanding.

Linda is President of MJM Grande Enterprises Ltd. and she operates out of Calgary, Alberta, Canada and Cabo San Lucas, Mexico. MJM Grande Enterprises is a diversified company that has several subsidiaries including consulting and publishing.

Linda, what more can you inform our listeners about who you are or what you do and how they can find you online?

Linda: David, what a beautiful introduction. Thank you so much. It makes me sound really, really, old. I think the one common factor throughout everything and I have enjoyed my time in petroleum immensely and in all the other endeavors.

The common factor comes back to people and relationships. That is truly the common thread with which I hope that I lead my life with and where I put all my appropriate priority.

David: Wow. You're also a published author, successful author. Tell us a little bit about that venture.

Linda: Oh, thank you for bringing that up. It was fun. It was a passion center. I love to share my table with people that I care about. I've written three national bestselling cookbooks and you can find out more about those at Cooking with Fire. It's all food with attitude. It's really about sharing time and space at the table with people you care about.

David: Yes, literally and metaphorically. Linda, you've been one of the people I reached out to for quotes on my "Break Through to Yes" book. You very kindly offered me something that touched my heart. Tell us a little more about that.

Linda: When you asked me for the quote, I was thinking on a more, I guess minute level, on a more micro-level. The more I contemplated what collaboration truly is, and you and I were able to collaborate on some brainstorming ideas, things that you hadn't perhaps thought of.

One of which was when you went out to your network and asked for their input to the covers on your book. I thought that was just a wonderful piece of collaboration, a wonderful test group of like-minded individuals that provided enough to verse input. Just little things that I've walked that walk before and it's such a joy to be able to share some of that knowledge and collaborate with you.

As we've done in many other ventures in petroleum and other ways we've been able to collaborate, share common themes and ideas because I think one of the things I did say is that collaboration requires a high level of respect for and trust in one another. That's something that I truly hold in very high quantity for you, David. I highly respect you and I highly trust you. That's a very critical element to many of our collaborations.

David: Very much so and Linda, you're one of the many people, special people that I walk away from a conversation with and think, "Wow. I knew that and she brought it to light. She brought it to heart." Thank you.

In a recent conversation that you and I had. We were talking about the world of global politics, global leadership. There are things that we want so much more of. What can you share with our listeners around the world today, Linda about what you hope for versus what seems to be most common?

Linda: Certainly, I'd love to expand on that. What I've been thinking a lot about especially in anticipation of this conversation, David, is right now and I don't mean to timestamp where we are at this moment, but we're right in the thrust of political, bi-partisan, and tri-partisan arguments, one-upmanship in both the United States and Canada.

What's really occurred to me, I was thinking of collaboration when we first started talking on a smaller level. I'm now thinking about collaboration on a much larger level.

I'm thinking that if our politicians, if the leaders in our countries focus more on the big picture and the real issues, release their egos, stop playing their tri- or bi-partisan politics and really work towards a solution that I honestly believe that we could impact significant improvement, change, and betterment in areas like the economy, poverty, crime, employment and unemployment, health care, social issues of all sorts, immigration, what's happening right now in the United States with Mexico, education which has become such a critical, critical piece around the world.

If our leaders could just focus on solving the problems instead of pointing fingers at one another and one-upmanship, I think we have so much brilliance in those people that we could actually, actually do some good if they work together and stepped out of their ego.

David: Yes. Now, Linda you have very special perspective because you have your heart in Mexico. You have your heart in the United States of America and you have your heart in Canada.

Linda: That's true.

David: You are given a very wide and international perspective. As we close out this interview, with that in mind, Linda what's one thing that you wish our listeners to become more aware of, to challenge themselves on?

Linda: The piece that I've come to, in contemplating more about collaboration, it is about trust. It is about respect. More importantly and the only way we can get to true and effective collaboration is if people work toward something bigger than themselves and literally leave their egos at the door.

David: Thank you so much, Linda Matthie, a great friend, mentor, and an international entrepreneur. Thanks, Linda.

Linda: Thank you so much, David. What a pleasure.

David: Today we've explored some of the collaborative wisdom of Viki Winterton, Tara Russell, Stephen Smith, and Linda Matthie.

Key messages today included:

1) learn to listen at several levels to understand what is really going on.
2) create sustainable social impact models by collaborating with people, governments, and corporations who you align through social impact visions. This is a strategic impact and your human impact journey.
3) collaboration requires a high level of respect and trust. Walk your talk every day. That's right, every day.

This is so important. Next week's guests on our radio show and podcast, this will be show number 11 of our 15-week series. They are: Dana Meise, Dana has walked farther than any man. He's walked the Trans-Canada trail from the Atlantic to the Pacific to the Arctic. We will have Dee Ann Turner of Chick-fil-A, VP-Human Resources. We will have Teresa de Grosbois.

With those people, we are so fortunate and pardon me. I skipped over Teresa's...four-time bestselling author now. Dee Ann Turner is a first-time bestselling author. Also, we have Doreen Liberto Blanck of San Louis, Obispo of Earth Designs.

Thank you everyone. Now collaborate. Have a break through week.

Chapter 11 Collaborate with Vision featuring Dee Ann Turner, Doreen Liberto, Dana Meise, Teresa de Grosbois

David: Welcome, listeners from across our planet. Welcome those that know we are truly connected and not separated by borders, beliefs, organizations or intentions. Now is our time to E.S.C.A.P.E. the tyranny of the communications and leadership barriers too often witnessed in our political, regulatory, media, and special interest groups.

In my book "Break Through to Yes," I set out ten steps that are essential to successful collaboration. This show's theme is Collaborate with Vision. That's step number eight of my ten. I'm delighted to provide you with the insights and stories of my collaborative network. I challenge anyone to show me where they can find the connection to 45 experts and do it so openly and on your time.

What I've decided to do and what my guests have allowed me to do is, I'm really excited about this, with the support of my 45 guests in this 15-week series, I will be publishing a book next year, an e-book, an audio set "Break Through to Yes: The Wisdom on the Podcasts."

This will include all the interviews plus excerpts of my talks and recent workshops. This is going to be so cool. I don't have to be the rock star. I just have to know an amazing community of wise people, collaborative leaders around the world.

Today's show features more wise people, friends of mine, people I deeply respect: Dana Meise, Prince George, British Columbia; Dee Ann Turner, Atlanta, Georgia; Teresa de Grosbois, Calgary, Alberta; Doreen Liberto Blanck, San Luis Obispo, California.

Today's key messages include:

1) your dreams will inspire others and inspire you;
2) collaboration is a key part of your successful organizational culture; and
3) how you are in relationship with others will define your future success.

Here's a quote from "Break Through to Yes: Unlocking the Possible within a Culture of Collaboration," "In the past we said, 'The sky is the limit.' With collaboration, producing multinational space exploration probes, we may say, 'The universe is the limit.'"

Consider my client and friend, Ron Fraser's thoughts on this and what he has to say about collaboration in my book. Here's Ron: "First we live in confusing times made more confusing by the tendency of more powerful people to speak for supposedly less powerful ones.

At every level of our human interaction whether business, medicine, law, education, whatever, why not discover the actual interest that people have? Why not truly discover with clarity by inviting real people with real interests to use their own voice?

Collaboration levels the playing field by reducing the confusion created by power. Second, collaboration is a behavior, even a liturgy that hold profound promise in shaping the deepest desires of human flourishing -- the desire to love and be loved. Collaborative habits can set the table for some of the most primordial longings that make us truly human.

A third reason is the hope that collaboration holds for learning. If finding and using one's own voice has anything at all to do with personal transformation, i.e. learning then collaboration holds the essential keys -- the practice of putting in to words, articulating what we mean, reshaping our horizons. When we speak and hear others, our worlds move.

The fourth reason and perhaps the most important one, is that collaboration becomes not just a practice but a way of being, a way of becoming." Ron Fraser, Director of Learning Services, the Alberta Bible College in Calgary, Alberta.

Leadership can connect your people within your organization as well as across the world in ways that we have not seen possible until now. Leadership is, also, about connecting with self.

Are you in alignment with your values in your actions and communications? What values does a collaborative leader hold? Are you in coherence between your head and your heart? Do you lead from your heart and your whole intelligence? Do you see your purpose as getting the right things done that serve the whole?

As a conscious leader, conscious business leader, what is your answer to I am, we are? Fill in the blanks. I am. We are. Take some time to think about this. Your answers as they're expressed in the moment and as they evolve over time inform your vision, purpose, community, actions, and relationships.

These questions were from a friend of mine as a collaborative effort took shape among 100 peers from around the world who contributed their wisdom to "Break Through to Yes: Unlocking the Possible within a Culture of Collaboration." Together, we will take our awareness, curiosity, and decisions to a much more profound and successful level.

Today we've got Dana Meise, the Great Hike specialist on the Trans Canada Trail. In December 2013, my friend Dana became the first person to hike across Canada from coast to coast, east to west on the Trans Canada Trail; huge accomplishment. He is about to complete 24,000 kilometers of that Trans Canada Trail. Dana is in Dawson City in the Yukon right now on his way to the Arctic Ocean.

Welcome, Dana.

Dana: Hey. It's good to be part of your show.

David: Dana, can you give our listeners a little bit of background to yourself and why you're doing the Great Hike?

Dana: I just had the dream to do it. I made a promise to my father who can't walk. You know a promise is a promise. A handshake deal is a handshake deal, in my world anyway. That's it. It's been nothing but dividends. It's such an amazing journey. All the people are so amazing and everything's remarkable. Yes, indeed.

David: You're an amazing person and an amazing man, Dana. I have a huge admiration for you because you've largely been doing this on your own and yet you've learned to collaborate along the way. You've borne everything on your own time and expense and yet you've learned that there are many, many people there that would really love to help you. Can you share a little more about that, Dana?

Dana: Interestingly enough when I first began, embarrassingly enough I'll tell you straight up, I was very egotistical in the sense that I don't need help. I'm independent. I'm strong. I'm a strong guy. What I realized was I was losing out on a lot of opportunity. People really, really wanted to be part of the journey.

It was just one of those realizations . "Oh, my goodness. I'm actually being a jerk here," in a sense that these people really want to be part of it and not for ego, not for recognition, just because what I did echo effected everything maybe, perhaps what they wanted to do.

I was fortunate to have some people in the beginning of my journey especially in Newfoundland, which is an easy place to get along. These people had really wanted to be part of what you were doing. I realized that I had the ability to give back.

Because when people offer you food or something, you think that they're just giving it to you. No. You're in their world giving them a story. I didn't realize the power of the story and the power of just getting along.

David: There's a big piece of this that many of us have got to learn more of from people like you, Dana where we think we have to do it all ourselves and that excludes others.

Dana: Yes, and that's such an awful way of thinking. That's where I went wrong. I went wrong at first and then I realized very quickly that everything I've done is like, "I have a gift. I'm giving back." Collaboration is all about give and take but your contribution can be something you don't realize you're contributing; like you inspire someone to walk down that street, to see a waterfall you've never seen before.

You inspire people all the time and you don't realize you're doing it. That's a dialogue you have with the people you're with.

David: Wonderful. We've got a couple of minutes left, Dana. How did people find out more about you in the Great Hike?

Dana: Just through Great Hike. I don't self-promote. I don't have somebody doing it for me. I really like the natural aspect of just meeting people along the way. While I'm on the Yukon here, the word of mouth is crazy here because people have a lot of flip phones. The point is people just love what you do and the word gets around and people feel like gold.

I don't know what else to say other than to say that people just tend to really resonate with somebody who's just following a dream and just out there doing what they got to do.

David: Yes. While you're a great Canadian and world-class explorer, I think you probably have the Guinness Records for the longest hike.

Dana: Yes, I do.

David: Wonderful.

Dana: I was also named one of the 100 greatest explorers of all time by Canadian Geographic which was for me honestly, when I read that, they don't tell you that, they just do it. When I read that, I was...just sat on my ass and was, "I cannot believe it!" I'm so grateful that people really, really thought that my journey's been that wonderful.

David: Do you have one final thing that you'd like to share with our listeners today?

Dana: Yes. I guess it's just all about...well, you're about collaboration, I mean the book and everything and what you're doing is remarkable because I really, truly believe that because I'm not anti-anything. I'm always pro whatever-makes-sense. I guess that would be my big thing, just listen to what your opponent has to say.

Many times, people don't always love my hike by the way. People would be, "You're living off the tax dollars. Blah-blah-blah." I always win them over because I'm like, "No, actually in fact, I did this on my own and I have sponsorship and I pay taxes like everyone else."

What ends up happening is I win them over. That's just by hearing their voice and understanding. I don't just walk away and be like, "That was a jerk." I don't do that. My whole goal with this journey has always been information. You never know where that can come from. It can sometimes come from one of your adversaries.

David: A solitary hiker over seven years is connecting communities and people and the nation.

Dana: All these years connecting all these communities and more often than not it's just an angry person. What happens is you speak with them and what happens is that I ask them, "Where are you from?" They'll be like, "I'm from London, Ontario." I'm like, "Oh, home of Sir Frederick Banting, right who invented insulin?

Imagine how many lives he saved as a Canadian. What an amazing life he had by the way."

Suddenly he lights up and he's like, "Well, yes. Yes, yes, yes! That's where I'm from. Yes, yes!" Even if he didn't realize that that's where he's from, it lights him up.

That's what the hike has done for me. It allowed me to open so many doors because I have walked over a thousand Canadian communities and I can just see them. When I meet people, I always say, "Where are you from?" Then we would talk. I would also get through with an amazing recall ability; meaning...

David: I'm sorry that for right now, we're going to have to end this interview.

Dana: No worries. No worries.

David: You light us up. Thank you so much, Dana for everything that you're doing. We will be in touch. We will find ways to celebrate your film, your book, and my book as well and my radio show in the future.

Dana: David, you have no idea. I would do anything for you. You are the true deal. I aspire to be, hopefully one day with your coaching I hope, at some point in your shoes.

David: Thank you so much, Dana.

Dana: Yes. Thank you, too.

David: Dee Ann Turner has worked for Chick-fil-A for more than 30 years and currently serves as Vice President, Corporate Talent. That's not Human Resources, Corporate Talent. Over the years, Dee Ann has played an intricate role in growing Chick-fil-A's unique and highly regarded culture while overseeing recruitment, selection, retention of corporate staff and recruitment of the franchisees.

Dee Ann's insightful knowledge and applicable tools to building an incredible and influential culture are revealed in her new book, her bestselling book. I'm so happy for Dee Ann. She is published November 3rd and immediately became a bestseller. "It's My Pleasure: The Impact of Extraordinary Talent and A Compelling Culture."

Dee Ann, tell our listeners a little bit more about yourself and how they can learn more about you.

Dee Ann: Sure, David. Thank you very much. We have enjoyed a tremendous culture at Chick-fil-A that was founded by our founder, Truett Cathy. I had the opportunity to do work with him side-by-side for about 28 of those 30 years that I worked for Chick-fil-A. His principle was all about people. He liked to say we're not in the chicken business. We're in the people business. The people decisions are the most important decisions we make.

From his guidance and influence, I chose to write a book about these experiences. In that book, one can learn about the essence of compelling culture, can learn about building a team that creates a compelling culture, growing a compelling culture within your team, and engaging your gift in a compelling culture.

All those things are about selecting the talent and about the principles and behaviors that cause people to stay with you a long, long time which has resulted in Chick-fil-A's not only a great sales path of double digit sales increases over most of the years we've been in business but also 95% retention rates of our corporate staff and our franchisees.

David: 95%.

Dee Ann: 95%.

David: Wow! Tell me more because that's just unheard of. That is unique.

Dee Ann: It started with Truett. He really believed that if you make the right selection then everything else would fall in to place if you just made the right selection. We invest a ton of time. It is probably average about 90 to 120 days average that somebody is in the selection process for a job or to become a franchisee.

The purpose of that is two-fold. One is obvious, to make sure that we make a really good selection. The second is we like for people to get to know us within that time period so they can make sure it's what they really want to do because we're looking for, as often as possible, long-term relationship. We believe that's helped make us more successful.

Really what's been behind that retention is that we make that we make the right selection to begin with. We invest the money and the time upfront to do that and then we don't have to spend as much money and time on the backend making changes.

David: Yes. Tell me about that backend. I've got a lot of experience in that. What I'm really hearing is, Dee Ann you're talking about making sure that it's you really do the work. You really get the right people and support them and engage them without treating them as widgets or resources. What happens at the backend? Your 95% retention, that's exceptional.

Dee Ann: The back-end for most people associated with Chick-fil-A is retirement because that's what most people do when they come here. They stay till retirement. If something turns out not to be a good fit, the first thing we do is performance-related. We've made a commitment so we work very, very hard to give every opportunity for someone who's struggling.

We do that through whatever coaching is needed, training that's needed, development that's needed. We really do everything we can to make it successful before we give up on it and hopefully the employee gives up on it. That backend is predominantly we're planning people's retirement, receptions versus asking them to exit the company.

David: Yes, that's so wise and great business because you don't have a turnstile coming in where you're selecting, re-training, doing all that and de-selecting. It allows you to be much more focused during that five-year or 50-year career I'm sure.

Dee Ann: Right. The selection process can be expensive but the turnover is...usually the average of any employee in the US is $15,000 to $25,000 to replace them. I think that's conservative. I think it's worth the investment and not to mention the distractions you don't have by keeping people in place. When you move people, that's a huge distraction to rebuild a team and in fact, it impacts your ability to collaborate.

David: Yes. For those people that have not yet read "It's My Pleasure," tell our listeners one big idea in your book.

Dee Ann: I think that there are many. There are several things in there. I think one of my favorite sections and people tell me what's a favorite section of mine, I talk about and it's really related to what we're just talking about, I talk about stewarding talent. I talk about stewarding emerging talent and stewarding seasoned talent because that works a little bit differently in each case.

Emerging talent they say they're looking for early opportunities like feedback, lots of early responsibility. They do bring fresh ideas to the table. Seasoned leadership which we have a lot of at Chick-fil-A obviously with the high retention, they bring context to the discussion, wisdom, lots of years of experience of saying what's worked and what hasn't worked.

Where we're truly remarkable as an organization is when we're able to leverage those emerging talent and seasoned talent together. Our organization really works at that to get those fresh, new ideas and I call it the momentum. When I think about seasoned talent, I call that the endurance. When momentum and endurance come together, that's where we create some really remarkable results.

David: Dee Ann, this is fascinating to me because oftentimes in my generation and I'm older than you are, my generation tends to get in the way. The older we get, the more it's important and what I hear you say, the more important it is to let the seasoned talent mentor, support, and encourage and be part of the training but not plug up the system.

Dee Ann: Yes, absolutely. I think that and, David I of course understand that after 30 years as well. I think the most important thing that I do as a leader right now is to provide the context to help people see the boundaries, to remove the barriers for them, and then let them go and encourage them along the path and let them come to me when they need help. The most important thing sometimes I can do is just stay out of the way.

David: Yes. I was at the Omega Institute and we're putting on a presentation probably about ten years ago, Dee Ann. One of the participants, Ann Begler of Pittsburgh. She said, "David, do you want to know the definition of respect?" I said, "Sure. Ann, tell me." She said, "It's not doing for others what they can do for themselves." I loved it.

Dee Ann: Oh, yes. That's great. That's very good.

David: Dee Ann, tell us a little more, I guess what I would like to do as we close this, in this moment what is the one thing you challenge our listeners to do or become more aware of to make their collaborations more successful?

Dee Ann: I think one of the most important things we can do is we want to leverage all the talent that's available to us. To do that, we must appreciate. We talked about the differences between the emerging and seasoned talent. There are all kinds of differences as they come to the table. If we really want to win with our businesses, we must be innovative. The way to be more innovative is to collaborate around differences.

We can bring that kind of diverse thinking and diverse experiences to the table and really leverage all of that. That's when an organization is really going to perform.

David: Wonderful. Any last comments? I'd like to continue this conversation for a long time but any last thoughts before we go, Dee Ann?

Dee Ann: I appreciate so much your time and I hope that your listeners will be interested in reading "It's My Pleasure."

David: I'll buy your book on whatever source you want.

Dee Ann: Just about any of them right now but amazon.com, at my website or at Barnes and Noble are some of the choices.

David: Wonderful. Thank you so much for your wisdom and your insight, Dee Ann Turner.

Dee Ann: Thank you so much, David.

David: In November 2015, I made a presentation to Synergy Alberta titled "Re-think Stakeholder Engagement in Regulatory Processes." I think we need to re-think simply because the processes diminish trust, innovation, relationship, respect, fairness, transparency, possibilities, community and they reduce collaboration. This is such a waste of time, such a waste of money, such a waste of innovation potential, and destroyer of trust.

The way we look at this is just not so fair. What I want to say is by re-thinking the whole process I want to create a vision of what's possible as opposed to forcing my clients, my province, my country, my world in to square pegs in round holes or round holes. It just doesn't work.

If you're a regulatory lawyer, a politician or somebody employed by the regulatory process or the professionals, mostly this works. I will admit. The outcome is they usually get it right. The process destroys possibility or at least diminishes it.

In my recent experience of defending clients who are faced with a mountain removal coal strip mine proposal in Alberta, I respect the International Coal Company. Good folks. We could communicate clearly. I respect the Canadian Environmental Assessment Agency, the AER, the National Energy Board, et cetera.

At the end of the day, you've got landowners right across the road from basically a mountain that's going to be destroyed, blown up, shipped away, separated. Who could go through six to eight years of process and not much recognition for what they're faced with?

When the money comes, it goes to the lawyers. It doesn't go to the landowners. When the companies make their applications, most of the processes were designed for short-term, things that can be resolved within weeks or months, not years. It separates. It really separates.

Let's look at who is rewarded or who gains from eight-year regulatory processes, millions and millions of dollars of process costs. Where is the public interest? When do we get to talk about shared value? When do we get to talk about the future?

In my presentation I talked about, with respect for the community, inclusion of the Piikani people of the Blackfoot Tribe, recognition of renewable energy initiatives, and a focus on economic, environmental, and community sustainability for this area and for Canada. Projects like this proposed mountain removal project are better served with a round table.

Earlier this summer I tried hard to get everybody just to sit down and say, "If we want the best for this area in the future, how do we create that together?" I challenged the listeners, the participants in my workshop what are the three things we need to re-think? How will we break through to yes? How will we proceed this way? These are all good questions and I want you to be part of the answer. Thank you.

David: "Living the life of your dreams takes action. Otherwise, you're just dreaming." That's a quote from my wonderful next guest, Teresa de Grosbois. Teresa is an international speaker sought by entrepreneurs and large corporations wanting to better understand how local word of mouth can suddenly turn epidemic. She specializes in topics including influence and success.

Teresa has a proven track record in understanding word of mouth epidemics and having taken three books to the bestseller status in only 8 months. She teaches business and marketing courses around the globe, including teaching classes to start-up entrepreneurs in developing countries.

Teresa is the Chair of the Evolutionary Business Council. That's the Evolutionary Business Council and leads an international, invitation-only council of speakers and influencers dedicated to teaching the principles of success. Go to her website, TeresadeGrosbois.com. You'll learn a lot more.

I learn a lot from Teresa. Teresa lives in Calgary, Alberta, Canada but she's a citizen of the world. One of the things that I mostly enjoy about the Evolutionary Business Council, its coaching leaders, it is a true collaborative where people can put an issue out and get influenced. Talking about influence, Teresa just released "Mass Influence: The Habits of the Highly Influential." Welcome, Teresa.

Teresa: It's great to be here, David.

David: Tell us more about you, your work, and the things that are important to you.

Teresa: I really have a lot of fun working with people who, everyday good people, everyday heroes that are just all about how do we teach the world better ways of being, better ways of thinking. I have a lot of fun helping regular people see that it's the everyday grassroots initiatives that really create the most change on the planet.

David: Yes. There's been such a shift, hasn't there? We have circumvented the mainstay, controlled processes of communication, connection, and learning. Through people like yourself, the Evolutionary Business Council and everybody in your organization and in your network, you make change.

I noticed that in my introduction as I was reading it, I'm curious more about the developing nations component of your work. I know that you travel a lot and you've done a lot. Can you share with your listeners a little more about collaborative leadership for the developing leaders and countries?

Teresa: If you really look at what's happening with a lot of the research on success and influence and leadership skills, there's an awful lot happening in the English-speaking world. A lot of the principles of success are really becoming everyday common knowledge in the English-speaking cultures of the world.

For example, we know that a lot of us create self-limiting beliefs in those earliest years of our lives often before we reached the age of six. Often those first failures in life create a lot of self-limiting beliefs that start running the show as we get older.

Most good successful leaders have had to overcome a lot of that hard wiring, overcome a lot of that negative self-talk to step in to leadership and influence. Yet, much of that research and much of that thinking is not making it in to other language cultures.

In fact, I personally believe that when we can find the folks that are teaching that and really help them, help get that knowledge out to the far-reaching corners of the world that actually is going to create significant shift in terms of not only fixing the economy of the poorest countries but shifting basic fundamental things on this planet like how much war we end up in and how much conflict and strife there is.

David: Yes, creating that global connection that we have, such the easiest access in the world to each other through the internet; for example, through telephones. I also want to come back to "Mass Influence." As somebody that I respect a great deal, you've published three bestsellers previously. You've just published "Mass Influence." As somebody that's keenly interested in what you do and how you do it, obviously I wanted to jump in on social media. I wanted to pre-order "Mass Influence."

What's happened since the release? Tell us about how you crowd sourced, engaged at a local level. What's happened?

Teresa: It's pretty humbling what's been going on with this book since release day. I'm deeply moved to see the response this book has had because the same day we launched, we hit the bestseller list in three countries, in Canada, the UK, and Germany. I have since hit number one in four countries. We're now in the bestseller lists in Canada and Australia as well. We hit number one in Australia yesterday.

It's interesting watching the response this book has got but it's very basic practical principles laid down in this book. Influence in my world is a lot like breathing. Breathing was a skill you had to learn in the first few seconds you were alive. If you didn't learn it, your life was going to be very difficult and once you learned it, you never really thought about that skill again. Yet, breathing takes up 24 hours of every day.

Influence is a lot like that. It's a very natural and intuitive skill. Once you learn it, you never really think about it again. You simply move through your day using the principles and using what you know to work. The learning of it takes something. It takes some paradigm shift. It especially takes confronting some of your negative limiting self-beliefs.

One of the reasons I wrote this book was that I really wanted everyday good people to get that influence is a skill of leadership that is worth having and it's a lot easier to attain than you might think.

David: You've gifted the world. You've gifted our relationship, Teresa. As we close now, in this moment what's one thing that you wish to challenge our listeners to do or become more aware of to build their collaborative success?

Teresa: I think one of the most foundational principles of influence is you got to give influence to get influence. Just like if you want to get respect, you give respect. Influence is no different than that. If you want to become influential, start acknowledging and recognizing the good work of other people. Become the raving fan of other people you respect and admire and in that act, watch what starts happening to your own influence.

I often challenge people to do a 30-day challenge. In fact, we give out a program that teaches people how to do this when you get the book. We're giving the book away for free right now by the way. If you want a digital form of the book, you can go to massinfluencethebook.com. I would say for the next 30 days, gift out influence 30 times and watch what happens to your own influence.

David: Fantastic. Fantastic. Teresa, thank you so much for joining us today.

Teresa: It's just my pleasure, David. Thank you.

David: I introduce you, listeners to Doreen Liberto Blanck. She is the owner, President and founder of Earth Designs. She is, also, a Director with me in our Collaborative Global Initiative. Doreen works in many places around the world, across North America. She has done some exceptional work in California. Her home is in San Luis Obispo, California.

Doreen's focus is land use planning, environmental analysis, public policy development, mediation, facilitation, consensus building, conflict resolution. She is a member of Mediators Beyond Borders as I am. She's on the national roster of Environmental Dispute Resolution and the American Institute of Certified Planners and Association of Conflict Resolution Specialties.

Doreen, I could talk about you because you and I met just a few months ago and I'm so impressed with the work that you do for community, for the Earth, and for making business work in the new ways. Rather me continuing to talk about somebody I have a deep respect for, Doreen introduce yourself and about your work and how people can learn more about you.

Doreen: Thank you, David for those kind words. I have about 20-plus years of experience as a community planner, environmental planner, economic development advisor, educator, and of course professional facilitator and mediator.

I taught Urban Planning and Collaborative Planning at one of the Cal State Universities for several years and have authored a number of articles. I was also on the San Jose Obispo County Planning Commission for six and a half years.

I have a graduate degree in Dispute Resolution from Pepperdine University's School of Law. I've mediated and facilitated in several multi-stakeholder projects as you've mentioned. I'm currently part of the Collaborative Global Initiative with you, David. I'm very proud of that and I look forward to many years of continued association with you.

David: Tell us. In the last couple of years, Doreen, give us an example of a very interesting project that you've been involved in.

Doreen: Probably one of the more interesting projects that I've been involved in and is indirectly associated with climate change issues. In California, we have a very progressive policy, very progressive program for climate change and how to address it. There have been some new laws for California where urban planning communities are encouraged to balance transportation with land use.

One project I've been working on in South Monterey County is also they have some multi-modal transit district or transit center. The interesting thing about this is to bring in together all of the parties number one, to bring the State of California into accepting that this is a location for a transit district, number one.

Number two, identifying the stakeholder so that we can begin meeting and planning on what type of transit center it's going to be. For those people who don't know what a multi-modal transit district is, it's essentially where you have rail stop, you'll have public buses, you have taxis, just a combination of modes of transportation to get people out of their car and get them into another mode of transportation.

The interesting part of this program, this collaboration is that we included Fort Hunter Liggett, which is a very large army base in Monterey County. The importance of that is that the army was very interested in having alternative mode of transportation because they were bringing many of their troops in single vehicles into Monterey area.

We've been working with the army. We've been working with regional parks. We've been working of course with the county, regional governments, just a number of stakeholders to make this multi-modal transit center viable, number one and number two, conceivable.

We're to a point right now where we have concept plans that we've developed for the site. We've worked with the property owners in the area. We're coming to a point where we're now going after funding and it does look like it's going to be very feasible.

This has been a long process, ten years of getting it from having the State of California to acknowledge yes, this is where we should have a multi-modal transit district, too. Yes, now it's going to be feasible and we'll have a stop there probably in about four or five years.

David: Wonderful. There's also a future series of events on the Climate Change Adaptation series that you and Kathy Porter really initiated. I'm working with you on it, Charalee Graydon. Many others are working within our Collaborative Global Initiative in association with Mediators Beyond Borders.

We're looking forward to meeting with Rhodes House in Oxford, England and the first of annual Adaptations Summits will be in Vancouver. As a visionary, as the co-visionary along with Kathy Porter, tell our listeners what the point of that, why are we doing that and what's the invitation.

Doreen: This is very exciting for Kathy and for me because we began talking in June about climate change issues and getting beyond the actual debates that are going on about climate change, at least in the USA. They're still debating about whether or not it exists.

Getting beyond that, getting beyond talking about scientific models or other evidence of what's happening, it's like we are accepting that this is an issue. Climate change is an issue. Let's now get beyond that and start talking about how can we make decisions.

What are the tools that are available to make decisions to resolve disagreements maybe between government agencies on what to do about climate change or to come to a consensus? Bring everybody together to come up with a plan on how to mutually address climate change issues.

This will be, as far as I know, the first time that there will be any conference worldwide and talking about getting beyond the discussion of climate change per se and then talking about how do we resolve these issues. What are the tools available to make decisions, collaborative tools available? It's really exciting.

David: I think it is exciting and I'm excited, also, for the reception that we're getting on this that business people are just as excited because business people will have assets and billion-dollar arenas and communities have...I guess the bottom-line is it gets way beyond this debate and in to how do we relate? How do we collaborate? How do we make things better together?

Doreen: We all have stakeholders in this state whether you are part of a sporting community where you have many people coming to your stadiums or you're a person living in a house. We're all part of the climate change issues. How do we bring everybody together to make mutually agreeable decisions? It is exciting to do that.

This conference will present ways to do that, present tools so people can go away and say, "We're going to take this back to our local community and we now know a way to bring people together to start talking about this issue."

David: That's right. Last time I got my analytics, we've had listeners in about 16 countries around the world. I expect some of them are going to be saying, "Wow! How do I learn more? Can I get involved?" How do they get in touch with you, Doreen or Kathy or just have an opportunity to read your blogs, to build their awareness about this series?

Doreen: Sure. I think probably the best thing is I'll give an e-mail address. People can contact me if they're interested that I can give them additional information. My e-mail address is doreenlibertoblanck@yahoo.com.

David: Wonderful. Now as we close this conversation, Doreen, in this moment, what's one thing you challenge our listeners to do or become more aware of to make their collaborations more successful?

Doreen: I think one of the most important things to do is to look outside of the ordinary people that are collaborating and look at people who are not represented as part of collaborations and include them into the circle of collaboration.

I've worked with many people and many government agencies, private who said, "We've always done it this way. We've always included the same people." As Albert Einstein said, "The definition of insanity is doing the same thing over and over again and expecting different results." If we truly want to do a collaboration, we need to reach out to groups and individuals who are not normally at the table and we need to invite them as part of the dialogue.

David: Thank you so much, Doreen Liberto Blanck of Earth Design and the Collaborative Global Initiative. You can check us out at colloborativeglobalinitiative.com. Thanks again, Doreen.

Doreen: Thank you, David.

David: Today we've listened to four more incredibly intelligent, committed, and visionary people in my network and now in your network. We've heard from Dana Meise, a man who's been on an eight-year journey walking the Trans Canada Trail, ocean to ocean to ocean mostly on his own but with great support from many. He inspires me. Hopefully, it inspires you.

We've talked to Dee Ann Turner of Chick-fil-A and a recent bestseller. She along with me worked with Elevate Publishing out of Boise, Idaho; great people. Dee Ann is just a great heart and now you know it. We've talked with Teresa de Grosbois of Calgary, "Mass Influence," her fourth international bestseller. It is truly about collaboration.

We've talked just now with Doreen Liberto Blanck in San Luis Obispo, California. Doreen does Earth Designs. We are working together on a Climate Change Adaptation series of summits starting in Oxford, England then going to Vancouver and then many nations we hope.

We're getting such positive feedback. Let's not argue about the shallow of the debate. Let's work together on the solutions and build community, build understanding, build innovation.

Today our key messages include:

1) your dreams will inspire others so dream big. I dreamed being a thought leader in collaboration by being a collaborator and it's coming true. What's your dream?
2) collaboration is a key part of your successful organizational culture; and yes, culture. Let me stop there. Culture, it's not an event. It's not a meeting. It's not a project. It's how you are, how you work together inside the organization and outside.

3) how you are in relationship with others defines your future success. Linda taught me that over and over and over. I put something out to her. She comes back with ideas and innovations. Challenge, love, respect. I hopefully do the same for all of these great guests. I really admire them. They are supporters of me and I would do most anything for them.

Next week, the theme is Now Lead, which is step nine of my ten essential steps. The guests include David Milia, Haskayne School of Business, University of Calgary; James Armstrong, CNOC Nexen out of Calgary, Alberta.

Bruce McIntyre and Don Simmons, I almost skipped over because they're close friends of mine and business associates; in Don's case for about a dozen years and in Bruce's case, it's been since 1996. People I deeply respect who lead with integrity. Charalee Graydon from Spain. She's the one that connects us to Europe and she has great wisdom, great contacts, and great integrity. Now Lead next week.

My call to action for you this week is be courageous and collaborate with audacious vision. Yes, audacious. What's your big hairy idea? Make it so. Check in. Who is your network? Who can support you? Who can fill in your blind spots, your gaps? Who has the resources and the network that would be useful to you and how can you be useful to them? Be courageous and collaborate with audacious vision. Let's make this world a far better place.

Thank you for your time, creativity, and collaborative awareness. Talk to you next week.

Chapter 12 Now Lead featuring David Milia, Don Simmons, Bruce McIntyre, James Armstrong and Charalee Graydon

David Savage: Welcome listeners from across our planet. Welcome those that know that we are truly connected and not separated by borders, beliefs, organizations or intentions. Now is our time to E.S.C.A.P.E. the tyranny of the communications and leadership barriers too often witnessed in our political, regulatory, media, and special interest groups.

Today is American Thanksgiving. Happy Thanksgiving, American cousins. Today think about gratitude. Who are five people you are grateful for their leadership in your life? Call them. Tell them soon. I'm grateful for all that are listening and dedicating themselves to collaborative leadership. Thank you.

In my book "Break Through to Yes" I set out ten steps that are essential to successful collaboration. Today's show them is Now Lead and that is step nine of the ten. I'm very excited. Today, we've got five great leaders from Canada and Spain, people that I've got strong and long-term connections with, who I've had many collaborations with, and I have a deep respect for.

They are Don Simmons, Bruce McIntyre, James Armstrong, Charalee Graydon and David Milia.

Key messages today include:

1) leadership demands leadership at all levels. Yes, at all levels, not just at the top.
2) building your culture of collaboration is evolutionary.
3) leadership is a profound earned relationship. It's not a status. It's not a title. It's an earned relationship.

Here's a quote from my "Break Through to Yes." "Effective collaboration requires this strong leadership brought about by such dimensions as clarity of vision, decision-making capabilities, emotional intelligence, and engendering of trust. A strong leader demands accountability from his whole team regardless of who is on the team.

Accountability fulfills purpose. What is your and your organization's purpose? What is the essential 'why' you were answering? If you and your organization failed, what would be lost to the outside world?"

We've talked about how and why collaboration fails or succeeds. How might you learn from that experience to enhance your probability of success in this your present work and future? Think about this. No one can sit idly by. Lao Tzu says, "When our group wins, leadership is when we say we did it ourselves."

Our next guest is David Milia. David is a management professional with proven success leading large multi-disciplined teams in meeting company short- and long-term objectives. That's really true. He's a collaborator. He's a visionary. He has broad progressive experience in general management, project management, strategic planning, and financial modeling. He's very good at cost reduction and innovation in complex environments.

I will cut to the chase. David Milia and I met probably 18 months ago and I've been a fan of David's ever since. He is a connector, a visionary, an innovator, and he gets stuff done. He and I have some great conversations about how to build sustainability, how to build shared value. I see David as a collaborative leader.

Just so people can get a better sense of how to connect with the work of David Milia, he is Associate Director-Centre for Corporate Sustainability and the Haskayne Energy Initiatives at the Haskayne School of Business in Calgary. Rather than me boasting about my friendship with David, how about...Mr. Milia, tell us more about you and what your work is.

David Milia: Oh, wow! Wow! Thanks for having me, David. It's a pleasure to be part of this and I strongly think you're doing great things with your show in sharing collaborative models and sharing with others wisdom from others. There's just no replacement for mentorship. I want to commend you on that.

There are so many things that I have my hand in. A lot of stuff I do on the side where I just love connecting people to other bright people and seeing how we can transition things particularly in the energy space. I have quite a heart for energy and the role that Canada plays in energy.

For me, my career for the last, about 16 years has been dedicated, predominantly in the first half I'd like to think, to oil and gas endeavors as a Project Manager and looking at engineering design and working with engineering firms to build things.

As I got to meet more bright people, smarter people than me, people that in their own right were visionaries, they had a severe implication on my career to move and to think bigger, to move towards something better, something not just local, but something national and global. That kind of took over for me.

My career about halfway in, I'd say the eight-year mark, I started asking tough questions. I had my date today and I anchored that with really looking at energy future for the world and for Canada and Canada's role in it. Really that's a high-level summary of everything that I do with my day today. Those opportunities come.

For example, to be at the center for corporate sustainability here at Haskayne to help disseminate knowledge, I welcome that. If we can have folks that have what they think is a competent view of one area, to understand competent view in another and come out more balanced or at least more understanding of where the other person's coming from, I consider that to be success in the work that I do.

I also have a strong stake on the ground trying to promote energy transition in the future founded on learning from the past, knowing what other leaders can teach us; looking at short-term endeavors, the energy position of Canada and the short-term with hydrocarbons and balancing that with long-term thinking, transition to renewables.

Finally, and one that is extremely personal to me that really pushed me to go in to the post-secondary space is how do we impact tomorrow's generations to be transitional leaders and visionary leaders?

I hope that answers somewhat of the question. I know I'm a little bit high level.

David Savage: That's a start. David Milia, you've been one of the hundred people kind enough to provide me your wisdom in to my book. I know you've got lot of experience on building cultures of collaboration within organizations whether it's Haskayne, whether it's Cenovus EnCana. Tell us something about your experience. How can our listeners start to build their culture of collaboration wherever they are in the world and whatever type of organization they're part of?

David Milia: Sure. Sure. That's a great question. I'd like to say that probably the first key is to be open-minded, to not be stuck in one thing that worked in one area. To be truly collaborative, you must be willing to be open to other people, ideas, and endeavors. Ergo, you must be able to listen.

Really the structure that I currently subscribe to and I tweaked over the years is valuing people and their ideas and positions and partner that with a strong competency and a RACI type way of looking at things.

For me, the way that I look at that culture is if you have competent people, even if the "leader" doesn't have the full competency in one area, that "leader" is able to bring this group in and through that RACI structure say,

"I may be accountable for something but I'm going to be respectful for those that are responsible in some areas to listen to their ideas. I'm going to enable them and be a champion and cheerleader for them to move that idea forward.

Likewise, should they fail I'm going to be the one, because of my accountability, to not be pointing fingers but to learn from those things and share those lessons learned going forward so that we can change gears." That's in the executionable space.

In the thought leadership space, it's much broader I would say. That is again, the willingness to listen but also be able to sit at the table of somebody, which you might think has the exact contrary position to yours or where you stand on a subject matter and be able to truly listen and be able to say, "Where can we find common ground? Where can we not necessarily pushing to get something done always but where can we really enable each other in areas that matter?"

David Savage: One of the things that I really admire about the work that you do, David is you're not looking for compromise. You're looking for more. You're looking for, "Okay, what's the better wisdom together we can find?" Tell us about looking for more. Where do you see shared value in collaboration working together?

David Milia: We all have what I call 'WIIFM', what's in it for me type of thing that tend to derail some of these conversations. I thought to enter into these collaborative spaces being aware that there might be a 'WIIFM' in the air and seeing how I can move our focus away from that 'WIIFM' and rather into that collaborative space where we get that personal connection done, where we really look at something authentically and in a trustworthy manner.

For me, it's a shared value implies in that collaborative structure that go hand in hand in my opinion is that you really care about something and that you're going to get to the core to why you care about it first. Once you get there, then depending which area you're tackling it from, you're respecting the other person's ability to provide competency and listen to what they have to say.

If say the target might be misconstrued that we need to garner a solution to something but really, it's not the solution but the problem has been misdefined in that conversation then I'll enter that space trying to define that problem so that we can finally sit down and have a safe space to authentically talk about it and strive for something good to come out of it for both sides not necessarily one side and draw out what those tensions might be.

David Savage: David, as we close this interview, what is one thing that you wish our listeners to do or become more aware of to improve their collaborative successes?

David Milia: The number one thing is being open to listening to others. There's so much wisdom from people in the world today that we take for granted or people that aren't willing to share it because we've created these norms where there's fear around sharing an opinion. There's fear around wanting to say what you really think.

If we can come in and really put away our ability to judge or quickly talk about something because we have one area of knowledge and put on our listening ears, that would be something I would encourage your listeners to try to do. It is a hard thing to do. It's hard for me every day, I tell you.

David Savage: Thank you so much for your insight and your collaborative wisdom, David Milia.

David Milia: Thanks for having me, David. It's been a pleasure.

David Savage: I am so pleased; especially pleased, today to have my friends and two presidents I've worked for; Don Simmons of Hemisphere Energy and Bruce McIntyre. Bruce and I worked together in five different ventures. What I want to talk to Don and Bruce about in this segment is to talk about styles of leadership, collaborative leadership versus top-down leadership.

I want to get their advice because they're both men, presidents of small oil and gas and mining companies in Canada and New Zealand who I have a tremendous respect for in how they lead. I'll put forward my disclaimer. I've worked with them both. I have a huge respect for them both and I do some business development work with Don at Hemisphere of which Bruce is the Director.

Let's start. Bruce McIntyre, we're going to start with you. Bruce is a professional geologist, has over 36 years of oil and gas experience and a proven track record of finding quality oil and gas reserves. He has numerous senior management and directorship positions in both private and publicly traded oil and gas companies. He's been an Independent Director of Hemisphere Energy since August 2008.

He is a member of the Canadian Society of Petroleum Geologists and served as its President in 2002. He has a Professional Geologists Designation with the Association of Professional Engineers and Geoscientists of Alberta and is a member of the American Association of Petroleum Geologists.

Bruce, let's start off. What else might you tell our listeners today on Voice America about your background and your style of leadership?

Bruce: I began my career with a large company from the States, Union Oil and progressed my career over the years going smaller and smaller and each time going to a smaller company realizing how much I really didn't know about the entire industry. When you get down to it, you can't know everything about an industry.

What I found is that it's better to draw on the skill sets of the team below you as to draw the best in them. In that way, they can assist you in learning the things that you don't know within a very complex industry.

David Savage: Learning together, figuring out your strengths, and where others can fill in the gaps.

Bruce: Exactly.

David Savage: When does collaboration work? What are the types of instances where you rely on collaboration versus just doing it yourself?

Bruce: I think you rely on collaboration for 99% of what you do in a business. At least, that's the way I've approached it. Ultimately, that 1% when it comes down to deciding, you must take in to account the information that you've gathered from the people that are around you and with that, move forward and make the decision.

David Savage: Yes. I know, Bruce that you gathered great people around you largely because of the respect and trust that they have for you. We'll say the same thing about Don Simmons who I'll talk to in a minute. When doesn't collaboration work? Can you think of some situations or with certain personalities on the other side where you just don't want to be collaborative?

Bruce: There are circumstances where people don't want to throw the ball back. In those instances, you really must deal with that. You call it a rogue in your midst. You need to be able to...they can be destructive to the team.

Those are the sorts of individuals that need to be, I guess, weeded out and that's where collaboration doesn't work. I think that's a call that's often made by the person at the top. It's not something that you really can collaborate on. It's a decision that pretty much so you must make on your...

David Savage: Right. I like the description of a rogue and that they are in fact the outsiders. Sometimes they have value but sometimes they need to be kind of penned up and put aside.

Bruce: Yes, or isolated.

David Savage: Isolated. Let's talk about Don Simmons now. In a minute we'll come back to Bruce and Don to get their collective wisdom on collaboration. Again, Don and I have worked together. Bruce introduced me to Don probably nine, ten years ago.

Don Simmons is a Bachelor of Science, Professional Geologist. He's also President and Chief Executive Officer of Hemisphere Energy Corporation out of Vancouver. Don has extensive experience in petroleum geology and a proven track record of discovering oil and gas in Western Canada and internationally.

Initially, Mr. Simmons...gee, I rarely call you that, Don, served as the Company's Vice-President, Exploration and became President and CEO in February 2008. Before joining Hemisphere, Don was a geologist at a private oil and gas, Sebring Energy, until its sale in 2007.

Prior to that, he spent five years with EnCana working on various projects in southeast Alberta and Ecuador. In fact, a prior guest in a couple of episodes ago has been working in Ecuador in conflict management. Alberta and Ecuador come together.

Don, tell us a little more about our company, your company, Hemisphere Energy and how people can find out more about that because it's obviously something that the three of us are very proud of and proud of the team.

Don: Yes. Hemisphere is a publicly traded company. We've been in existence for quite some time. As some of the initial people are part of the team, we started and restructured the company in 2009. It's really been a growing company since then.

We've certainly added to the growth and to the production of the company as an oil and gas company. A big part of that growth has to do with the team that's been built around it. I think part of my career all the way through it, I'm lucky enough to be involved in companies and teams that were great experiences and really led to my philosophy on how to lead I think.

We're fortunate here that we've got a great team we've put together, works very well together. I always believe that surrounding yourself by good people that have the skills to do the job, that you trust and respect, and that trust and respect you are the ways to really build a team in a successful company.

David Savage: We've been talking about working together and Bruce talked about sometimes as the president, you don't know it all. Of course, many presidents don't think that way. We got a great team. Let's names some names. Who are the people that you've brought together to collaborate within Hemisphere?

Don: Some of the people that have joined the team as we've grown, on the engineering side, Ian Duncan, our Chief Operating Officer; Ashley Ramsden-Wood came on as our Vice-President of Engineering; Andrew Arthur, Vice-President of Exploration.

All are people with various experiences in oil and gas. Again, some of the key parts of these people are the fact that they know they don't know everything and they're not afraid to pick up the phone and ask people. They're not afraid to get together as a team and debate things.

These people were added to a team that existed with our CFO, Dorlyn Evancic; some of our key supporting people that have been at the company for a number of years, Annalisa Whittle and Christine Franz, very key. They are a huge part of our team on a supporting role.

David Savage: Viana Luk who greets us and keeps us all put together.

Don: Absolutely. Viana is our latest person to join the team, almost a year ago and again, plays a key part in supporting the entire team.

David Savage: Both of you have worked for very large companies. I tried my best throughout my career not to do that and to start or be part of small groups. Let's spend a minute, Bruce and Don. What's the difference in big and small companies? Some of our listeners might think, "That's really great when you work in small ventures that you control and you can pick." Is collaboration not possible or is it even better in medium to larger corporations?

Don: If I can take a crack at that first, my experience at a large corporation where I started right out of University at Alberta Energy Company which merged to become Canada's largest independent oil and gas company to form EnCana.

I thought the collaboration was extremely good most of the time. However, it's the way the culture of the company, it's the culture of the management. EnCana and AEC before that were really run as small companies within a large company. There was a lot of focus put on the team of a specific area.

I think being able to move from a big company to a small company for myself personally was somewhat easier and the fact that we really did work as a direct team -- a geologist, an engineer, a geophysicist, the drilling engineers; we really worked together; the land people just like you do at a small company.

There are other larger companies I haven't worked at I know have different management styles and maybe not quite as collaborative and may not be as successful.

David Savage: Thanks, Don. We've just got a little less than a minute now. Time just evaporates so quickly. I'll ask you both, Bruce if you could first and then Don, what would one thing that you'd want to challenge other company presidents to do with respect to collaborative leadership?

Bruce: I know many CEOs and I know their styles can vary considerably from the styles that I've seen with Don and myself. I think what we need to do is get out there and listen to the people you've got under you or at least working with you. Listen to them. They are there for a reason. They are there for their skill set. They're not simply there as a support mechanism for the CEO. They're not just a sycophant or a yes-man for the CEO.

David Savage: All right, Don. You get the last words.

Don: Yes. I think I can just expand a bit where Bruce was headed there. I agree that the presidents and senior managements of companies I think, they need to look at their team not only as the support of yourself but you need to get out and support that team. Be there for them. Listen to them. Really work with them closely because the team as the team goes is how you're going to go and how the company goes.

David Savage: Thank you so much, Don Simmons, Hemisphere Energy and Bruce McIntyre -- two men and leaders that I have the utmost respect and admiration. Looking forward to all the collaborations. Thanks, Bruce and Don for helping us with your wisdom today.

Bruce: Thanks, David.

David Savage: Before the break we talked with Don Simmons and Bruce McIntyre. They are presidents who are widely respected and attract the best people around them. Their challenge to us is, you remember this, "Get out there and listen to your team. They are not syncopates or drones. As the team goes, the company goes." Yes, great quote. Thanks, Bruce and Don.

Companies led by big ego personalities abound. Too often, they do not focus on the development of their team. Too often, these big ego leaders leave their companies after a few short years and before their shareholders start to see the longer-term destruction inflicted on their team. Yes, longer term. They look like rock stars initially but boy, they destroy.

Leadership is team. Leadership is not separate. Collaboration is an organizational culture, not an event. I've developed an online 360 assessment tool to help you identify how collaborative your team is. Yes, check it out at my website.

With the assistance of SVI and Laura Hummelle, I have developed a very detailed assessment that we offer to you in service of the progression you are choosing to make.

Often, business leaders need to solve pressing problems like, "How do I deal with the political and power-driven agendas on my team? How do I get my team to stop being negative and help me solve these challenges?" Contact me for answers.

Charalee Graydon is our next guest, listeners. Charalee and I have a long relationship starting at the Calgary Chamber of Commerce. We were both Chairs of the Appropriate Dispute Resolution Committee. She's someone I've had in high, high, high respect and regard. We're doing some things with respect to Rhodes House right now, Climate Change Adaptation.

Charalee is somebody that I just find that we show up in each other's lives when we need to. There's a little more introduction. Charalee Graydon was born in Alberta, Canada. She holds degrees in Arts and Laws and she's a Rhodes scholar. She pursued both post-graduate legal studies at Oxford, England and has held academic positions in England, New Zealand, and Canada and practiced law in Canada.

She developed programs for students, judges, and the public and published academic works on legal issues, crime, and punishment. She has created courses at the University of Alberta on Sentencing and given many radio and television interviews on this.

She's a writer as well as being a lawyer and Rhodes scholar. You can find out more about Charalee Graydon at charaleeg.com and on Facebook, The Judgment Game. "The Judgment Game" is one of her two recent books. It's about generating ideas, brainstorming, creative thinking. It's also a book of fiction.

Charalee, the last two books you've published and congratulations, "Let's Play the Game" and "The Judgment Game," tell us more about you and what your purpose is, what you're doing with your books and your world.

Charalee: Thank you very much, David for the very nice introduction. I want to say it is nice to communicate with you after several years away from Calgary. Now I'm here in Spain and living in France. Yes. The work that I'm doing, I have moved from the legal world and the academic world in to a world that is, I'm not going to say less real, I've moved in to a world of writing. I'm writing in fiction but fiction that is very much based on reality.

Fiction has now taken me back to the world of alternate dispute resolution, which is where David and I first met at the Calgary Chamber of Commerce. That's what I've moved back to with the last book that I've written which is "Let's Play the Game," which is an attempt to deal with common social problems such as domestic abuse, alcohol and drugs, all these things that we read about daily.

I'm giving it to the people, giving it to people to work together, to collaborate and see if we can come up with some, I'm not going to say we will resolve every issue but it's a matter of communication. I hope that gives you an idea of where I now am.

I'm very excited, as well, to be involved with the work that's taking place with the climate, the adaptation, the climate change world that is happening with this summit in Vancouver that is upcoming in 2016. There you are. We've sort of gone in a circle but back to a world that involves law, involves communication, and collaboration. I hope that answers the question.

David Savage: Yes. Thanks, Charalee. Just for our audience, this is an exciting time for Charalee and I, Kathy Porter, Doreen Liberto Blanck, Jeff Cohen, Duncan Autry, Sara Daitch, and many others where we're coming together with universities, with corporations, with not-for-profits, with environmental groups to say, "Let's not debate anymore about climate change. Let's focus on when extreme weather and unusual weather happens, how do we plan for it? How do we communicate? How do we collaborate? How we do we ready ourselves before and during and after extreme weather events?"

It's been very well received. I'm delighted with the doors that Charalee has opened for us. One of the things that Charalee has is exceptional global respect and contacts. I want to come back, Charalee and talk more about you. You've done something very powerful. You're combining storytelling with collaboration and fiction and conflict resolution. Tell us more about that.

Charalee: Thank you, David because that's one of the things that I feel I'm not the only one that is doing is. It would be really nice...I know when my editor read "The Judgment Game" for the first time, he said, "This is really quite a great initiative, this book. It hasn't been done before. It's asking people to engage in the book. The reader takes an active part in resolving the issues that are posed in that book."

It's been done before. When I went on to the internet, you will see networks that are talking about collaboration and story writing. Again, it hasn't been done before. What I would say is we have a great opportunity in our world to use fiction because again, it's not something that is now being created.

We have ancient forms of communities that are using stories to tell their people about what's happening in the world. I believe that's where we are now. We're doing the same thing.

For example, I borrow very much from the First Nations people in Canada. One of the projects that I recently handled was in Madrid. That was a collaborative project at the Madrid Mediation Summit called Empowering Youth in the 21st Century.

That seems like a pretty big topic, a pretty big issue to try and grapple with but I worked and collaborated with an elder from the First Nations in Canada and a singer-songwriter and educator in Canada and this is me in Spain collaborating with people across the world.

We put on a very good presentation at the Madrid Conference and it was well received from people around the world -- Malaysia, from Papua New Guinea. Again, the world is reaching out and looking for solutions. Sometimes, and I'm going to say we can deal with those solutions by using the world of storytelling.

That's really what I'm doing and hopefully, that will be something that I can continue to do with the group that David mentioned.

David Savage: As we close, Charalee, in this moment, what's one thing you'd challenge our listeners to do or become more aware of to build their collaborative success?

Charalee: What I would say is start your meeting, if you have an issue you're dealing with, start the meeting by telling a story about what brought you to this meeting.

That will be a good way to break the ice, a good way to start the collaboration as was pointed out by the man, I'm going to give you his name, Seth Cohen, "The Power of Storytelling is a Jumpstart to Collaboration," which is a book that dealt with collaboration for change, using it as a change initiative in business and a very effective manner in handling issues such as change in business.

That's one thing that I will say. Start your meeting with a story.

David Savage: Thank you so much, Charalee Graydon from Spain.

David Savage: James Armstrong is an energy professional with extensive experience in commercial negotiations, joint ventures, agreement drafting, strategic acquisitions and divestitures. James has an in-depth understanding of unconventional assets such as oil sands, liquefied natural gas, shale gas, and tight oil.

In addition to his Canadian and U.S. experience, James has worked internationally living in the Middle East for over two years. He has a passion for teaching and teaches a class at the University of Calgary and has taught an Executive Education class at Georgetown University in Washington, DC for oil and gas professionals on Global Energy Policy.

James, I admire you because I try to promote next generation leaders. You're in that demographic and you're already leading. You've got recognition within the North American oil and gas community. You've got expertise in the Middle East. You and I have known each other for, I don't know, 15 years and you really get it and you teach me.

Tell our listeners a little more about yourself and what your work is and what you believe about collaboration.

James: Very well. Thank you very much for having me here, David. You're too kind and I think you're my number one fan. It's been a wonderful relationship you and I have had over the years. I look very much to you as a mentor and someone who's helped sort of guide me to sort of what is important in leadership or even in management. I thank you for the time you spent with me and that as well.

Formally, thank you very much, David. I don't think I'll be here without your coaching and leadership over the years to date. I like your listeners to hear that because I think it's important for them to know.

David Savage: Thank you.

James: Most welcome, most well deserved. Anyway, just to elaborate a little bit more, I have over 13 years in oil and gas. Early in career, I worked overseas and lived in Yemen. I was living in the capital city of Sana'a. I was working with our commercial team there in getting approvals from the government to help progress a lot of projects. We had a joint venture with them in Sana'a for a development block.

Following that, I returned to Calgary and I worked various basins mostly in Canada but also in the United States. I have a little bit of experience in the legal world in Alberta. Throughout that time, I've progressed in my leadership role. Initially when I started off I was the Technical Professional that I've developed in to having a team. Now I run a department.

My focus with the department is on the commercial aspect obviously. We do have many joint ventures throughout the world and the ones that are in Canada are the focus of what I do on a day-to-day basis.

David Savage: James, you've got a unique perspective because I know you've got a passion for teaching internationally and locally and in the oil and gas community and to land men specifically. I also know that you've worked in various company cultures. You've worked with Canadian owners and boards and management teams. You've worked with American ones. You've worked with Asian ones.

Tell me about your experience in those cultures and how you seek to build a culture of collaboration. Make me a compare and contrast where it might be something one can...main theme where you can say, "This is what I think works."

James: That's an interesting question, David. I haven't spent a lot of time reflecting on that from my personal perspective. I would say that each culture is unique, even the ones within North America whether that's Canada or the US. They do approach things differently.

If Canadians...maybe the old adage we're all very nice to each other but I do find that the Canadian culture is quite collaborative. That's not to say the others aren't but they do have a different perspective on things.

For example, in the US when we're working on a project, a lot of the mandates were sort of presented. "Here's what we're going to do, A, B, and C." We kind of worked through those to see what's appropriate whereas a similar situation in Canada would be like, "Let's come up with these mandates together and let's form this together at the onset rather than starting with a framework." You're kind of building up a little bit more from the bottom up.

With the Asian exposure that I've had, one thing I would say is they are very interested in learning, sort of, what is it that we do up here. They are quite patient and they are very engaged in understanding what it is that we do. I think some of the different perspectives that I've encountered with has been on maybe the approval side of things.

That's been a little bit different on the timing side of stuff whereas you do work with them to come to an agreed upon consensus but the timing of getting that final approval can get very close to the ultimate deadline and that can cause a little bit of anxiety and stress.

David Savage: You are a collaborator. I've worked on several volunteer industry initiatives with you, James. What is collaborative leadership in your mind?

James: It's interesting because it's a wide used word and sometimes I question whether people really understand what it really is. I'm a huge proponent of it because I see the other extreme of that. I had to deal with all our commercial litigation when we just can't get a collaborative result and we have to go to the courts to get us there.

In my experience with that is that nobody wins on that but I guess the lawyers. They do quite well with that but the two commercial participants do not. Again, I think it's a little bit of a mentality. It's like if I win, you're going to lose. If you lose, I'm going to win kind of thing.

It's not necessarily having a definitive outcome on one end. You don't want to get there. There are ways of working your way through some of these discussions to avoid that.

At the end of the day, the most important factor in business is going to be money. Being able to collaborate and get to a consensus or a decision on how you want to progress something is going to ultimately be a positive benefit for the organization and ultimately the shareholders.

David Savage: Not only reducing costs and tightening up timelines but also creativity and innovation that you can get from the collective wisdom.

James: Yes, absolutely.

David Savage: Before we close this interview, James, what's one thing you wish our listeners to do or become more aware of to improve their collaboration success?

James: When I teach my students at the University of Calgary, one thing that I say to them is that in my career I have never received the feedback, "You communicate too much. You talk too much. You provide too much insight and perspective."

I think that's so important is to always be clear as to what you're thinking because that could be the real death of a discussion or a venture is an assumption. You assume that somebody thinks this or mean that without clarifying because if you think somebody else is thinking something else, chances are you're incorrect. It's always good to get to the root cause and clarify what that is.

Just on sort of a final point, another thing that we really emphasize is it's so important to have those one-on-one and those actual face-to-face meetings. There's so much that can be lost in interpretation with written communication. Now with technology there's just an infinite number of different venues to hide behind something.

When you must sit down with somebody face-to-face, it can really change a lot of perspectives and relationships are extremely important. I think that's something that it is for the softer type of discussion but it is important and I cannot overemphasize that you'd really do get results when you build those relationships.

David Savage: James Armstrong, thank you so much for your wisdom today.

James: Thanks so much, David. It's been a real pleasure.

David Savage: This show has featured five great leaders from Canada and Spain: Don Simmons, Bruce McIntyre, James Armstrong, Charalee Graydon, and David Milia.

Our key messages today included: one, leadership demands leadership at all levels; two, building your culture of collaboration is evolutionary; and three, leadership is a profound earned relationship, not a status.

Next week, our theme is step ten. We make it through our tenth of ten steps. That is Make It So. Featured guests are: Michael Hill, a world-leading neurologist and stroke specialist; Atul Tanden, former Head of World Vision; Johanne Lavoie, Executive at McKinsey and Company; and Prabha Sankaranarayan. Prabha is President of Mediators Beyond Borders.

Our call to action as we leave this week on this American Thanksgiving: think about gratitude. Who are five people you are grateful for their leadership in your life? Tell them. Look for those that lead without being asked and without the title in the organization. Thank them, too.

Thank you for your time, your innovation, and your collaborative leadership.

Chapter 13 Make It So featuring Michael Hill, Johanne Lavoie, and Atul Tandon

David: Welcome, listeners from across our planet. In my book "Break Through to Yes," I set out ten steps that are essential to successful collaboration. This show theme is Make It So and this is step ten of ten.

This show features four great leaders with business connections across the planet: Prabha Sankaranarayan, she's the President of Mediators Beyond Borders; Atul Tandon of the Tandon Institute and former Head of World Vision; Johanne Lavoie of McKinsey and Company; and Michael Hill, one of the world's leading stroke and brain specialists.

Our key messages today include:

1)   examine and change the existing ways we do things to capitalize on the collaborative process, outcomes, and the organization's rules of engagement. Yes, examine them and change them.
2)   as a human being if you are forced to collaborate or act, you do it without life energy. Make collaboration yours; and
3)   collaboration is the highway where all people can be linked and honored. That's right, all people.

Here's a quote from my book "Break Through to Yes: Unlocking the Possible within a Culture of Collaboration" on the topic of Make It so. "To make it so, you will need to design and follow through on:

a) accountabilities;
b) reporting;
c) continuous improvement. Post mortem, what worked, what didn't, how are we together now, what's needed for the future?

d) building a collaborative muscle in your organization;
e) learning from successes and failures;
f) using accepted evaluation tools; and
g) integration, changing the existing ways we do things to capitalize on the collaborative process, outcomes, and the organization's rules of engagement. Build your culture of collaboration according to the circumstance and your need."

Now we'll go to an interview with my good friend, Dr. Michael Hill.

Dr. Michael Hill is a Professor for the Departments of Clinical Neurosciences, Community Health Sciences, and Medicine and Radiology at the University of Calgary. He is Director of the Stroke Unit for the Calgary Stroke Program, Alberta Health Services.

Michael's research interests include stroke thrombolysis, stroke epidemiology and surveillance and clinical trials. Epidemiology is a mouth full. Hopefully, my brain is a little more agile than it seems to be in this moment.

Michael recently completed the E.S.C.A.P.E. trial demonstrating the benefit of endovascular stroke therapy. He is funded by the Canadian Institutes for Health Research and holds the Heart & Stroke Foundation of Alberta, Northwest Territory, Nunavut professorship in Stroke Research.

Michael, I could go on and on about your accomplishments, your heart and what you've done. What I want to say is oh, I think it was about a year ago or 18 months ago, you were looking to move the E.S.C.A.P.E. trials forward and we had some conversations about how we might work together, what we might do.

Since that time, you've made huge successes and made an incredible announcement about four months ago. For our listeners, what I'll say one of the things I care most deeply about my friend, Michael Hill is he's the one in our Heart and Stroke Foundation Board meetings that invites us to his cabin in the Kananaskis wilderness area in Alberta and he ensures that we have walking meetings. He walks his talk literally.

Michael, tell us more about you. What is the E.S.C.A.P.E. trial and what's the success there?

Michael: As you said, I'm a neurologist and I'm interested in clinical care and trying to make outcomes better for my patients and obviously the patients that my colleagues treat and stroke victims around the country and even around the world. The E.S.C.A.P.E. trial was one way of our attempt to move the bar in how you treat stroke. Stroke has multiple manifestations and different types.

This trial looked at a specific treatment for some of the most severe types of strokes. It's not for all strokes by any means, but those patients who are afflicted with a major stroke, we were able to show convincingly that it's a team approach to therapy, and I really emphasize the team approach here, with using advanced imaging and then using catheters to remove clots and open up blocked arteries was a highly successful way of treating stroke patients.

Certainly, for some people we took them from being completely paralyzed to walking home out of the hospital in a couple of days. The results were dramatic and they have ushered in a new era for stroke therapy not only in Canada but around the world.

David: Tell us how many universities, and researchers, around the world, that are working together to create this E.S.C.A.P.E.?

Michael: When you do clinical trials, it really is a team effort, not only in your local team but you need to recruit like-minded colleagues and teams from other hospitals and other centers. We did that. We recruited about 25 sites to be involved in the trial in Canada, United States, Europe, England, and South Korea.

In the end, it turned out that because our results were so dramatic, the safety board that was monitoring our trial advised us that we should stop the trial early. Only 22 sites enrolled patients in the study.

That was exciting and that was a big part of the collaboration was working with people from around the world who were able to achieve the same fast, speedy, and team-based stroke therapy that resulted in these great outcomes.

David: You've had lots of challenges to get to this success. Tell us one or two of your biggest challenges.

Michael: Getting enough sleep. There were lots of challenges. I think the first challenge we had was to convince people that our concept of how we should be treating these patients was the right one. It did take some convincing.

There are some moral-suasion, arguments, and a lot of academic and scientific discussion why the approach that we were proposing was the best one and why they should work with us to prove that this was the best one. That took a lot of work.

We argued that case in the academic literature. We wrote articles about it then we argued that case one-on-one in formal presentations. We argued that case one-on-one in any informal presentations over a beer. Perhaps that latter was the most important aspect of convincing people.

The second part was getting funding to get the trial done. That's what, as you mentioned in the introduction, that is one of the things you and I had spoken about 18 months or 24 months ago.

How to fund this kind of an issue that the funding of investigator-led or investigator-initiated clinical trials is very much a very conservative environment where the public funding agencies that we have and even the charitable ones with peer review, it's conservative such that it's rare that you will get funded on the first go-round of a funding cycle.

That means that it takes often a very long time to get independent funding to make something like this happen. The nature of what we were able to do was to get...we had a consortium style funding. That was the way we were able to achieve it in the end.

David: I really empathize. This is such important work; such important work for me and others in the "yuppie" generation because this is our future. I hear in a particular circumstance where governments aren't funding like they used to and the public and the governments like to have quick hits and stroke research just isn't that way. And, you can't be contaminated by your source of funding. You need to be so clean and clear.

One of the things I particularly wanted to talk about before we close, Michael is what's next? You've developed some things, some outreach opportunities to say, "Okay, what's next to connect funding to researchers, to build on your work in the E.S.C.A.P.E. process that you've already successfully rolled out?" What's next?

Michael: Maybe two answers or two aspects to your question -- one is you're right about the funding side. It's appropriate in many levels to be conservative particularly when you're dealing with public money from taxpayers or even if it's charitable donations for organizations like the one that we're both participating in, the Heart and Stroke Foundation in Alberta.

We're interested in using some of the novel ways of things have been funded. For example, crowd sourcing -- the kick-starter kind of model. If that could be organized in a way that would make sense for people to either donate or give funding towards these kinds of developments.

We're interested in trying to figure out a mechanism to do that because there is an issue of speed whereas running a large clinical operation is very much like developing a new start-up business from the ground up, you can imagine that the tempo of how you do it and the momentum you build is important. Without that momentum and tempo, often things fail. That's an important feature.

The second aspect to your question is where might things go next for stroke treatment and I guess I would say there are two key things. One is to be able to implement what we have shown to be effective.

We showed it to be effective in a highly organized, 22 highly organized centers in the world and to now be able to translate that therapy to multiple hospitals and sites across Canada and even within Alberta where we are and round the world is going to take a lot of effort.

It is a situation where the therapy works but it only works in a highly organized and efficient setting. That's going to take a lot of teaching, a lot of practice change. We're doing that.

The second thing is a really important one to recognize that although we did have success in this trial and it's terrific that we have, I think moved the bar, we all acutely and I acutely recognize that only half of our patients had a really good outcome which means half of our patients did badly.

There was still significant mortality from the strokes that we were treating. We have a lot of work to do to try and improve that. We're looking to continue with our efforts in clinical trials and try to find new therapy so that we can help more patients.

David: We do have listeners in at least 12 countries around the world. There are going to be some of them, Michael that are saying, "How do I find out more? How do I connect? I've got an idea. I'd like to put some money behind this process." How do people contact you or your group?

Michael: You can certainly find us easily on the web. We have a website at the University of Calgary. It's easy to find us, ucalgary.ca or you could look up through the trial. That's exactly as its spelled and sounds. You could access through there. I'd also encourage listeners who are elsewhere, whether you're in Europe, Asia, United States or in Canada to look at your local source information.

In Canada, that's the Heart and Stroke Foundation of Canada. There's a good website which describes some of the activities including the research activities that are available through there. In the United States, the two organizations are the American Stroke Association and the National Stroke Association. Both of those groups are key.

I think in other countries, it will be specific to that country. There are lots of resources out there available. Many of them are easily accessible through the web.

David: Before we close, Michael, what's one thing you wish our listeners to do or become more aware of to improve their collaborative success?

Michael: I would say that probably the biggest lesson I would take from or I guess that we tried to implement in the E.S.C.A.P.E. trial process was that there's just nothing like one-on-one meetings and pressing the flesh to talk to people and explain your ideas to them in detail. It's just not enough to use electronic media or to assume that other people will think the same way you're going to think.

I think a lot of our success related to the fact that we went to visit everybody on their turf at their sites. We had a meal with them. We had a beer with them and worked through all the issues. It's a qualitative thing, observation but I think it was one of the key reasons why the trial went so well.

David: Thank you so much, Dr. Michael Hill.

David: Atul Tandon, our next guest is a serial entrepreneur, not-for-profit leader, humanitarian, and author with a 30-year track record of successfully birthing, building, scaling, and turning around some of the world's largest, best known and impactful for-profit and non-profit enterprises.

Atul has really got a track record. He has impacted industries including consumer banking, e-commerce, consumer marketing, microfinance, humanitarian relief, and development and donor engagement worldwide.

In 2011, Mr. Tandon launched Tandon Institute, a global advisory firm serving select non-profit and social sector organizations worldwide capacity to rapidly accelerate their impact, revenues, public engagement, and leadership effectiveness. Atul will tell you that he really can't separate those. These are not strategies. This is his way that he coaches us to do.

Atul currently serves on the Board of Wycliffe USA and CLA. He has been named one of America's Most Influential and Effective Fundraisers by the Non-Profit Times and was a catalyst for the ONE campaign, which has brought more than 3 million people together to fight extreme poverty and diseases.

Atul, thank you so much for offering your wisdom today. How else could you introduce yourself, your work, and how people, our listeners learn more about you?

Atul: Thank you, David. Thank you for inviting me to the show. I'm so excited. Thanks for the introduction. I must say listening to all that, people have been talking about global village for a while. I feel like I've been a construction worker on site for the past 30 years and the work still continues. I'm so excited for that.

It really is a testimony to so many people who have come before and presently engaged and will come down the road as we build a global community where not just thousands but hundreds of millions of people can enjoy a thriving life and future.

Where can you find more about me? Wikipedia has a profile of course. Otherwise, our website tandoninstitute.com. Your listeners can definitely go to either and learn more about me.

David: I'll quote a little bit about what Wikipedia tells about Atul. "Tandon's foremost contribution has been in developing and gaining industry-wide acceptance for a charity's two-sided mission: one that seeks to impact its beneficiaries and the other that seeks to change hearts and minds amongst its donors and supporters. These ideas around Supporter Transformation and the ethics of engaging donors are now gaining widespread recognition."

Tell us more about that, Atul.

Atul: Thank you for that. David, that came to me as I came from the world of global banking, consumer banking to the world of non-profits about 2000. One thing I noticed early on was that the non-profit community, the folks tended to focus on the impact side of its mission.

Arguably and understandably, activists who are excited about a cause whether it was helping children in

Africa or it was cleaning rivers in America, they got together and they launched these organizations.

By design, they were focused on the impact that they're going to have. Almost accidentally, they really looked to me, almost had their backs towards their donor and lean toward the beneficiary but really the back is to the donor.

I thought to myself, "Really, is that the right role and posture for these organizations? Should they be different? Are they really should be sideways?" In one hand, they hold the beneficiary and the other the donor and they're the connectors. They are bridges between the two.

If you use that bridge metaphor, David then the stronger the bridge the non-profit leaders and communities can build, there'll be more traffic. You can have a tiny bridge that a bicycle, rickshaw will make one at a time or you could have a two-tier, double-decker, six-lane highway.

Really, that's the charge of the thing the non-profit community has is to build those six-lane highways on two tiers between the beneficiary and their donors and make both realize their dreams, not only one.

David: Yes. It is true engagement, true connection not only to the cause and the outcomes as you say because when not-for-profits have their back to their donors, in a very judgmental thing I might say they're thinking about the check as opposed to the vision, the dream, the leadership that they can do together in collaboration.

Atul: Indeed. The case it's almost like you start to treat your donor like a checkbook or an ATM machine. Really, that donor is coming alongside the non-profits. We see the non-profits as a way to help them accomplish their dreams and their desires for a better world. At least from what now neuroscientists tell us, in fact the process of giving generates a sense of personal fulfillment and wellbeing in the donors.

At the same time, not the process of receiving but the process of engaging in improving their own lot for the beneficiary helps beneficiary become stronger and more courageous and in many ways actually more collaborative when they find non-profit partners that want to work with them not as a handout but really, they are to give them a hand out, if you will.

David: Yes. So much of your work, Atul speaks to oneness, speaks to spirit, speaks to respect and love and also speaks to way more profound business. Tell us a little bit about how this all comes together for you.

Atul: Thank you. Talking about oneness and let me just recount a little bit of the story of the ONE campaign that hopefully answers some of your questions. David, the way that the group of us, I think it was in the summer of 2003. Marklin Brogue was at that time with us in Washington. He's passed on, great loss to all of us. He brought us together and said, "Hey, we've got to work."

These were non-profit leaders from I think eight to ten organizations -- World Vision, CARE, Doctors Without Borders, the International Rescue Committee, and there were several others. We all got together. How do we change the mindset of the American public about international aid and humanitarian assistance?

It was a huge, huge task and we were just eight small people, if you will and getting together in a coffee shop and we didn't have a clear idea what we have decided yet. Mark said, "We got to work together, find a solution, find a way."

We all put our brains together and said, "The way to get attention and leverage it is," somebody said, "There's a presidential campaign happening next year. What if we could start to ask in the early poll states?"

What if we were to start to ask community organizers in those states to really start to raise the question of what do the candidates think about improving, helping people who are around the world who don't have it as good as we have it here in America?

That idea it got to poll. I think it was the IRC folks who had access that placed refugees in many of those communities. We got them organized to get foundation give us a small help to really feed it. We got them on board. Off we went. Eight of us, our organizations give us, they give the sign off, "Sure. Let's do this. It helps everybody, our country, our communities, the organizations." It was a win-win and turned out we were successful.

We got a whole bunch of young people excited in those states. When we did the polling after the primaries, clearly in those states we had a very discernible bump. This was the Bush-Kerry campaign and eventually that led to...as this work increased, it's almost like a snowball. It kept on increasing in size. Jamie Drummond that time was part of DATA. He was talking to the ONE campaign with Bono.

Some of our leaders were chatting with Jamie and we all got together and said, "From what they're doing there in the ONE campaign, what we are doing makes sense for us to frankly come together. The founder team, Bono and Jamie had a better chance of succeeding with this and taking it forward than we do in our small collaborative. Let's really merge with them." Off we went and you know the rest of the story.

It's really from a small coffee shop and to campus of University of Washington down to the ONE campaign. So many years later, you can see the trail. That trail, that track is frankly of a small group of people thinking about, like you said earlier, completely audacious part, unimaginable if only one of us individually. Having the courage to follow through and more that the desire to collaborate is when we work together, we can achieve great things and really focus on the common good versus the personal good.

When we focus on that common good is what the ONE campaign has showed us personal good results down the road. I've been very excited to be part of that initiative and many others along the way, very similar. We could show the rest of the story.

David: Thank you so much, Atul because your heart starts from India and goes to America, to the world, to Africa. I'm so glad that you have audacious vision. In this moment as we close this interview, what's one thing you would challenge our listeners to do or become more aware of to make their collaborations more successful?

Atul: Here's what I would say. I would say three things. Each of them are challenging, frankly but I think what it takes to be successful. One, listen first then speak later. Two is when we are speaking, engaging with somebody, really try hard to understand their motivations. The answer, what's in it not for me but what's in it for them. When you find, when you heard that, you'll understand their motivations.

Look for areas of genuine overlap that you can help each other, work with each other. As you identify those areas, that's when you start to work. Instead of focusing on the not's, focus on the have's. Be genuine about that. Be a genuine listener. Be genuine about understanding who they are, what their visions are. Be genuine about this is how we can work together.

Work together not only for mutual benefit but for the benefit of the larger whole. It's that thing, that shared vision and really a courageous servant leadership, strong processes, and a people-focused culture is where real change, lasting change happens.

David: Thank you so much, Atul Tandon, the Tandon Institute.

Atul: Thank you, David and my very best.

David: Johanne Lavoie is a partner at McKinsey and Company. After spending the first decade of her career working in the fields of post-merger management and large-scale transformations in manufacturing and service operations, Johanne focused the last 12 years of her career on next generation leadership and the human dimensions in transformational contexts.

Combining two decades of applied business experience with in-depth expertise in organizational and adult development and people-intensive system change, my friend, Johanne helps individual leaders and executive teams of global companies facing transformational change. There are lots of that going on right now.

As such, she spends a significant part of her integrating innovative approaches to influence profound changes in mindsets, behaviors, interaction dynamics, and stories in business contexts. Johanne is a leader at McKinsey Leadership Development and the Dean. Pardon me. Divine, I almost said there and it's probably true, Johanne.

You were the Dean of Centered Leadership Program. I want to also mention specifically to our listeners, Johanne co-authored the book "Centered Leadership: Leading with Clarity, Purpose, and Impact" and published March 2014, a great resource, a great leader, a divine leader. Let's just throw it out there.

Johanne, how can our listeners know more about you? Where can they look you up in addition to buying your book? Tell us more about you.

Johanne: Now that you've set me up as a divine leader, let's live up to. I guess, for those who are interested in "Centered Leadership," the book was written as a practical field guide to help leaders find their own divine energy and connect with their own divine self and essence.

It's rich with stories of leaders in all domains, but also practical applied exercise in reflection that you can do on your own. It's not a book that you read from A to Z. It's just something you pick up, do a bit of reflection, do a few exercises, go back to. That's my offer for those who would like to explore it more.

David: You and I have talked about collaboration being an evergreen topic. Why is it so relevant today in the corporate world?

Johanne: Yes, collaboration. I don't think I have one client who doesn't want more collaboration, more trust-based collaboration in the organization. It is the topic that just never goes outdated. It is ever more needed. I think it comes from the increased amount of complexity that we must deal with. There's no linear problem, no simple problem anymore.

Everything is interconnected. It's systems, dynamic. It's big. It's complex. You do something. You create unintended consequence. It's tough to handle such complexity and agility without enabling people to collaborate together to create positive and life-affirming change.

I think it's something people are grappling with a lot definitely in organizational life and in public and private sector. I think our old ways of looking at collaboration has been through formal structure. Now you want people to collaborate differently. You'll put a structure. You'll do a reorganization structure. You'll change something. You'll change incentive. You'll change systems and process and reporting line.

In a way that's necessary because you don't want this to be impeding desired collaboration. These are enablers but they're so insufficient and if we only lead with structure what we get is compliance. You don't get that form of heart-based collaboration where people are going really the extra mile because they're fully committed and engaged.

What my work has been focusing on is looking at collaboration and trust and agility and all these big, big words as outcome of enabling not only the formal structures but the formal structures in service of bigger vision that you want to create. Maybe that's what I can talk a little bit more about to make it more concrete.

David: Yes, let's do that. Before we do that, I've got a question, Johanne. You talked about something that I find a lot in my clients and in organizations that I've been exposed to and part of -- the compliance behavior versus the heart-centered leadership. How do you help your clients? How does McKinsey help your clients go beyond that compliance and this-is-the-way-it's-got-to-be-done?

Johanne: It's an interesting topic. It's easy for us to...I think it's the compliance and the drain of energy is the unintended consequence when we only work formal structure. As a human being if you're forced to behave a certain way or forced to collaborate or forced to comply to something, you do it but you do it without the life energy that comes with it. It's not you. It's something you're doing to comply.

It's much more how do you actually engage people's life energy to bring their full self to create something that is not what it should be. That's where to me the intangible structure, the informal is so much more important. That's where things suggest vision and things suggest creating intimacy in relationship becomes so much more important.

It's easier if I give a couple of examples for that.

David: Yes, great. Thank you.

Johanne: Maybe I'll start with vision, vision and other big plus words. I was talking recently to a client of mine and she leads a big co-op-based organization. I was asking her. I said, "What's the difference between a network and a community?"

She paused for a minute and she said, "The difference between a network and a community is that community shares the same flame and network is the network of relationship." She says, "In my job as the leader of this co-op is to light the flame in the hearts of people and to connect this flame."

I asked her, "How does that show up?" She says, "There's nothing that I don't do that I do without making sure that as I go and visit a customer I take one of my leaders with me, one of the Vice-Presidents with me or one of the General Managers with me. We'll find a way to talk about what matters and what's important and how that connects to the vision." She said, "That's how you light the flame."

That's what I do all the time is that I talk to community; to listen and to talk about what matters and to connect people together around what matters. That to me is at the heart of collaboration is how good are we at lighting the flame, a flame that connects with something that matters to people that we call sometimes vision? Vision and meaning is something that matters to us, something that is not that we want to see happen, something that we want to create.

I think that has a lot to do with creating an outcome of genuine heart-based collaboration. That component that I think is important because that's a uniting energy if you want. The second component is our ability and the courage that we have to be intimate with each other. I have the privilege to work with a lot of executive teams.

One of the biggest challenges, we have to re-learn to be human together and simply to create that base of intimacy where we're willing to be vulnerable with each other, to open up a little more deeply about what we're truly valuing, fearing, worrying about, talking about fears with each other. Very powerful, talking about what matters to us, about legacy, very powerful.

Being able to listen to another individual and suspend for a minute the filter of the judgment and stay with genuine curiosity. "I don't agree with you but help me understand what you are worrying about, what you are fearing, what is it that holds us back right now."

I find that is one of the straightest routes to collaboration is the ability to self-disclose and to be more vulnerable and intimate with each other. The power and the gift that come through this relationship is a really genuine collaboration because you pick up the phone to help each other and you cut through the structures that will never be perfect.

Maybe that's why every time I work with a senior executive team, I always ask, "Can we do a dinner first?" The dinner is always the same thing. In a dinner we share crucible childhood stories; stories in our childhood that polished us and tried us and formed who we are today.

My experience is that this is always the high point moment. It's a moment where all of us and real trust happens and then we can talk more openly about what really matters and vision. What you said is different.

David: Thank you, Johanne. You can see me. I can be open with you. I know that we have each other's backs. As we close this interview and I wish we could go on for another hour, but in this moment what's one thing you challenge our listeners to do or become more aware of to make their collaboration more successful?

Johanne: In relation to what I said is to what extent am I pausing to stop and ask the question "What really matters here?" Now we're talking about something. What really matters? Am I truly listening and getting curious about what's the fear that may be underneath, the behavior that I'm not accepting of that other person versus quickly judging them as incompetent or wanting to get up in the morning and do bad in the world?

Am I generous with my genuine listening? Am I open with my own fear and my own limitation, my own vulnerability? Am I connected with what really matters? Am I even asking the question? Not necessarily just once a year but every day, every moment in the middle of meetings, in the middle of family disputes or when engaging my teenager. Reconnecting on what matters.

I think creating space for reflection is important and asking those connecting back to these questions and that was my motivation in wanting to write a book that helps ask some of these questions that we could go back to because I think we lose in our days we've lost sometimes the ability to just pause and be silent and in stillness to ask if the new knowledge come up or the knowledge that wants to come up to come out.

David: Yes. Our listeners are witnessing you right now that you are on purpose. When I ask a question, there is a pause. You're thinking about that question in several different ways and levels around your purpose. Johanne Lavoie, "Centered Leadership," McKinsey and Company, thank you so much for your wisdom today.

Johanne: You're welcome and keep doing your great work.

David: Today, it was my hope that I'll be able to interview a woman that I have great profound respect for, Prabha Sankaranarayan, the President and CEO of Mediators Beyond Borders. Prabha just contacted me shortly before this show and was not in a position that she could participate. I know she really wants to. I'm going to tell you a little bit about Prabha, Mediators Beyond Borders and one of the Climate Adaptation summits that we are planning together.

MBB, let me go here. I'll just introduce you to MBB. It's an international non-governmental organization whose mission is to build local skills for peace and promote mediation worldwide.

Prabha is a conflict transformation practitioner who has mediated, facilitated and trained in Europe, Asia, Africa, and the United States. Her public and private sector work includes conflict analysis for public and private partnerships, consultation and assessment for industrial development zones, design and implementation of trainings for multinational corporations, inter-faith dialogues as well as facilitation of multi-stakeholder mediations.

Prabha is truly international and global. Mediators Beyond Borders serves projects in Turkey, in Ecuador, in New Orleans. She speaks English, Tamil, and Hindi.

I'll just tell you a little more about Mediators Beyond Borders. It's a great peacemaking community. I was at the founding meeting in Colorado eight, maybe even nine years ago when the visionary Ken Cloke who has been on this podcast on one of my early shows and many others set their intention. I'm still a member today.

MBB designs and implements strategic and highly targeted projects in global initiatives to advance peace through mediation. Projects and initiatives are operated across MBB's three areas of focus for capacity building, promoting mediation through advocacy, and providing consultancy services.

There are long-term initiatives that are carefully reviewed and approved by the board and are continually assessed for effectiveness. They really believe in capacity building. They do great work and they continue to do great work.

In addition to Mediators Beyond Borders, me, David Savage, I'm also a founder of Global Collaborative Initiative. CGI and MBB, just using those acronyms, and others are collaborating to convene Climate Change Adaptation summits at Oxford, England, Vancouver, Canada, and elsewhere.

Here's a quick look at what that looks like. This is really exciting stuff I want to share. I think Prabha would be fine with me sharing this. Other key people are Greg Walker, Charalee Graydon, Kathy Porter, Doreen Liberto Blanck. You've heard everyone other than Greg and Prabha on this podcast.

Climate Action Summit: Tools for Collaborative Decisions. Let's get beyond the debate. Is climate change real, not real? Who's to blame? Who pays the bills? Who do we separate and judge?

Let's go with the impacts and how we prepare, adapt, react, and change and collaborate around extreme weather events and changing weather. Let's go there.

While there are many climate change events being conducted around the world, there are few opportunities to move beyond dialogue to begin to explore the application of collaborative tools; collaborative tools to form a consensus on climate change issues.

Governments, businesses, and the public need to work together to make timely and effective decisions on climate adaptation. Yet, often key stakeholders or decision-makers are left out of the conversation.

The very first Climate Action Summit: Tools for Collaborative Decisions will be convened in Vancouver next year. The summit will provide examples of methods to dialogue and collaborate on climate change issues. Applying the tools will begin the conference. Puzzle groups will be invited to actively engage with experts to begin, to use in a collaborative fashion.

We hope to have fun puzzle groups, people that will have key questions that matter that need to be answered give them some funding so they can work on how we work together, how do we deal with climate change, extreme weather, how do we make sure this works.

Just as an aside, one of the conversations that one of our groups had reached out to a very, very wealthy individual who has an interest in social license to operate, an interest in climate adaptation, and an interest in reducing his risk in vulnerability when he has a billion-dollar stadium at sea level.

This is for us all. This is not a selective group or finger-waggers. This is how we're going to work together. In my home city of Cranbrook, I'm pretty safe but in my life city of Calgary, Alberta, we got the heads up in 2013 when most of the downtown was under a foot or two of water. How do we prepare for that? How do we engage? How do we react? How do we reduce litigation?

Often, it is same like-minded groups and individuals that are at the table with the same types of decision being made repeatedly. Who should be at the table? That's what we want to do. Decisions are being made to spend millions and billions of dollars based on the same underlying economic drivers and there's little or no effort to step back and take a good look at the overall system.

Collaboration is complex, requires effort, and does not fit within the crisis management response continuum. I hope that you'll get involved wherever you are. E-mail me, david@davidbsavage.com and I'll keep you up to date on the Climate Change Adaptation summits.

Today, this show has featured four great leaders with business connections around the planet. Prabha wasn't able to join us but I hope that she's satisfied that I've given a bit of a reflection on her great work and the great work of Mediators Beyond Borders; Atul Tandon of the Tandon Institute. He's now in Seattle and grew up in India; Johanne Lavoie, McKinsey and Company; and Dr.

Michael Hill, one of the most brilliant and collaborative neurologists in the world.

Key messages today have included: one, examine and change the existing ways we do things to capitalize on the collaborative process, outcomes, and the organization's rules of engagement; as human beings, two, we are forced to act and please don't do that if you're forced. Get engaged. Get people engaged; three, collaboration is the highway where all people can be linked, honored, and served.

Next week, our theme is Leadership and Team Awareness. This is going to be so cool. Featured guests are two experts that I hold in high regard. I think all 45 of my guests I hold in high regard. These two with respect to leadership and awareness is Ginger Lapid-Bogda of the Enneagram business and Bob Anderson of the Leadership Circle. Bob's book "Mastering Leadership" is just coming out right now, right this week.

Call to action this week: examine one aspect of how you work with others and co-create a better way.

Everyone, thank you for your time and your commitment to make it so.

Chapter 14 Leadership and Team Awareness Bob Anderson and Ginger Lapid-Bogda

David: Welcome, listeners from across our planet, our beautiful blue orb. I appreciate your attention and feedback. I'm a proponent of awareness of self and awareness of the group. I've studied many methods and techniques including the Leadership Circle, the Enneagram, and the Nine Domains.

I quote from the Nine Domains website, "Experience indicates that teams, like individuals, can be more or less healthy and functional. Teams, like individuals can be freeing, supportive, encouraging, and growth-full places in which to work.

On the other hand, teams can also show varying degrees of negativity, ego-driven behaviors, and serious but hidden pathologies that make working in such an atmosphere difficult and counter-productive. At their worst, teams can be so negative and pathologically destructive that they threaten the health and well-being of everyone in them." Yes, I think each one of us have had a taste of that.

"Having a way of objectively measuring these different states is extraordinarily useful and incalculably beneficial both for employees and for the organization as a whole."

Today's show theme is Leadership and Team Awareness. We're using the Leadership Circle and the Enneagram in Business as our feature models, assessment tools, process. This show features two of the most insightful and open experts on personal and team awareness in the world.

I have been taught by Ginger Lapid-Bogda and Bob Anderson and look forward to more opportunities to learn from them. Check out The Enneagram in Business and The Leadership Circle online.

Key messages for today:

1) awareness of myself and how I am in relationship with my team allows me and them to be more effective;
2) at our foundation, we must start by understanding our values and ethics;
3) keep on developing and growing your consciousness; and
4) access powerful and evolutionary assessments and tools for reflection and assessment.

Now let's go to our interview with Bob Anderson.

Bob Anderson is the Founder, Chairman, and Chief Development Officer of The Leadership Circle, LLC, and the Full Circle Group, LLC. Bob and I believe in circles and not squares and rectangles. Bob is the creator and author of "The Leadership Circle Profile." This is an awesome integrated and innovative leadership development tool.

"The Leadership Circle Profile" is used by companies worldwide. It's heralded as a genuine Break Through in the field of leadership development. When I was led to that is it's inclusive. It integrates so much and it's such a powerful guide to leaders as to how I am in relationship, how I lead, how other people see me, how they see me lead, and how I encourage and incite them to their own leadership.

"The Leadership Circle Profile" and assessment-associated tools are used by thousands of organizations around the world. Really exciting times, Bob is co-author of the book "Mastering Leadership," a work that I believe I know will be the next seminal work in the leadership field. I believe that's true. I am so delighted to have Bob on our show today.

Rather me continuing to grovel at your feet, Bob, tell our listeners more about you and your initiatives.

Bob: I had the good fortune early in my career through deliberate choice but getting connected with a lot of thought leaders in the field and work with them closely. What I noticed early on, this goes back in to mid-1980's, was that the field was a random collection of really good stuff, good theory, good research, good models and frameworks but partial and un-integrated.

I set about, not really consciously by choosing to do this but it ended up that way, trying to integrate and I kept trying to integrate. 20 years later, I had created an integration of the field and then I created Leadership Circle profile to begin to measure and assess and provide 360 Feedback out of that model and framework.

When I put it out, people started to say, "This is the first unified or integrated or universal model in leadership we've ever seen." Pretty much that's been my 30-year career.

Along the way, I partnered and merged businesses with my co-author, Bill Adams who's one of the best consultants I know and has taken this framework and really given it business relevance and practical application. We write all of that up and wrote "Mastering Leadership" which is about to come out.

David: How would people find out more about the Leadership Circle and how to learn more? What's the website? How do they connect with you online?

Bob: leadershipcircle. There's a lot of information there, lot of position papers. Of course, the book comes with a free self-assessment, which is "The full Leadership Circle Profile" assessment but only the self assessment, not the 360. You can turn it in to a 360 if you want to.

The book thoroughly describes the underlying model framework. The assessment is a rendition of the model. Looking at research and case studies through the lens of "The Leadership Circle Profile" is a lot of what the book is about. The book itself will be a great way to connect with Leadership Circle.

David: What are a couple of the key ideas that you've got in your new book "Mastering Leadership?"

Bob: First, we build the core argument, kind of business argument that we're making. Now it's getting real traction around the world. We asked most leaders if...second, is in leadership matters, they all agree in businesses; with effective leadership out to form businesses with ineffective leadership.

We define a business with this conscious competence. If you just think about how will you describe a leader that's unconscious versus one that's conscious? Is there a relationship between conscious leadership and effectiveness? Everybody would say, "Yes."

We present some groundbreaking research and looked between stages of adult development or the evolution of internal maturity or consciousness and effectiveness in leadership. The research is quite compelling. The core argument of the book is that the inner game runs the outer game.

The inner game of leadership can evolve, if it evolves through progressive stages or levels of maturity and development that usher in higher levels of capacity and capability to meet complexity. If leaders were all dealing now with escalating complexity, is our internal operating system mature enough to meet that complexity?

That's the core argument of the book. We build a whole framework on how do you develop both the outer game of capability and competence while you're developing the inner game of consciousness and maturity to get greater effectiveness. That's the book.

David: Tell me, one of my passions with my book "Unlocking the Possible Within a Culture of Collaboration" is the subtitle, how do you build that culture of collaboration, Bob? How do you build that culture?

Bob: It's a really interesting question because when I was thinking about it collaboration feels like a really soft, fuzzy word, and easily dismissed in a way and yet very hard, very hard to accomplish.

We'll often ask leaders to describe the business that if it existed will put them out of business. Once they create that description, we'll ask them, "How ready are you to meet that to go up against that business? Is it that you're not strategically ready or that you need to be able to work together more effectively in order to that?"

Usually, we need to work together more effectively in order to do that, collectively effective. Then I ask, "How hard is that?" They just nod and say, "That's the hard stuff."

Most leadership teams that we encounter, we're talking extended leadership teams, don't optimize collective effectiveness, probably 95% don't focus on it. When we focus on leadership, we focus on individual effectiveness, not collective.

We think that the collective effectiveness of a leadership team is the effect of the organization. It defines business performance. The organization won't perform at a level that's higher than the collective effectiveness of its leadership. That plays right in to collaboration. How well do we show up together, engage in difficult conversations, cross boundary conversations so that we can lead effectively?

That requires a very high level of authenticity, high level of capabilities and get the un-discuss-able conversations on the table in a great way. When you do that, you immediately move in to a culture of collaboration. We must work more collectively effectively on issues that are cut across all lines in the business in order to really have the business perform at a high level. Collaboration is right at the heart of it.

David: As we close this interview, Bob, what's one thing you wish our listeners to do or become more aware of to improve their collaborative success?

Bob: When we work with leadership teams over a long period of time, a year or two, the difference they say that really made all the difference was that "We can now tell the truth to each other."

The ability to get difficult conversations that are politically-charged or have sacred cows associated with them, to get them on the table and cut through complexity and the complexity of those issues in a great way is really, central to our ability to collaborate and create the kind of culture as we want together.

David: Bob Anderson, the Leadership Circle and "Mastering Leadership," a brand-new seminal book on leadership, thank you so much.

Bob: You're welcome. It's great to be with you.

David: Our special guest is one of the women that I just love because the leadership and business combination, the self and team awareness she brings, Ginger Lapid-Bogda. Talking about the Enneagram, Ginger and I have been talking just an advance of this interview saying, "It's hard to describe the Enneagram that people have dedicated an entire lifetime to," including Ginger.

I've devoted about three months of my time to taking courses, et cetera. It's hard to do that in such a short period of time. I strongly recommend our listeners around the world to go to the theenneagraminbusiness.com.

Just a little bit of a background to the Enneagram; the reason I think it's so great is Ginger's Enneagram in Business, the Nine Domains, others are just insight-filled pathways to self-awareness of leaders and assessment of the levels of development for teams.

Background of the Enneagram comes from the Greek words and this is from theenneagraminbusiness.com. Ginger has a ton of resources there. I don't want to make it too difficult for the listener or for Ginger. I'll just do a quick introduction.

"The word enneagram comes from the Greek words 'ennea' or nine and 'gram', which is something written or drawn and refers to the nine points on the Enneagram symbol. The nine different Enneagram styles, identified as numbers One through Nine, reflect distinct habits of thinking, feeling, behaving and with each style connected to a unique path of development.

Each of us has only one place, or number, on the Enneagram; while our Enneagram style remains the same throughout our lifetime, the characteristics of our type may either soften or become more pronounced as we grow and develop."

Let's go there. Enneagram is believed to be several thousand years old. Many of our listeners are comfortable with Myers Brigs and that type of stuff. I think the Enneagram is so much deeper and so much more.

As another easy access point, listeners for Ginger's work is if you go to Google Play or iTunes, download Know Your Type, which is the app. Know Your Type, that's available for Apple and Android and Kindle Fire devices. It's just a great and very easy way to illuminate the Nine different architectures of human personality.

Ginger, one of the things that you've given me is a wonderful quote. It's a life lesson. "Love what you do. Be good at it and make yourself easy to work with." Do you notice, listeners? Easy to work with.

Ginger Lapid-Bogda is a PhD is an Enneagram author and teacher and an organizational development consultant, trainer, and coach for over 40 years. Ginger works with organizations, leaders, and teams around the world to create vibrant, productive, and sustainable organizations. This is not a quick fix.

Ginger's written five great books on the Enneagram in Business. The newest one is "Consulting with the Enneagram." She also offers global certification programs that enable coaches, leaders, consultants, trainers to use the Enneagram. For more information, got to theenneagraminbusiness.com.

She has amazing multinational corporations as her clients: Whirlpool, Medtronic, Genentech, Nestle, Kaiser, et cetera, et cetera, et cetera.

Ginger, thank you so much for your time today. I've spoken enough. Tell me more about you and your work and let's just start there.

Ginger: My work at this point is focused on how to utilize the Enneagram integrated with other change technologies, leadership development models, change strategies, behavior science models because these particular models without the Enneagram are quite powerful but when you include the Enneagram with it, you get to see how individuals show differences in terms of how they might utilize one of these models to make themselves, their teams, their leadership more effective.

I wonder, David is I should go through the Nine types very quickly...

David: Yes. Please.

Ginger: So that some of your listeners may find themselves. Not as you said a quick fix, but sometimes it's just helping people anchor themselves a little bit. Would that be a good idea?

David: Yes. Thank you.

Ginger: The Enneagram types or styles are numbered One through Nine. There are Nine different styles, each with a particular worldview, patterns of thinking, emotional response patterns, and behavioral responses that are related to their thinking and their feeling patterns.

Ones are sometimes called the perfectionists. They think that they're looking, seeking a perfect world knowing that it will never be perfect but what's important is that they're constantly trying to improve themselves, each, all of us in the environment. It's a continuous search for perfection.

Twos are people who like to be liked. They're very relationally oriented. They are highly intuitive, tuning in to the needs of other people and they like to kind of orchestrate or arrange things or make good things happen behind the scenes preferring that to being highly visible.

The Threes are focused on goals and success. They appear very confident and competent in order to gain both respect of others, their own self-respect. They're kind of the people who get stuff done.

Type Fours like deep connections with their own interior world. They love the deepest connections with other people. They feel most alive and most real when they're engaged with others in a very deep way and they're authentically expressing themselves.

Fives are people who thirst information and knowledge. They thirst everything they can possibly can about the things they think are important. They engage in emotional detachment automatically keeping themselves re-spilling resource because they find emotional interaction highly draining. They like to keep their interactions with others to a minimum even though they're very curious about people.

Sixes have insightful minds. They tend to engage in the anticipatory scenario -- building, preparing, hoping for the best and preparing for the worst or things that might be obstacles. Sometimes they see themselves as sort of mega problem-solvers but they're constantly wanting to be prepared to increase the best-case possibilities and decrease the worst-case scenarios.

Sevens are craving stimulation, people, ideas. Their minds go faster than a nanosecond. They're always connecting disparate things, things that may not seem connected to the rest of us. They like to keep all their options open feeling like nobody has a right to restrict them.

Eights like the truth. They want to keep everything just and under control. They want to make very important things happen so they tend to move to action when mad, when they're sad, when they're anxious, and when they want to do something. All of this is also partly to hide their vulnerabilities.

Nines seek harmony, peace, positive, mutual regard. They're very sensitive and it's sematic actually to conflict so they can't get resolved, to tension and to ill will. They're fantastic at facilitating conflict resolution between others or amongst brothers but they sometimes leave themselves or what they want to say or their opinions in the background for the sake of group harmony.

Those are the Nine types. I'd say that in business leaders, that's our main entree. Actually, it's very interesting. It's the business leaders that tend to bring most of the people who are doing work with the Enneagram into organizations because they know there's a leadership shortage worldwide. It's been very hard to know how to groom people internally or even how to bring in people laterally.

The Enneagram is the most persuasive and profound way to develop leadership capabilities because your leadership style is directly an outgrowth of your Enneagram type and then you could see what the predictable strengths and the predictable development areas are.

Leaders can work on their development before it becomes a cause of stress to them and the organization. It helps them develop more kind of lateral skills and processes and a deeper understanding of themselves so that they can handle all the complexities much better.

It's fantastic for team development, enhancing communication skills. The applications are, I'd say, rather endless in terms of the Enneagram's applications in the business setting. That's kind of what's being embraced a lot globally by leaders and companies and Human Resources people around the world.

David: Some of the sense of the other type being where your personality type is you're going to put people in a box. In my knowledge about the Enneagram says in fact it's the opposite. It's making us much more comfortable with aspects of all Nine types, with aspects of making sure that our organizations have a great balance of perspectives and types and tendencies.

Tell us more about the inclusive aspect, the holistic aspect of the Enneagram for business.

Ginger: It's inclusive because the idea is that there's not any particular type that's particularly adept at any particular job but that each of the type can bring different things to the job as long as they have the required and necessary skills and experience and that they have the diversity of experience and perspective that each of the type brings.

As people develop their self-mastery, they can create much more innovative organizations. That's much more interesting and it's more embracing. I think that that aspect of it is extremely important.

I think the other part of it is that you said the thing about the box. One of the leaders in one of the companies I worked with said, "Other systems tell you what box you're in. The Enneagram shows you the box you're already in. Instead of boxing you, it helps you break out of the box."

Because the Enneagram is fundamentally a developmental system; once you know your type, there are specific activities for developing specific areas that are going to work for people of your type but wouldn't necessarily work for people of other types.

David: If we simplify and oversimplify, oftentimes companies, boards of directors, and investors will look for a type Three, an achiever to be in charge of their company. What's the problem with just having an executive or an executive team that is too heavily tending towards type Three or type Eight?

Ginger: Or any of the types that they might be biased?

David: Yes.

Ginger: It's not the type that's going to make you a successful, effective leader. It is your level of self-mastery, your self-acceptance, your self-knowledge, your willingness and ability to change and grow. That's going to make you an excellent leader.

I would say that people who had been in the Enneagram for the first couple of hours and they say, "Shouldn't we hire by type?" I say, "No. You want to hire people who are self-mastering, who are engaged in their self-development because these are the people that are going to be flexible. They're going to be easy to work with. They're not going to expect everybody to be just like them and they're not going to want everybody to be just like them."

I have seen some organizations where they have got the same type like three or four levels down of the same type and they might feel like they have a similar work style but they have the same problems and the same blind spots.

There are blind spot sides to every single type. If you have a variety of people types, you don't get those blind spots because you get people saying, "What about this? We could think of it this way." It's sort of the anti-cloning methodology, if you will.

David: Yes. Ginger Lapid-Bogda, the Enneagram in Business, she's been talking to us about self-mastery, level of development for teams, how to avoid blind spots.

David: We're back now with Ginger Lapid-Bogda, the Enneagram in Business talking about the insights and the profound self-awareness and team development possibilities when people really use this tool.

Ginger, what's going on in the business application of the Enneagram globally?

Ginger: I work globally and a lot of my colleagues do. I would say that the Enneagram is being used in businesses globally, every major continent, every major country. It's used in every industry. It's being used in health care. It's being used in hospitality. It's being used in banking. The cars, Toyota is using it. On and on it's just quite remarkable how many different applications there are in how many different industries.

I think there's a trend towards sharing and being more collaborative. I have an Enneagram business network, about 85 different people from all over the world. We work in a collaborative way either in small groups or pairs. We have two levels. One is, senior members and those are people I work with directly and to whom I refer work.

There are associate members who get mentored by senior members. Senior members love the mentoring so it's a very developmental process. They're required to be in either of them, senior or associate to agree to what we call Blue Ocean ethical guidelines taken from individualized, professionalized with the Blue Ocean strategy that's so useful in working the strategy.

It has to do with being honest and not misrepresenting yourself in any way; about respecting intellectual property; about sharing information with others; about not competing for the sake of competition but to collaborate in an egalitarian way to keep your prices fair.

If money is involved, to have that not be your primary motivator; to realize that there's kind of enough to go around so you don't have to take work away from others; focus on relationships and people; and to also agree to treat each other with respect and the way we want to be treated.

Also, we don't say things about each other or other people and even in the Enneagram or the Enneagram business world or other consultants that would be disparaging of them.

David: Those sound like profound rules of engagement that any team could adopt radically and make theirs and customize. That's a great set of awareness tools for anybody to work together collaboratively.

Ginger: I think the Enneagram has sort of ethical integrity, values-based to it. If we're not using it in organizations and encouraging our clients to use it that way, we're out of integrity with the whole, really underlying essence of the system.

David: Ginger, what are your hopes for a collaborative future?

Ginger: You mean globally or with the Enneagram?

David: Either one or both.

Ginger: Let me get up a little bit in the sky here but we have so many global problems and challenges and although the Enneagram is not the solution to all the challenges, there is a way that the Enneagram and people's self-awareness, it's sort of a level of consciousness; when you work with the Enneagram, it has the capability to help individuals, teams or organizations be conscious.

Entities and people like that, organizations like that, institutions like that can only help address some of the world's global problems where the high level of consciousness is needed. I guess that would be my biggest hope -- that we have a role to play; not an overstated role, but not an understated one either.

David: Yes, recognition of our self, recognition of others. I know one of the things that's personally useful to me, seems like every day is when the hair on the back of my neck is going up, I can recognize it right way. I can recognize my tendencies and I can remind myself what would be creative, what would be inclusive, what would be in love, and what would be useful for my company and my clients.

Ginger: I use it a lot, the quote from Viktor Frankl about the space between stimulus and response is your life quality. I'm misquoting but it's close. "In that space is an opportunity for choice and in choice of our alternative, we have freedom."

The Enneagram not only helps people observe themselves and create that space which is pretty amazing because it shows you where to create that space but gives you a way to understand your current reaction, how it relates to your type, and helps you bear what your development is. Is that a chronic response? It gives you more options for choice in that space. For me, it's all about choice and freedom.

David: Ginger, as we close this interview, what is one thing that you wish to challenge or encourage our audience to do as they collaborate?

Ginger: It's to be yourself, to respect yourself and to respect others as much as you respect yourself and to keep on developing and growing and increasing your consciousness both as individuals, as teams, as organizations. That's a lifelong journey for all of us.

David: Thank you so much, Ginger Lapid-Bogda, the Enneagram in Business. I know, the little that I've known, I've learned in the last ten years about the Enneagram, the more and more insight it provides me. Thank you, Ginger.

Ginger: You're welcome. Thanks for asking.

David: By using the Leadership Circle, the Enneagram and other insight-filled methods, you'll advance through success through becoming more conscious, connected, and collaborative.

Here's another quote from our new friend, Bob Anderson. "When the leadership system functions effectively, performance improves. The leadership system is the essential organizing system that must deliver on all functions owned by the top team or C-suite.

These functions include and require that leadership become cohesive, define the future or vision, set the direction, create and execute strategy, ensure alignment, communicate clarity, engage stakeholders, develop talent, manage performance, build accountability, ensure succession, allocate resources," that is often missed. Most often missed and something I truly believe in, "and craft the culture." This is a culture.

Here's a reading from my book "Break Through to Yes." "The Enneagram is believed to have made its appearance more than 2,000 years ago in Egypt, Persia,

Spain, and the Middle East. Unlike more widely known personality assessments, the Enneagram invites us to un-type ourselves and connect with others in a more meaningful and productive manner."

The Golden Rule that we were taught in our youth is 'Treat others the way you wish to be treated.' You've heard that. In the Biblical language, "Do unto others as you would have them do unto you." I really like the Platinum Rule -- "Treat others the way they want to be treated." Makes great sense to be with others in their way rather than expect them to be like me.

The Enneagram informs me of several important things. What are my tendencies and needs in relationship? What are my tendencies in conflict? What are my tendencies and needs of the other in this relationship? What are the tendencies, their tendencies in conflict? What are their and my underlying fears? What language and behaviors light them up and shuts them down? Pretty critical stuff. How do I get more of what I want?

When I have a stronger sense of these then I can connect, communicate, and act in ways the other person understands and prefers. Whether in communication, negotiation, mediation or collaboration, be with the other first. That's right. Be with the other. It's a more effective way than waiting for them to come to me. Being with them builds connection, respect, and trust.

In collaboration, awareness of the people you choose to engage is critical. The Enneagram and the Leadership Circle gives us an invitation to the appropriate mix of personalities and styles in to our collective.

On my website I've built a graphic that I developed to illustrate the strengths of the Nine types. As negotiators, each type has its strengths and weaknesses. To bring the balance mixed together gives far better rudder and more balanced perspective. Conversely, the right mix reduces the risk of tunnel vision and groupthink.

I'm a certified believer in another great method, the Nine Domains in levels of functioning. Check out the Nine Domains as well. This is really good stuff -- consciousness, being aware of the other.

In a way, you can look at it in many ways. What's the purpose of me speaking English when the other person speaks Arabic? What's the purpose of me simply talking at them? Listen first. Find out their language. Once you do that, you'll see how quickly the communication, the trust builds.

Remember the movie "Avatar?" "I see you." So powerful. Let's do that. Let's look at how we see each other. Let's go back. How do we see each other? What does it mean?

Remember Ken Cloke's interview, one of our earliest episodes? Here's a quote from Ken. "What is the deepest level of our collaboration? What's the highest achievement that we can make in this field?"

I think we begin to think in those terms, we begin to see all of life completely differently. What we then, I think see is that the collaborative project, if we can call it that, is one that has been building over the course of human history and has yet to realize complete fruition.

Here's another before we close for the break. Here's Ken's brilliant metaphor. Ken Cloke, "It doesn't matter whose end of the boat is sinking. We're all in this together. We have to realize that we have to take responsibility for it and start working on our problems together. It doesn't mean it's easy. It just means it's truth."

David: Here's another quote from my book "Break Through to Yes: Unlocking Possibility within a Culture of Collaboration." "Most readers are crafting their skills to collaborate better on initiatives which often are within and outside your organization with known processes, resources, and roles. This may give you a sense that it may be easier than collaborating on a startup and that assumption may hold you back from challenging all the rules and all the relationships.

There are costs and benefits to each manner of collaborative initiative. Ensure you're conscious of the fact there's a play and design with the end in mind. To build your skill and network, start with specific challenges and opportunities within your organization or organizations. Start small and build the confidence of your team. That collaboration works better than the other approaches to getting things done and achieving goals.

What is one challenge or opportunity that I can commit to break through and capture by using a confluence of people, organizations, resources, and structures? Confluence? That's a coming or flowing together, meeting or gathering at one point.

Given this intention and objective, forgetting for a while our own structure, resources, and limitations, what is the optimal confluence of people, resources, processes, and global networks that will achieve this success?"

Wow! Can you imagine? Yes, let's imagine. When I speak of walking in circles, often a successful collaboration takes a long time to occur. Unlike simply calling a meeting on a specific task, successful collaboration requires the participants to have the awareness and skills to collaborate. Sometimes we must accept baby steps even when we know much greater steps are possible.

That's something Laura Hummelle and I have experienced in our Kootenay Rockies area. Leaders there are taking the steps that they know that they trust.

They're not familiar with bigger picture. They're not yet ready. They will be ready. We're ready. We're learning and we're happy to co-create with them.

With this book and this podcast, I want to create a better bridge between the vision and the action. Effective collaboration is evolutionary. Every time we work together, we are developing our own story, our own network, our behaviors and possibilities for future collaborations. Yes, it's a collaboration. It's a pathway. It's an evolution.

Depending on the perspective we take, the movement is different. When I talk about walking in circles with the view looking down, the movement is round and round and seemingly without progress. Yet, if we looked at the same movement from the side, it may seem as a spiral rising upwards as we move.

If we keep the effort of collaboration smaller and controlled, we will keep having the same small and controlled result. This is not brainstorming. This is not another meeting. This is how we work together, inside and outside reaching out, not limited by what you have. Everything is possible. Everything.

Are we getting enough courageous participants who challenge the ideas? Is collaboration designed as well as it could be? Does our reward system support the people? Do we incent collaborations by our compensation packages and other ways? Oftentimes we don't. Busyness is incented, results sometimes. Collaborative culture, rarely. Collaboration is not an event. It is a culture.

My friend, Tina Spiegel from Australia told me the reason to use collaboration is a process is because it holds key elements which we as relational beings treasure. Think about old technology. Yes, think about that. How does it get significantly improved?

There are reports across the globe on how when the windows and doors of an organization gets thrown wide open, there are all the answers to challenges and find solutions that were not happening in the closed shop environment.

Think about Tesla breaking the rules and giving away its technology. Open sourcing builds better vehicles, increases loyalty, and leads to higher profits. Playing within your organizational silo and collaborating small is understandable yet.

The leaders who are developing their collaborative leadership networks and aspirations have a great advantage. Those that only play within their own organization are missing. They don't see what they can't see yet.

Think about doing more with far less. Think about not brick buildings and procedure manuals. Think about evolution, innovation, flow, flexibility, high performance, teams. Then, access collective intelligence. Yes, start small.

Learn together. Build trust. Empower the group. Celebrate success and learn from your failures. Dream big. To recycle a phrase, think global and act local. We are only separated by two degrees of separation in this world, this digital world today.

Consider also these words from my good friend in New York, Everett Cox. "The first collaboration for every human being is in the womb. The first collaborator for every human being is a woman. When that first collaborator is dishonored in any way, the entire social fabric that began at the womb is threatened, weakened, and endangered." How are you in relationship to your organizational womb? What do you choose to consciously create?

This show has featured two of the most insightful and collaborative experts on personal and team awareness in the world, Ginger Lapid-Bogda, the Enneagram in Business and Bob Anderson, the

Leadership Circle. Look at them. Look at their teaching, their learning, their curiosity, their opportunity, and their invitation.

Key messages today have included:

1) awareness of myself and how I am in relationship with my team allows me and them to be far more effective,
2) at our foundation, we must start by understanding our values and ethics, interests and intentions, reflection, claiming, platform, foundation, our base.
3) keep on developing and growing your consciousness by accessing powerful and evolutionary assessments and tools for reflection and assessment.

Next week is the last of our 15-week podcast series in the fall of 2015. As we complete this 15-week series, we turn to the future because the future is what really matters, our shared future, leadership as if the future matters. Next week, our theme is Next Gen Leaders and some highlights.

I'm delighted and proud to tell you the featured guests, the next gen leaders that we have: Dan Savage, video game developer, Infinity Ward, Los Angeles, California; India Sherret, World Junior Ski Cross Champion, Cranbrook, British Columbia at Canada; Sarah Daitch, member of the 2015 Governor General's Canadian Leadership Conference and founder of the Collaborative Global Initiative. Sarah's working out of The Hague in the Netherlands.

Somebody that's not as young but youthful in heart and spirit and intelligence, my good friend, Susan Brady, Linkage in Boston. I also want to encourage you to come back and listen to Chuck Rose, "Win , Win, Win or Walk Away" and "We are One," those two amazing songs that Chuck sent my way for this podcast. We'll talk about some highlights and challenges.

As we close today, my call to action is what gets measured gets done. What gets measured over time with expert support creates evolutionary cultures of collaboration and leadership. Investigate the Leadership Circle, the Enneagram in Business, the Nine Domains, the assessment app on my own website. Whatever you choose, choose one and move forward together with your team. Move forward. Build your culture of collaboration.

Chapter 15 Next Generation Leaders and our Future feauring Dan Savage, India Sherrit, Sarah Daitch and Kevin Brown

David: "D-Day, June 6, 1944, Operation Overlord, the long-awaited invasion of Nazi-occupied Europe began with allied armies from the United States, Britain, and Canada lining on the coast of Normandy. On D-Day, the 3rd Canadian Infantry Division landed on Juno Beach.

The Canadian assault troops stormed the shore in the face of fierce opposition from the Canadian strongholds and mined beach obstacles. The soldiers raced across wide open beaches swept with machine gun fire and stormed the gun positions.

In fierce hand-to-hand fighting, they fought their way into the towns of Bernieres, Courseulles, and Saint Aubin and then advanced inland securing a critical bridge head for the Allied invasion. The victory was a turning point in World War II and led to the liberation of Europe and the defeat of Nazi Germany.

14,000 young Canadians stormed Juno Beach on D-Day. Remember, the population of Canada was about 15 million at that time. Their courage, determination, and self-sacrifice were the immediate reasons for the success in those critical hours. The fighting they endured was fierce and frightening. The price they paid was high. The battles for the beach head cost 340 Canadian lives. That's 340 Canadians and another 574 wounded.

John Keegan, eminent British historian wrote, "Six armies in Normandy state the following concerning the Canadian 3rd Division on D-Day, 'At the end of the day, its forward elements stood deeper into France than those of any other division, any other nation.

The opposition the Canadians faced was stronger of that than any other beach save Omaha where the Americans were fighting. That was an accomplishment in which the whole nation could take considerable pride.'" Check out more on junobeach.info.

Let's look at command and control versus collaboration on D-Day on Operation Overlord. It was hell on Earth. Field generals did not give the authority to those in the battle. They commanded from the top.

What's worse, the top two generals in the Nazi army, they had all the assets. They outnumbered. They have the bunkers, and the Panzer divisions. Yet, on June 6, 1944, those leaders decided they were going to spend a couple of days in Paris with their girlfriends. Yes, can you imagine?

The people that saw that Operation Overlord coming, wanted to react and were in the fierce battle, didn't have the authority to engage the Panzer divisions that were a distance away from the beach. Even worse, Hitler insisted on absolute command and control. He was said to have sneeringly referred to by some of his army as "that Bohemian corporal." Command and control.

Hitler is said to love to have midnight to 3:00 am rants where he just ranted at his generals and then he would take drugs so he could sleep. He would often sleep until noon. Sleeping until noon on June 6 was a major catastrophe. Tanks, aircrafts, armies were not directed to move until Hitler woke up.

Does this sound like any boss you work for? Command and control. Think if the Nazis actually had a flatter structure where the people in the battle could actually react and respond to that battle. Think about what could have resulted if they properly had a system that engaged all that everybody felt part of and there was deep comradeship.

My father, Alexander Gordon Savage, I want to talk about him in this show about the next generation. Dad's father died when Dad was 15. Dad went off to the University of Alberta, met my mother May Miller and played on the varsity football team.

Think of this: a year before you were to graduate, your country says, "You've now graduated. We need you in the war. Come now." Dad earned his rank of "Leftenant," that's the British pronunciation of Lieutenant. He led 75 men at age 24.

Think about youth and leadership in the war and at D-Day. Think about that. These were not men in their 40's, 50's, 60's, and 70's that we see as leaders today. These were men in their teens and 20's and women. Yes. In that war on D-Day, Dad made it through.

Back in September of 1944, he was on his way to Calais when he was on a road at night leading his men in the dark. They didn't know that the Germans could have the technology, but the Germans saw them.

Dad was machine-gunned all the way down his left leg. He rolled off the road and into a water-filled ditch and had to wait bleeding until sunrise. Working together 12 hours later, his men got to him and got him out. Bravery, commitment, comradeship, working together, collaboration.

During World War II, Gordon Savage served with the 6th Field Company at Royal Canadian Engineers as

Lieutenant and was wounded by machine gun fire in France during the attack on Calais courtesy of the Canadian Military Engineers Association. Dad was 24. The young are our focus today; the young, our next generation of collaborators. PS: if you want to learn more about Juno Beach, read Mark Zuehlke's book "Juno Beach."

Welcome to our listeners from across the planet. I appreciate your attention. I appreciate this. During this 15-week series we've featured 45 guests from Canada, United States, the Netherlands, India, and Spain. Everyone has offered their insights.

According to our analytics, welcome to our listeners in Australia, Austria, Belarus, Cameroon, Canada, China, Germany, France, Italy, Iran, Jamaica, Japan, Mexico, Mongolia, Morocco, the Netherlands, Romania, Russia, Saudi Arabia, Singapore, Spain, Sweden, Thailand, Turkey, Ukraine, United Kingdom, United States, and Vietnam. Hello and thank you for listening.

Today's show features Kevin Brown of Spain, World Mediation; Dan Savage, Infinity Ward, Los Angeles; India Sherret, World Junior Ski Cross Champion of Cranbrook, British Columbia; Sarah Daitch, Collaborative Global Initiative, The Hague, the Netherlands; and music by my good friend, Chuck Rose "Win, Win, Win or Walk Away."

Key messages today:

1) you must make certain that every cog in the machine is working well together to move forward;

2) getting involved in collaborative initiatives and teams across generations. Build skills, understanding, and opportunities; and

3) it takes a village to raise leaders. Be there in support of our next generations of leaders. That is plural, our next generations and our shared future need you.

Now we move to the global connection and dialogue. I'm very pleased to introduce you to Kevin Brown. Kevin is the owner and President of Mediation International. Go to his website, mediationinternational.eu. Kevin is executive organizer for The 2nd World Mediation Summit in Madrid 2015 and is senior roster expert with the United Nations for mediation and ADR facilitation.

Kevin provides conflict management services locally as well as on an international basis while being based in Madrid. His services include: ombudsing, mediation, group needs analysis, conflict coaching, training courses, organizational systemic issue analysis, facilitation, and much more.

Kevin has worked and does work for the Canadian, US, British, German, Irish, Israel, Afghanistan, Palestine, and Egyptian embassies in Madrid, Spain.

Kevin, I'm going to let you tell our listeners and me more about Kevin Brown, Mediation International and your work.

Kevin: Thanks, David. It's really great to be here and to participate in your show. As you've mentioned, I am the owner and the President of Mediation International based here in Madrid and operating across Europe. Mediation International has the distinction of being one of the 30 companies worldwide that has been accepted as a qualifying assessment program with International Mediation Institute (IMI).

I'm also an internationally certified mediator with IMI and currently am organizing The 3rd Annual Mediation Summit here in Madrid in 2016. I'm a roster expert with the United Nations Development Program for Mediation and ADR Facilitation. The work I do includes everything you've mentioned including of course, organizing the annual World Mediation Summit.

My background includes a Master's Degree in International Conflict Analysis and Management with Royal Roads University from Canada. I'm currently working on my Ph.D. in Conflict Management and Mediation. I have well over 25 years of experience as a mediator, designer of ADR training programs, and well over 4,000 hours facilitating ADR training programs.

As you mentioned, I do love to work with the embassies here in Madrid. Most of my work is outside of Madrid because mediation really isn't all that mainstream here in Spain yet. Some of the work I've done internationally include Afghanistan, Thailand, Georgia, Belgium, Ukraine, Romania, Spain, and, of course, Canada where I first began doing my mediation.

David: Our purpose in this show is to encourage the Next Generation Leaders. I am very excited to have you talk with us, Kevin, because there is underlying interest that we all have in helping our next generation to be even better at conflict management, about negotiation, and about alternative ways of resolving conflicts.

For me, I got very involved in the early 1990's having gone through a marital breakup, and having raised my kids on my own. When you get surprised in life and when you've got these amazing children, it's important to learn how to communicate effectively and encourage the next generation.

Any comments as to your why? Why is this so important to you?

Kevin: Really great question, David. I, too, have had a very diverse life. With my first marriage, I had two daughters and I now have a two-year old daughter who is growing up very quickly. It's really important to me to pass on the mediation information and mediation skills to my children. One of my daughters is a mediator now with the Canadian Military. I'm just thrilled that she's involved in this.

One of the things that we're doing is the World Mediation Summit. The whole focus of that is to promote mediation to people who have not heard mediation or aren't familiar with mediation. When I moved to Madrid a few years ago, it became very obvious to me that mediation really is still in its infancy here in Spain and it's going to take a while before it becomes mainstream.

For this reason, we organize these summits and we're going to have our third summit in 2016. We invite people from across the world. Our first two included ambassadors, diplomats, judges, lawyers, mediators, providers, users, students, all sorts of different individuals that are interested in mediation.

David: There's a place to convene. I'm actively considering and hoping I can find a way to participate and support your initiative, Kevin.

Kevin: Yes. That's wonderful.

David: As we close this interview, in this moment, what would you challenge our listeners to do or become more aware of to build their success as collaborators?

Kevin: Great question, great question, David. To be a collaborator, one really needs a lot of skills, life skills, not just mediation skills; skills that involve utilizing other people from all different venues in life. I use collaboration in so many ways both professionally and personally. So many factors are involved -- working together, inspiring others and being inspired, sharing and learning, dialoguing, listening to people, consensus building.

In my opinion, when we work collaboratively, we're engaging others equally and find the results that well, not work for everyone, making the implementation process much smoother. Collaboration, it's a method. It's a skill that is very much like all of mediation skills. It's one that we use in all aspects of our life.

At the World Mediation Summit for example, we have collaborators that are academic members, users, providers, media, all of us working together to build an amazing summit not just for us but for all the attendees.

David: We are right up against our commercial break. Thank you so much, Kevin Brown, World Mediation. I invite our listeners to check Kevin out, the World Mediation Summit in Madrid out, and find a way to build our skills together. Thank you, Kevin.

Kevin: You're very welcome, David.

David: We've got India Sherret today. She is a young ski cross racer from Cranbrook, British Columbia,

Canada. Growing up in the Kootenays, India grew to love the mountains; of course, a as we all do in the Kootenays; I live there, too, and all the possibilities that the mountains give to us.

India started skiing at the age of eight and racing at ten. Her first taste of ski cross, that's right, ski cross, came when she was 13 and fell in love with it instantly. From there she began racing ski cross full time and competed in FIS Nor-Am races with the Alberta Ski Cross Team when she turned 15. At 18, India qualified for the Canadian development team and hopes to make the Canadian National team within the next two years.

India has represented Canada at many international events including the 2012 Youth Olympic Winter Games and World Junior Championships. Yes, Youth Olympic Winter Games and World Junior Championships. She's earned the titles of 2015 Canadian National Champion and World Junior Champion. In her free time in cross training she enjoys mountain biking, rock climbing, hiking, and camping.

I've asked India today to join us, listeners because she has such a commitment and talent and passion. Of course, ski racers, those high-performance athletes also need our collaboration.

India Sherret, welcome to our radio show. What would you say to our listeners to help them get to know you a little better and be able to connect with you after the show?

India: Hi. My name is India. I'm from Cranbrook. If you feel like contacting me after the show, you can reach me at 250-417-5315 or e-mail me at india.s.ski@gmail.com. As far as getting to know me, born and raised in Cranbrook, skier for life, essentially. I'm not much special really. I train hard, work hard and I have a pretty neat job.

David: I think you're very special, India because I think what you bring is just such high performance. I'm thinking for our listeners, some of them may not know what ski cross is and specifically if you could tell our listeners what ski cross is.

I'm interested in your comments where in fact you're racing with three others. In a way, it's high competition and in a way, there are key elements of collaboration there. Can you explain that a little more for our listeners, India?

India: Yes, for sure. Ski cross is a really exciting sport. There are four competitors racing down the course at the same time. It's very similar to motocross, snow cross, that sort of thing.

We have a drop gate start and there are courses full of jumps, berms, rollers, that sort of thing and with of course, having four people on a pretty narrow place you can really get into some tight situations with; too many people in the one turn, that sort of thing.

With the collaboration aspect of it, all the time, you'll end up in heaps with your teammates, your countrymen or your friends or anything like that and something that while it's an individual sport, if there are two of you in a heap together, the first two move on to the next round. You're really trying to work together as a group to try and push each other through the format.

David: What are the speeds that you're going downhill in ski cross?

India: Oftentimes, we reach between 60 and 80 kilometers an hour.

David: Yes, just incredible courage to do that, India. When you finish that ski cross race and well before it, years before it, how do you work together? What's the team mean in ski cross?

India: There are a lot of aspects to the team with us. There are your athletic teammates but then there's a whole team of people behind us. Say our development team, it's about eight athletes. What people might not know is there are 20 people or more that are pushing us. There are people that make us accountable for all our decisions and everything we're doing. They help us along the way.

They say, "It takes a village to raise a child." Well, it certainly takes that many people to raise an athlete. We have physiotherapists, strength and conditioning coaches, on snow coaches, support staff, medical staff, really pretty much anything you can think of. We have mental staff. All those people really just help us in every aspect to be the best athletes that we can be and the best people.

David: I want to find ways for our village to support you and the many athletes around the world. India is a Junior Ski Cross World Champion. I'll say that for our listeners again -- World Champion. What are some of the ways for people to collaborate with you and support you? It's a lot of hard work and it's not very well paying. What are your needs from people that might choose to support you?

India: I'm always looking for people to sort of help me out financially. Any sort of donation really, really helps out. In a $30,000 season, every dollar counts. Last year I ran a crowd funding campaign and I raised over $6,500 I think. It meant the world. I came out of last season debt-free. If anyone out there is interested in supporting myself or the Canadian team, feel free to contact me or Alpine Canada.

As far as something more than just contributing those, I'm not a sponsored athlete. I am always open to looking over contracts and building relationships with businesses, sort of what I can do for you and what you can do for me.

David: Wonderful. From a global perspective, India, I haven't shared this with you but a few years ago, I coached a cross country skier representing Iran which is kind of an oxymoron but it happens; a wonderful man, Justin.

If you were to say anything for the global athletes beyond ski cross but those that are committed to sports excellence and championship and leadership, is there one thing that just thinking about it now, India that you could challenge our listeners to do or become more aware of with respect to collaboration and your world, your experience, your profession?

India: I think when you watch high performance athletes say, in the Olympics and that sort of thing, you don't look at them and think that they're an unreachable standard. Yes, there's a lot of work put in to that, but sort of collaboration with yourself.

A lot of people are inspired by high performance athletes to be better versions of themselves. See us on TV and don't be afraid to push yourself physically. Get out there and bring someone with you. Bring a friend. Get out to the gym.

David: Thank you so much for your encouraging us all for our own greatness and challenging ourselves. Even if it's ourselves in a road bike or cross-country skis or ski cross, whatever that is, get active and get involved and get together.

India: Exactly, yes.

David: Any last words before we close the interview, India Sherret?

India: No. Thanks, David. I really, really appreciate the opportunity to speak with you today. It's been great.

David: Thank you very much.

David: Our next guest today is Dan Savage. Dan's been in the video game industry for eight years spending his time at Neversoft where he worked on the Guitar Hero series. When Infinity Ward acquired Neversoft, he went on to develop Call of Duty: Ghosts.

During his career at both studios, the games he's developed have sold over 50 million copies world-wide. 50 million copies. Dan is currently the lead vehicle artist at Infinity Ward and lives in Woodland Hills, California. I'm also very proud to say Dan Savage is my son.

Dan, what would you like to share with our listeners today about you and the work that you do?

Dan: I guess I want to clear a few misconceptions people might have about game design and just discuss how people collaborate in a very creative field that usually takes hundreds of people over years to create that. It's one stop and you get experiences.

David: Yes. There's a big difference there, isn't there where oftentimes you get contacted. "I want to be a video game developer," and thinking that's, my judgment, sitting in a dark room for hours a day by yourself playing games and that's not it at all, is it?

Dan: Yes, I get that a lot where I tell people what I do and they, depending on who the audience is that I talk to, I'll say, "Oh, it's so cool. Let's talk a few more games," or they'll kind of roll their eyes and say, "Oh, you're one of those guys that sits in a dark room in a cubicle eating Doritos, drinking Red Bull, play video games, and that's how you make video games."

I just want to kind of clear up that misconception. That's not video game development. Yes, you must test the game for sure to make sure that it functions, squash bugs, but we're not in to video games and video game developers, we're not working with the controller in our hands, sipping on that Red Bull. It's a lot more collaborative and creative than that. It takes a lot more than just holding on to your controller.

David: Each of us works in different small teams, larger teams, big teams, bigger teams. What can you describe as to what your work environment at Infinity Ward looks like in those ever-expanding circles?

Dan: Right now, 250 people, such a large ship to steer and you break things down in different departments -- creative department, weapon department, field front, just for art. You have environment arts for single player and multi-player. You have programmers. You have designers. You have effects guys making sparks fly in your lighters, stickers, riggers, animators.

Some of that you have the QA (Quality Assurance) guy who actually does play the game to squash bugs to the Chief Creative Officer who's trying to steer this huge ship. A ship with that many people moves kind of slow. You got to make sure every cog in the machine is just in the right order to make sure you get to move forward making creative content.

David: As a lead, how do you collaborate? How do you get stuff done?

Dan: For me, I had some transition from going from a senior artist to a lead artist. As a senior artist, I create content all day long. We worked in a dozen programs that are different proprietary in-house programs or professional programs.

As a lead, let's just say I spend a lot less time creating content and more time sitting in meetings, working through programs to track assets, e-mailing the team constantly that could go easily to 400, 500 e-mails a day. They're kind of very important for how the day went.

What's the day's asset? How big is it? Who's going to work on it? What needs to be on standby? Who needs to implement the assets and games? It's got to be big, small. You got flies. You got static and so on and so forth. It's non-stop running around collaborating with people and just keeping the communication open.

David: Tell me, Dan what's one thing that hurts collaboration when the impact that you want to have, the progress that you want to make on a game, something that people tend to do that isn't useful?

Dan: Too many cooks in the kitchen for sure. It's meant to try and have a democracy when you're designing your games, but it's very often we have way too many cooks in the kitchen.

I've had experiences as a senior lead where I'm sitting there working on the assets and I have four art directors hovering over my shoulder, all trying to get their requests for this outfit that are each in their unique ways on their own levels. It's just not collaborative. It really hurts the process.

What I found is what one art director may want a resident of a level is completely contradictory to a different level. You really need to have a hierarchy structure that works top-down.

David: Yes. I'm thinking also I know that you're very committed, dedicated and you're always looking for ways to lead better and more effectively. In the next few years, what are you working on to develop your collaborative leadership, Dan?

Dan: Luckily, the field I work for really does invest in it's a great place to work. We do have training for leads. Not all leads are alike. Try to become the best leader that you can. To get the best from people, realize how you treat one employee totally different from another one based on their skills and their strengths.

I'm going through as much conscience and connection as I can to become a better lead, learn how to collaborate. If I find someone has stuck off then they come in and talk to me, how can solve this creatively and get the best out of what we want for this game.

David: Yes. That was a challenge. You often get asked by people that want to become video game developers or parents that are reaching out to you to talk to their schools or talk to their kids. What are a couple of things that you want to do to help foster their interest but make it useful?

Dan: That's a good question. It's usually important, just because someone enjoys playing video games, they might not make the best video game developer. I would point that anyone who's interested in video game development there are lots of free programs out there. Autodesk and others have free student programs and then the Unreal Engine and Unity Engine are now free to use.

Someone who is interested can start making maps of the video games. They can start making their own small games or big games, just kind of get in to the content. There are a lot of tutorials online where maybe someone who makes lots of video games has more fun programming. They connect to that experience. Maybe they want to do the art side of things.

There are just tons of content. There are a lot of documentation to really start things going. Definitely challenge them. Just look up online. Unreal Engine, Unity and look at other products because that's how you get your foot in the door, really get the juices flowing.

David: Thank you for that, Dan. I know one of the things that has been successful for you isn't necessarily your digital art. It's your leadership. It's being team captain and assistant captain on many sports, your world view, and your ability to bring people together. That's not a "me" leadership.

As we close, I wanted to acknowledge you on that, Dan. I think the world of you, love you. I want you to, in this moment, what's one thing that you wish to challenge our listeners to do or become more aware of to build their collaborative success?

Dan: I definitely challenge them to look inside their own homes. Your listeners I'm sure have children who play video games. Instead of looking at them with a negative connotation, "Oh, my son or daughter are wasting their time and melting their brain." This could be a creative time to collaborate. You get what your children like playing.

What challenges them when they're talking with friends? Is this just a hobby? Is it more? Find out what intrigues them. See the art of the game, maybe art class for kids who lean towards that in video games. If they like the programming, there are lots of programming classes in summer camps now.

These are things I challenge listeners to kind of started talking to their kids what video games and see how they can work together, children and parents so they kind of see, get the creative juices run.

David: Wonderful. Thank you so much, Dan Savage, Woodland Hills, California, Infinity Ward. Thanks again, Dan.

Dan: Thank you.

David: So far, so great with the wisdom and youth and leadership of Cranbrook's India Sherret, my son, Dan Savage, Los Angeles, whom I'm so proud of, and starting off the show with Kevin Brown from Madrid. I want to express my profound appreciation for all 45 guests on broadcast during this 15-week series.

My friend from Calgary, Monelle Fraser tells me that she listens to our show in parts so she can ponder each guest's wisdom and think about how she may use those insights in her work and in her life. Many guests tell me how much they have enjoyed collaborating with us on Break Through to Yes.

We are building a new network of collaborative leaders globally. Yes, 30-plus nations. Yes, I believe it's from six nations. We are all connected a little closer. I'd love to have a 2016 series where you're a part of this. Each listener has a voice.

We're only separated I believe by two degrees or even less. Last week, I Googled my name, David Savage, to see who's out there. I found David Savage who is a leadership coach, trainer, teacher, and outdoorsman. He works with businesspeople in Australia on collaborative leadership. Wow! My twin in the Land Down Under.

I embrace and I'm very encouraged by the leaders of our next generation. Today we are focusing on three such leaders. I love and I'm grateful to Chuck Rose for his gift of my theme song "Win or Walk Away" and "We are One." Go to chuckrose.ca to listen to them and connect with Chuck.

I'm a huge fan of Heather Gemmell, Cranbrook, British Columbia. She's a fantastic young musician, performer, artist, an individual that is equal to anything coming from the mass media.

Let's circumvent the mass media, the mediots, the system, the process, the politicians, the social mediots. Let's seek out in your community and globally who are the next generation of artists, leaders, innovators, and connectors in your community and around the world. Like never before, we can do this now.

David: Our next guest is Sarah Daitch. Sarah is a mediator, facilitator and public policy consultant, and former member of Canada's national cross-country ski team. Raised in Inuit, Dene and Métis communities in the Canadian North, Sarah works with governments and not-for-profits facilitating multi-stakeholder collaborative processes.

As a certified mediator with a BA in International Relations and an MA in Dispute Resolution, Sarah is dedicated to collaboration through dialogue to address natural resource conflicts at home and abroad. Sarah was a 2013-2014 Action Canada fellow, member of the 2015 Governor General's Canadian Leadership Conference. So cool, Sarah.

I could just keep talking about your accolades. You got so many. What I will say is you're also a member along with me and several others of the Collaborative Global Initiative. You're a Canadian working in The Hague, Netherlands now and for the foreseeable future. What else would like to tell about yourself, the work you do, and how people can learn more about Sarah Daitch?

Sarah: Thanks, David. It's great to be here on your radio show. I've been listening over the past few weeks, just some interesting interviews with collaborative professionals from all over. I think one thing I'd like to share today is to just mention a little bit about the role and organization I'm working with currently. It's called the Access Facility.

They focus on acting as a resource to help companies and communities solve problems collaboratively together. They're a multi-stakeholder platform and they want to increase the uptake of mediation to resolve problems and challenges that occur between companies and communities globally. That's what I'm focused on for the time being.

David: Fantastic. Great work. I'm envious of the work that you do, Sarah. You got right into it so quickly. I found out about you through our mutual friend and fellow in the Collaborative Global Initiative, Duncan Autrey.

You and Duncan and others I consider the next generation leaders where the role of my demographics we mostly need to support, encourage, and facilitate getting you out front. What can you share about how our next generation, how your generation can better do that through collaboration?

Sarah: I think one thing that's been important to me in developing my career and my skills in collaboration and mediation is to really look to the people who've been out in the field doing this work for decades. That was one big draw for me to join the Collaborative Global Initiative with yourself, with Kathy Porter.

These are people who have been working on multi-stakeholder process, bringing different parties together to solve problems for many years. It's very useful for the younger generation, for Duncan and myself to be exposed to this and to learn from their skills.

I've had a couple of other great mediation mentors through Mediate BC in British Columbia, the small claims civil dispute resolution through the court system. I had a great mentorship there through Ben Ziegler.

I also had an opportunity through an American conflict resolution organization called Resolve to have some really good mentorship. Tate Capishki is another mediator I worked with who has been solving natural resource disputes in different far-flung regions of the world for years.

It's so useful and valuable for me to have the chance to collaborate professionally and personally with people of our own generation but also the previous generation. Hopefully, together we can create more sustainable outcomes for the generation to follow us.

David: These are tremendous skills that you teach. You walk the talk, Sarah. You're the first one in my program with Métis, Dene, and Inuit community background. Any comments about that? Is there something that is different or is this really the same work wherever you work?

Sarah: I think for me, I learned a lot from growing up in those cultures. My own parents immigrated to Canada and they settled in the far north, in Baffin Island originally and then later in Fort Smith, Northwest Territories. I grew up around indigenous cultures.

I think what I learned to be around the Inuit was the importance of flat hierarchy. Clearly your generation and your age matters in terms of your status and your role. To be socially accepted, it's important to make yourself equal with the people around you. Oftentimes, it's done through humor, through self-deprecation.

I think some of those lessons of inclusion and making yourself equal to the people around you have really stuck with me. I feel very grateful to the communities I grew up for teaching me some of these good lessons and just teaching me more how to communicate and be comfortable across different cultures.

David: Thanks, Sarah. Now as we close, in this moment, what is one thing that you challenge our listeners to do or become more aware of to make their collaborations more successful?

Sarah: I think collaboration rests on if you're going to open the door to have a dialogue with different people about what kind of future you want to create or what kind of problem you want to resolve, it's important to have people in the room or at the discussion table who are affected by the decision.

A good example I can think of is I've worked on a project in my home region in the Northwest Territories about how the revenues from diamond mining would be managed. We had a dialogue that brought together parties from government, from indigenous organizations, from NGO's, different levels of government. What they said to us was, "We never get together and talk about these things."

That was eye-opening, because they were all working together in a relatively small community on a similar topic but just being in the same room, it opens all sorts of other possibilities and solutions. It's important to get all the parties who are going to be affected by a decision at the table to explore what solutions can look like.

David: Thank you so much, Sarah. Thank you.

Sarah: Thanks for having me, David. It's been a pleasure.

David: Today we've had: Kevin Brown, World Mediation, Madrid, Spain; Dan Savage, Infinity Ward, Los Angeles, California; India Sherret, World Junior Ski Cross Champion, Cranbrook, British Columbia; Sarah Daitch, Collaborative Global Initiative, The Hague, the Netherlands; and music, "Win, Win, Win or Walk Away" by Chuck Rose.

Key messages from today's episode and this will be the final in this series are:

1) you must make certain that every cog in the machine is working well together to move forward;

2) get involved in collaborative initiatives and teams across generations that builds skills, understanding and opportunities. Learn from the next generation. Mentor the next generation.

3) it takes a village to raise leaders. Be there in support of our next generations of leaders, next generations and our shared future need you.

Like my 24-year old father on D-Day, I salute the next generation of leaders. This series is for you. This series is also for my children Melissa, Heather, Dan, Claire, and Patrick and their partners Steve, Tyler, Nicole, Jamie and for you my grandchildren Quinn, Sarah, Bailey, and Charlie and to our next generations of great leaders working together. Over to you.

My call to action and my final call in this 2015 series is please lead from love.

Thank you. Have a break through week.

Chapter 16 Book Release Celebration featuring Anna McHargue and David Milia

David Savage: My journey in writing the stories, creating the ten essential steps to collaboration and including the real wisdom of over a hundred people in my book has evolved over the last three and a half years. March 22nd, 2016 is a huge day for David B. Savage and a whole bunch of folks including those who help me create it and our two guests today Anna McHargue and David Milia.

I'm very proud of the book, *Break Through to Yes; Unlocking Possibility within a Culture of Collaboration.* It is a collaboration from around the world. In this podcast on Voice America, you'll also hear portions of two songs that my good friend, musician, performer, speaker, Chuck Rose created for this radio show and podcast. Today, I've asked two key people in my writing, speaking, and publishing and learning journey over the past year to join us in this celebration of the book release. Anna is the person largely responsible for turning my hopes into wonderful language. We also have David, the person who collaborates with me to build the shared value and sustainability conversation in Calgary, Alberta, Canada and the world. Thank you for listening to us today on Voice of America. In our past episodes, we've reached people just like you in 30 different nations. We celebrate Break Through to yes, let's Break Through together. Now quick introduction of my two guests as executive editor of Elevate Publishing, Anna Marie McHargue has been solving complex language problems as a professional editor since 1989 when she won the editorial leadership of the year award. Anna is fantastic. She saw what I was trying to write and made it sing. Anna, how would you introduce yourself to our listeners?

Anna: Well as you said, I am an executive editor and I've been editing for about 30 years now and I absolutely enjoyed learning all about collaboration and working with you to ensure that your voice and your message came through strong and clear. I think we were very successful with that.

David Savage: Well thank you, I'm so delighted with Anna's work. Kirkus Reviews gave us an incredible review. " A treatise on collaboration." Anna, how can people find out more about you and your work?

Anna: Well, you can easily look me up on LinkedIn. That gives you a little history of my editing and my books as an editor in the past 12 years.

David Savage: Thanks Anna and now I turn towards my other friend on the show today. David Milia, associate director, Center for Corporate Sustainability and Haskayne Energy Initiatives of the Haskayne School of Business at the University of Calgary. Welcome David, please introduce yourself to our listeners.

David Milia: Oh hi David, thanks for having me once again on your show. I thoroughly enjoyed the first time you had me as a guest and it's a great to be here once again and have a conversation along with Anna Marie. What I try to do I guess, I was thinking about how should I say it this time I would be a little bit more impactful and recently I had somebody tell me about what I happen to be doing is what you described about what I hoped to be. What my "why" statement is personally is to be a champion and disseminator of knowledge around anything that's sustainability minded, energy minded, and that involves people. That involves collaboration, that involves us creating solutions together so that's what I hope I could say about myself as my brand apart from what you said is my day-to-day job, I guess.

David Savage: Wonderful and listeners, just be aware, if you look at the episode description on VoiceAmerica and on my website, you'll find the LinkedIn profile links and more. So, let's get started and this will just be an open conversation. I've got a few questions that Anna and David have heard about before, but we're going to go wherever this takes us probably even before that. Let's make it free. David or Anna is there anything else that you'd want to share with our listeners before we get into the few questions that I proposed?

David Milia: Well, I guess I would want to share what I'd like to get to the folks that come to my seminars, which you have attended en masse, David and we're very thankful for that. That is to listen to us with an open mind. Everybody has a whiff of my "what's in it for me" so to speak when they're listening to a topic or a series of topics and as we speak, please take what you will as good and challenge where you stand on the things that we're going share, but most importantly, become into it with an open mind to be open to say, "Hmm, what will they share? What will be open to me today that might help edify my position at work and in my personal life."

David Savage: Wonderful and Anna?

Anna: Yes, I was going to that along the same lines and to listen with humility and understand that we don't all know everything and that's what the beauty of collaboration is and I hope that is communicated today as well.

David Milia: Yes, absolutely.

David Savage: Yes, thank you both because I really truly believe that the best leaders are the leaders that don't know. That are realizing, express their openness to learning. Now, they may know most of what I might tell them, but even they're asked of me, includes me in the conversation. One of the things about our book, I will call it and the missions that both of you share with me is to change the culture in corporations so part of that inclusiveness will go to moving away from—I want to get my way with you and convince you and call that collaboration and moving to what's out shared vision?

What are our values that we share and how do we create shared value? That's great work that David and I and Dan Clarke of CSV Midstream will be talking about at Haskayne April 14th in Calgary. It's also great work that Anna and I have done and I am hoping that Anna will agree to work with me in the future on future books, future offerings because there is more that I can learn, more that all of us can learn and one of the things that Anna is particularly good is helping us craft stories that really resonate, that take us to that future state so that's a bit of a Segway into well, book's coming out March 22nd. What do you think? Anna and David, what do you think?

Anna: I look forward to sharing comments about this book because I think that as I said, once you imagine yourself in the situation as a leader where you are willing to offer humility. You're willing to offer a sense of not knowing I think that people will really find themselves in a position they haven't been in before. Usually, you go into a meeting and you know that your boss or your leader would like you to do one thing or the other, but I think after reading this book, perhaps a leader will find that his idea is not always the best and in the spirit of collaboration, the goals will be far more easily met and far more exciting and meaningful to everyone in the room instead of only the leader.

David Milia: Wow, geez, I want to say ditto just about immediately, but I'll dovetail a little bit more onto that as well. You know, I was fairly impressed with your book, David and I was very blessed to contribute a little case study to it. I think the part that spoke to me specifically out of your book that I could and to what Anna Marie has already said is that message accomplishing more together than we do apart. That is a hard thing to learn in corporate environment of action sometimes.

Particularly with leaders who are passionate to get things done and look at the objective, but sometimes don't take a good look around to say people matter and how we get there is just as important as getting there. I can say that in my walk I'm still learning that to this day and it initially and early on in my career, I would have benefited from having a book like yours to help guide for a few best practices on what I could do better particularly when I was a young manager and first promoted to say what does true collaboration look like.

How do I take the linear things that I must do at work and apply some critical thinking to them in collaboration with everybody within my team, understanding that although I may be accountable for something, everybody has a responsibility to make this successful and if we are all in it together, it's much better that I'm just leading it by myself and pushing forward bullishly. I failed many times to be too much of a bull without listening and I can tell you the difference between finishing something, accomplishing something when the group is all in far outweigh the times where I've gotten something accomplished and just moved onto something else with a team of not all in.

Anna: I understand why and I would like to add that, you know, I think part of that is that you're able to hear each and every voice at the table and understand what is being shared and the cue what is not being shared and I think that once that happens the start of collaboration is forced forward even more.

David Savage: One of the things that you both know and our listeners when they listen to, buy, read the book *Break Through to Yes* will be, the amount of failures I have had a time I have write out their—there are a whole bunch of cases where I go through and say, gee, this is what we started hoping to do and this is what happened and in the lens of collaboration, collaborative culture and our ten essential steps in the book, I analyze where those went wrong. Where they went right and that to me is building a culture of collaboration where it's a continual learning, continuous improvement and engagement.

Chuck Rose's Win, Win, Win or Walk Away lyrics;

Say you've got to win at any cost.
No golden rule, no line you haven't crossed.
Who cares if Mother Earth's in tatters, you're the
only one that matters.
Sorry buddy, you've already lost.
I have a dream that there's enough for everyone
and it's not about who's lost and who has won.

It's so simple it's wise, no defeating, no
compromise. It's the future it's already begun so
find a win, win, win, and walk away. Everybody
wins or find a better way. No exceptions, no
excuses, no one loses if someone loses. It's a
brand-new game and that's the way we play.

Confrontation's a mistake that we've outgrown. I
know I'm better off with you than on my own.

When we change the way we start, the intention in
our heart makes us more than we could ever be
alone. Though it's greater than the summer of all
the times. It's a game that we've all won before it
starts so let's choose the very best together will
break this with yes when we lead with love and
follow with our hearts so it's a win, win, win or
walk away.

Everybody wins or find a better way.

No exceptions, no excuses, no one wins if someone
loses, it's a brand-new game and that's the way we
play. It's got to be for everyone, it's not for just a
few. The only way that I win is you will win it too.

It's more than economics, it's not taught in any
schools, this game of life is ours and we're
changing all of the rules so find a win, win, win or
walk away.

Everybody wins or find a better way.

No exceptions, no excuses, no one wins if someone loses.

It's a brand-new game and that's the way we play so find a win, win, win or walk away.

Find a win, win, win or walk away.

Find a win, win, win or walk away.

David Savage: Win, Win, Win, or Walk Away. That was a song beautifully crafted, performed, recorded, and given me permission by my friend Chuck Rose, ChuckRose.ca. Now Anna and David, we were talking about collaboration. I ended the last segment of this show about revealing a number of my failures in building collaborative organizations, some of my successes and part of the reason I wrote the book. I'd like to ask you both what's you experience? What's your wisdom that you can share with our listeners about building a culture of collaboration within an organization team, not for profit family.

Anna: I am happy to jump in here. As an editor, I have learned that over the years, the best work that I have been able to put my name on is work that I have co-shared with my author. The projects where I've, you know, forced my opinion or demanded an outcome have been works that I haven't been proud of and I also think they've been works that are—my authors haven't been proud of. The best work that I've had have been pieces where the author and I are in sync, where we're working together, where we understand each other's goals, where we understand each other's hearts, which I find to be the most important and with that just follow on success because there's a goal that has been met by each of us and that has been the most meaningful.

David Milia: For me it'll be somewhat similar, but I'll say through the best instances I've had with creating collaboration has been where—as a team, we've been able to sit down and have at least a high level of understanding of what objective we're trying to get to. Not necessarily the designed steps to get us there so what I mean by that is if the objective was to you know, increase production, I come from the oil and gas sector or whether it was to increase profits or whether it was to create a community engagement piece. Whenever the team, that was around the table was able to first agree that this objective was worthwhile doing before we got into the personal bullishness of wanting to do it our way, our personal way.

That was one key step and then that closely followed with what Anne Marie expressed earlier, which was everybody's respected, there is no voice that's higher than another. There's just people fighting to get us to that objective and passionately going after that and then once alignment is created and relationship was established and the best example I've been exposed to, there was also an intrinsic authenticity of relationship that also led to empowerment of teams. Let me explain what that means. A lot of the times we'd have a group of managers that were talking about things and each of them wanted to leave to mark and providing the services as to their expertise for that matter and when the person whose idea turns out to be the one that after talking about around that table was accepted as the one that is worthwhile pursuing. Those leaders, those other managers whose idea had not garnered that acceptance would go to their teams and down the line also express how they were aligned collaboratively to that idea even though those teams might say well, I thought you were going into that meeting, "Fighting for X, Y, Z for US?"

Instead of saying, well, no I lost that fight, they would say, no I went there, and I saw this and this makes more sense and we are going to back it up. When that's happened, and I'll say it's happened very few times, but when it's happened, we've really had significant positive outcomes both on the project we were handling on the authentic relationship between teams to make that project happen.

Anna: Why do you think that happens rarely as you said?

David Milia: Well, in my environment, we have multiple—in that environment that I gave that example, we have multiple disciplines and approaches of doing things from an engineering standpoint and so each of them always wants that their specific discipline be the one that be the focus of how we're going to do the projects. Say you had an electrical component, or a mechanical component, or a structural civil component, each of them wanted to ensure that that project would absolutely have that part be the focus of excellence over the other ones.

David Savage: Now I want to jump in here and say that it takes time and that's we wrote this book and offered this radio wisdom that it is a culture. It is an event. It's not a one time, one off, let's do this quickly. Building that trust and respect and integrity takes time, takes learning, takes failure, and what both of you have shared is in building that culture, it's an on-going process. I will share a couple of instances where in my past, in my business past, I've found that boy it's been difficult to get people to the table to collaborate and when we get to that sweet spot of collaboration, the outcome is far better than what I ever expected so my message here is, if I would have got what I wanted it would have been less than what I got after I collaborated.

David Milia: Yes.

David Savage: I think one other aspect of this is creating dialogue with our Collaborative Global Initiative in the United States and Canada. We're creating dialogue that really circumvents the conversation, the regulatory, the political, the community, the outreach conversation so we are convening dialogue with respect to rebuilding the environmental assessment process. What would that look from the indigenous people? What would that look like for the environmentalist, for the business people? Because the way that it looks now destroys that a lot of value and a lot of relationships. Another one is the expiration of a nuclear power plant permit and starting to plan eight years in advance through community inclusive dialogue with all the stakeholders, all the interest groups to say the process will be the process. What can we do to circumvent it and make it more efficient and I think that's a powerful invitation again.

David Milia: Right so as you know, David, I'm working on part of that energy future, there's a—we like sometimes, I'll say to put things into boxes, perception based boxes of us versus them or this group representing and us representing that. I like to always reference Simon Sinek's *Start with Why* and I think I've probably done this to death with you, David, but his notion of having a "why" statement, people buy why you do things. Not how and what you do, but that "how" and "what" also is fairly important for having an avenue to get you there so when I look the problem that I sometimes see as a perception based tug of war, whether it be regulatory or the way we look at first nations and engagement or whether it be environmental, NGOs versus oil and gas, which is one of my favorite perception based tug of wars to play with. I always ask what is the "why", the "how," and the "what" that each has.

If one has a fairly strong "why," but is missing the "how" and the "what" and the other one has a strong "how" and "what" and is missing the "why". Instead of entering into conversations where we have the good guys and the bad guys based on wherever you stand, I like to think I'm going to help one group to help them establish a "why", I'll help another group to establish their "how" and their "what" and they're both keen on providing a future energy, a future engagement model, a future collaborative working style that will bring prosperity to the country. That's our big sort of objective and under that we focus on where the gaps are instead of focusing on us versus them.

David Savage: Right, Anna what are your thoughts?

Anna: Well I was actually thinking that was a beautiful segue to get us back into the book because there are so many examples of how this—how your ten steps in particular really are can be used across any industry, any government agency, any non-profit, even in your home for that matter and I think that that's something that's incredibly valuable to remember that the beauty of this collaboration that you've shared with us and put forth is something that we can take across all of these industries. You've shown us how to do that so clearly. I think that that's going to be a giant benefit for anybody who has a moment to research the ten steps.

David Savage: Anna, I want to—I'll ask this question of David after the next break, but before this break, I'd like to ask you, in this moment if there was one thing that you had challenged, encouraged, pushed our listeners to do to improve their collaborative success what might that be Anna?

Anna: I think I've stated this already, but I do indeed believe that this is the most important and that is to act in a sense of humility. When you're acting in a sense of humility and you're showing your team that you're willing to be humble, I think that changes the game. I think that that shows your team that you are part of them and that they are part of you and that true humility you can get so much more done than you could have ever imagined.

David Savage: Yes, I was thinking about your process of being diplomatic with authors, being a challenger to authors, being somebody that loves authors, and helping us as authors work collaboratively with you for better words, better stories, better outcomes. Do you have advice, wisdom? How do you do that without saying David, this work is crap? Or wow, this is so awesome, you know, how do you help people like me move forward?

Anna: I think the most important thing is what you, yourself has taught me or reminded me and that is that when you establish a strong relationship with a person, you want all of the best for them and I usually try to get to know my authors first so that I understand where they're going, what their message is and what their goals might be, but also, I like to understand what their voice is. Once I understand those things, I don't want to tell them that their work is terrible. I want to tell them that it could better and let's figure out a way to make it so. I also feel that when you're working so closely with someone, you know, you and I worked together for a very long time, I feel that we get to know each other and you understand the way I like to work. I understand the way you like to work and when we respect each other's boundaries, we respect each other's expertise because clearly, I'm not an expert on collaboration. Clearly, you're not an expert on editing or else you wouldn't need me so we respect each other that way and because of that, we're able to forge ahead. I think that's the most important thing.

David Savage: Well, listeners, I want to share with you something that over at a three period, I wrote about 600 pages then I had all these input from a hundred people around the world and Anna crafted that into a hundred 184 pages and crafted it into four parts.

Part one, Why I Believe in the Urgency of Collaboration,

Part two, The Discipline of Collaboration,

Part three, The Essential Steps to Collaboration and

Part four, Break Through

There is a huge win, win for me and working with people in Elevate, especially Anna. Before we sign off, Anna, I know I've only been able to get your time for this first half hour, the last few minutes, the last minute is yours before the break. Any last comments?

Anna: Well, thank you David, yes I just I want to say that I think this book is special in that it is going to touch people in a way that they hadn't been touched before. I don't see a lot of people, even though they're talking about collaboration, you can hear that almost every day, I don't see a lot of people really doing it and so I think that this is going to be a tool that you know, many of us as leaders will have the opportunity to dig into, to learn from and to really challenge our teams with and so it's going to be a great benefit.

David Savage: Well, thank you so much Anna Marie McHargue, you have been incredible.

Anna: Thank you for having me.

David Savage: Partner and collaborator for me and I highly recommend anybody that can capture your interest to collaborate with you. Thank you.

Anna: I appreciate that. Thank you.

David Savage: We're back with David Milia of the Haskayne School of Business. David and I and others are really working on building the courage, the vision and the success in collaborative leadership, sustainability. Now that's the three pillars, people profits and planet, not just green. It's all three and shared value. Share value being what can we generate together. We've—earlier heard with Anna and David talking about not trying to get my thing approved. Not trying to push my agenda, but see what's really needed, see what our collective Y is. Now, we're back with David. David, I want to ask you the question that I asked Anna just before the break is if there was just one thing in this moment that you'd really like to challenge, encourage, and invite our listeners into to improve their collaboration. What would that be?

David Milia: Right, so she talked about humility, which is usually believe or not, my number one, although the hardest thing to do in my opinion sometimes as well. What I would add to that is really golden rule type based things, David. If you're going into a collaborative sort of session, but you're going in and your mind is not open, if you're going and you're not willing to listen or have respect for others in the room then should you really expect them to have respect for you and be open to what you have to say? Applying that golden rule, which lets you know, do unto others as you would have them do unto you.

I believe that we have control or most control or influence over ourselves before we can over anybody else so if we want others to be respectful towards us, to listen to the positions that we might have, we have to show the way by our actions during those times to say, I will be respectful. I will be a listener and so some of us have to learn that more than others. I'm a fairly bullish get it done kind of guy, David. It became apparent early in my career that I needed to find ways to listen and so a way that I—a rule that I had particularly with meeting with my team was that I refused to talk first regardless of what the agenda item was to make to make sure that I had listened to those around me because otherwise, I had the propensity as you well know to talk and talk and talk and I really needed to do more listening rather than talking.

David Savage: Yes, I want to talk about mindfulness and presence and self-love, self-appreciation, all of those things because it's important that I be present for myself and what's going on for me, allowing others in. You talked about the golden rule, another way of stating it is treat others like you'd like to be treated.

David Milia: Yes.

David Savage: I think we both prefer the platinum rule, which is treat others the way they'd like to be treated and that's the way, that's an invitation to say welcome. I will find out the language that invites you in. In some of the work that I've been studying lately, I realized that all of this especially you David, you're a pillar in the western Canadian arena of collaborative leadership of Creating Shared Value and sustainability. I'm realizing that often times, when I speak to groups or when I coach executives, mostly it's about getting their to do list done as opposed to their "To Be" list and that's B-E, not just a To Do. It is so important and as a collaborative leader. Out of those collaborative leaders, the ones that you bring together, University of Calgary and throughout your career, those are the visionary people that I find that when we look at how people fit into an organization, there are the people whose sole task is to look at the entire forest, look at where the wind's blowing, look at what the threats and opportunities are and those people in particular will be interested in this conversation and my book I believe.

If you want strategies and tactics to get your way with other people, this isn't the book so I want to go back, David to what you and I and Anna and others I believe is let's hear all of the voices, let's hear those that disagree with me, that speak out to me and they're valuable if we ask a thousand about what is collaboration and ask them to put a check mark beside one of the next ones, collaboration is an event, collaboration is a system, collaboration is a culture or option B, collaboration is a mistake, what's your wisdom around those, that kind of a survey David is that an event, a system, a culture, a mistake, maybe it's all of the above. Maybe it's none of the above. Tell me your thoughts.

David Milia: Sure, I would say that collaboration could take on many forms depending who's in the room of that can lead to success and true collaboration, but I think that regardless of whether you look at it as a system, an event, or even a mistake. What will its ability to be successful is the culture so without culture, I don't think you can have the platform to create a system that will work or event that will work and that you'll end up going into a huge mistake. Those things can happen readily in business, particularly when there are strong positional people in the room that have authority over you and who have not shown a culture of respect or openness or humility and very quickly fear can take over those types of environments and that culture, it doesn't intend to lead to good things either sooner or later. In particular, it doesn't breed the grounds that alluded that we both love, which is a critical thinking landscape and it tends to lead to something that we call group think, which is the leaders speaks and everybody else follows.

I often wonder again when I was a young leader and I was in a room, I wasn't very good at this, the opportunities that I missed for not being a better leader and not being a better collaborator, not being a better listener, where and I definitely have examples where this occurred where everybody told the lie based on what I thought and then later as we faced new challenges, came back to tell me oh, yes, I saw that that you know, you look so confident, you look so this so that and pushing it forward, but I didn't want to say anything. I see that as a big failure in my leadership because had I been able to listen, had I leveraged the people in the room, had I been humbler, we would have had a better outcome overall and the people within my team would have felt better about the relationship that they had with me so I carry both of those to this day and I feel like I still make mistakes every day to be quite honest.

David Savage: Well I've published a lot of my mistakes in my book. That's why I call it a culture. I agree sometimes it's a mistake, sometimes it's just an event, but I think it is the corporate collective relationship. It is our rules of engagement; how do we work together? How do we make it better each time? I think that often until I trust you, until I see your ability to stand up to me, until I allow myself to recognize that you've got a brilliant concept that I didn't even know about and you're sharing it with us. You know, that's a beautiful evolutionary organization that allows that to happen. The flipside is too often I believe around boardrooms around the world is we look for hero leaders. We look for the rock stars that will be the hard hats, the drive at home, make the money. Well increasingly, they repel community repel those of us who think bigger. Margaret Wheatley, another one of my favorite people and I've interviewed her for my book and for my videos. She has a great quote where she said, "While we're driven most often to strong personality and those hero leaders." We, these aren't her words, it's off the top of my head, but those walks are hero leaders. We want them and then we kill them because they're trying to do too much.

David Milia: Yes, that's quite true.

David Savage: A complex world, too much in an area where there is none duality. There is none certainty. They just many shades so we end up setting them up for failure because we're not there with them.

David Milia: Reality that I've heard and that our friend Daniel Clarke shared with me because I definitely shared and what you've said, we've often heard the analogy of be where the puck is going to be, right? That's where you want to be in business. Not where it is, but where it's going to be David sometimes visionaries like us are so far ahead of the puck that we're on the other side of ice by the goal keeper, wondering why there's two guys still fighting for that puck way over there where they should be over here ready to score because we're too—too far ahead of that puck and sometimes.

Even though we might be visionaries, we need to go back a little bit to get the hook into coming to the other side of the ice by influencing a little bit as to what's happening on the other side. You know, that stuck with me due to the challenges I faced after being a visionary leader, after caring and still failing, but always caring to be better, right, always wanting to have a teachable spirit. Always thinking that the more that I know, the more I realize how little I know. The more experienced I get and still wanting to drive value forward for country and energy and sustainability so I don't have a full answer of how I can affect things because for me, it's one thing to talk about it. It's another to drive action and of course, I'm an action guy. I can't lose that part of that's what makes me, but how do I open up to other areas that make action more pragmatically better for all those aspects? That's the part that I'm always tweaking with, always working with.

David Savage: Yes, there you have my ten steps, the ninth and tenth are now lead and that truly is getting into that leadership role, hold the accountability, the game plan, the measurables, the metrics, the success, really get into that behavior, but before you get to step nine, now lead and step ten, make it so. You must invite others in otherwise it's just my show. David, before you leave what else would you like to share? What last comments would you like to make to our listeners around the world?

David Milia: Yes, well the big one, that I want to reiterate more than anything, is how much I wish there was a book like this when I was younger in my career and I was so hungry to be better, but felt so incompetent in trying things. A book can help, people can help, mentorship can help, and the big thing I want to leave your listeners thinking about is just try. Don't always just look for perfection. Use guidelines and try and by trying and getting better and having that teachable heart, to always want to drive it forward, being okay when you fail as long as you've learned something from it. That will inevitably create better collaborative situations create better relationships and better outcomes.

David Savage: Thank you so much David Milia.

David Savage: Wow, I'm so grateful to the Annas, the David's, in my life. Off the air I was just telling them both thank you for your friendship, your leadership, and your mentorship. I learned so much and I hope I teach so much. That's the invitation that I'm making with *Break Through to Yes; Unlocking the Possible within a Culture of Collaboration* is to say in 2016 and beyond in 2026, this is the era of collaborative leadership.

Organizations that create shared value will succeed and out pace, out race, out be embraced by communities and all stake holders versus the hero led ones, the bully led organizations that just want to push their agenda on the rest of us. That just doesn't work anymore. It might work for a while but ultimately, those hero leaders, those rock stars, those rapidly advancing share prices, they crash. They're not sustainable.

I invite all of us to look at, okay, what do I value? What is my dream for my community, my business, my planet, where do we want to be five years from now? Ten years from now? How do I bring the health, abundance, and opportunity to my grandchildren, to your family, to Sarah and Quinn, to all our grandchildren.

Therefore, we're collaborating, therefore we're figuring out these difficult, challenging, complex times together. To Bailey, to Charlie, all my grandchildren, all our global family, so when you have a dream use my ten essential steps to collaboration to create the container, to create the safety, to create the innovation and creativity, the inclusion, the invitation, use it. I invite you I invite you to build on it. I invite you to considering whatever your dream is, your project, your initiative, think about, think beyond the box that you're in, the saddle, the corporate tour, the organization or the family and say if I wanted to accomplish this, who are the people inside and outside, who are the people in the Middle East, in Asia, in China, in Greenland, in Argentina, who are those people that I could reach out with in this digital age that will help me, that will challenge me, that will help hone my initiative and my success.

How can we work together, how do we design that collaboration? There are resources, it's not just corporate money or Angel Funds or charities. There are many people.

My friend, Richard Schultz of Wisdom Ways. He challenges me and invites me and mentors me and leads me and is taught by me. He's introduced me to a fellow by the name of Eric Leeman of Sandyhook Area, New York State, Connecticut, pardon me. Eric's got a global initiative to make our children's experience of the world less violent. All of the sudden, through Eric I'm connected to some big hearts, the visionaries, powerful people in Paris and Germany. All of the sudden through Eric's relationship to me, he is connected to the video game industry and the future looks very positive and it doesn't look like anything that we know today. Dream it make it so and from this point on, I hope you read my book. I'd like to reach out to you and build our community. This is my purpose, this is my "why," I'm no longer prepared to put up with Mediots. Those that outrage and engage us, that lead us down rabbit holes, that makes false promises, that destroy the Earth, that destroy our future, destroy our communities. Now is our time, now let's lead and make it so. Thank you so much and this is just one step into many steps of evolving our global culture, our national culture, our organizational culture, our family culture, to work to better, together better, forever and for better. Thank you, talk to you again.

Break Through To Yes: The Collaborative Podcast Series
by David B. Savage

Book 1: The Foundations for Collaboration
includes eight 15-minute podcasts originally aired on the
Tenacious Living Network. The chapters are;

Finding Your Truth
10 Essential Steps to Collaboration
Great Leaders Know That They Don't Know
Global Book Release Celebration
EGOS
How Collaborative is my organization?
Collaboration is the Way; Shared Value is the Destination
Building Your Collaborative Culture
Thank you to Tenacious Living Radio for originally
producing these episodes.

Book 2: The Collaborative Guest Podcasts
offers three podcasts where David B. Savage was a guest
on Barry Wilson, Bob Acton and Duncan Autrey's
podcasts. The chapters are;

Fractal Friends Duncan Autrey,
      -talking about conflict resolution, communities,
      activists and collaboration
Mastering Leadership with Bob Acton,
      -exploring negotiation, collaboration and
leadership
Collaboration and Cumulative Effects on our Land with
Barry Wilson,
      -sharing ideas on how we collaborate on the true
      cumulative effects of our construction, capital
      projects and communities.

Book 3: The 10 Essential Steps of Collaboration
provides you with 16 podcasts originally aired on Voice
America in 2015 and 2016. The chapters and guests are;

Why Collaborate
   Chuck Rose, Denise Chartrand
Collaboration Gone Bad
   Kathy Porter, Duncan Autrey
Our Global Campfire
   Jeanne McPherson, Allan Davis
Set Intention
   Patricia Morgan, Don Loney, David Gouthro
Be Aware
   Ken Cloke, Cheryl Cardinal, Ryan Robb
Embrace Conflict
   Esther Bleuel, Jeff Cohen
Seek Diversity
   Joan Goldsmith, Amy Fox
Design the Collaboration
   Richard Schultz, Laura Hummelle, Colin Campbell
Come Together
   Donna Hastings, Rob McKay, Art Korpach
Listen Deeply
   Tara Russell, Linda Matthie, Viki Winterton,
   Stephen Smith
Collaborate with Vision
   Dee Ann Turner, Doreen Liberto, Dana Meise,
   Teresa de Grosbois
Now Lead
   David Milia, Don Simmons, Bruce McIntyre,
   James Armstrong
Make It So
   Michael Hill, Johanne Lavoie, Atul Tandon,
   Prabha Sankaranarayan
Leadership and Team Awareness
   Bob Anderson and Ginger Lapid-Bogda

Next Generation Leaders and Our Future
	Dan Savage, Sarah Daitch, India Sherret, Kevin Brown
Book Release Celebration
	David Milia, AnnaMarie McHargue

Book 4: Unlocking the Possible with Collaboration
provides you with 14 podcasts originally aired on Voice America in 2017. The chapters and guests are;

Collaboration and Leadership
	Bob Acton, David Mitchell
Collaboration and Sports
	Tristen Chernove, Martin Parnell
Collaboration and Organizational Culture
	Mike Thompson, Stephen Hobbs
Collaboration, Company Dispute Resolution and Mindfulness
	Julie Murray
Collaboration and Critical Thinking in This Age of Lies
	Doreen Liberto, Chuck Rose
Collaboration, Europe and Rotary International
	Elisabeth Delaygue Bevan, Florian Wackermann
Collaboration and Human Sexual Trafficking
	Lance Kadatz, Cliff Wiebe
Collaboration, Human Resources and Global Networks
	Amy Schabacker Dufrane, Japman Bajaj
Collaboration, The Secret Marathon and Going the Extra Mile
	Kate McKenzie, Shawn Anderson, Martin Parnell
Collaboration, Leadership and Disruptive Technologies
	Jim Gibson
Collaboration, Negotiation and Mediation
	Jeff Cohen
Collaborative Global Initiative Tool Kit

Barry Wilson, Doreen Liberto, Jeff Cohen
One Yes, One Thing, One Dream
Deva Premal and Miten, Klara Fenlof, Robert
Stewart, Sara Amos and Quinn Amos
Unlocking the Possible
Ken Cloke, Duncan Autrey

I hope you enjoy the Break Through To Yes: The
Collaborative Podcast Series

Acknowledgements

Thanks to;

a) every one of my guests from around the world on my 2015, 2016 and 2017 podcasts.

b) VoiceAmerica (Book 3 and 4),

c) Tenacious Living Radio (Book 1),

d) Obair, CE Analytic and Autrey (Book 2) for originally producing these podcasts.

e) Dawood Taiwo for editing and cover.

f) Vladimir Krstic and Pete Stover for audio production on the audio books.

g) Ginger Wilmot for transcribing the podcasts.

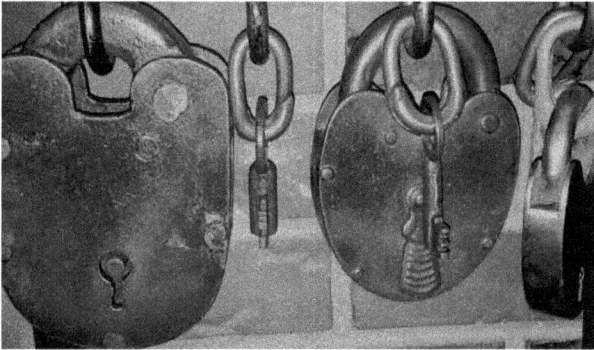

Unlock the Possible within a Culture of Collaboration

SAVAGE
MANAGEMENT Ltd.

"David B. Savage's *Break Through to Yes* provides the key for real success – collaboration!"
Marshall Goldsmith, *Thinkers 50* #1 Leadership Thinker in the World and Top 5 Management Thinker 2015

"Written in a manner that illustrates collaboration in action, *Break Through to Yes* shares decade's worth of knowledge and a structure that outlines what true collaboration looks like."
David L. Milia, MBA, CET, Associate Director, Centre for Corporate Sustainability/Energy Initiatives Haskayne School of Business

"David Savage is deeply insightful and highly intuitive. He is a skilled and highly regarded practitioner with a strong sense of ethics and values. He has a profound commitment to personal and organizational transformation and can be counted on to be honest, resourceful and supportive. I recommend him highly."
Ken Cloke, Founder Mediators Beyond Borders

"David is a brilliant leader who is the expert when it comes to understanding the power of collaboration and creating an open culture/ open door environment for all. His ability to share information, target the needs of the audience, and engage their perspective was seamless.
Denise Baril, Founder, Workplace Speaker Network

"Savage reminds us of who we are and what is most called for in our organizations. He brings qualities, values and intentions to the core of our professional work."
Gloria Boogmans, Independent Business Woman.

About the Author

David B. Savage, BA (Econ), PLand, CPCC
**Collaboration, Business Development
and Negotiation Specialist**
Savage Management Ltd.

Savage brings over 42-years expertise, experience and leadership in oil and gas, renewable energy, health care, entrepreneurship, stakeholder engagement and conflict management. Over a ten-year period, David and partners, collaborated to develop 5 companies and 4 not for profits. Since 2007, Savage Management has focused on build capacity, innovation and accountability in people and in and between organizations and communities.

David Savage works with leaders and organizations to advance their success through collaboration, negotiation and business development.

CORE COMPETENCIES:

Negotiations and Agreement Building, Business Development, Acquisitions, Management Consulting, plus   Strategic Planning & Execution, Sustainability Engagement and Organizational Development, Management Leadership and Team Building, Stakeholder Engagement, Business Development, Conflict Management, Executive and Team Coaching plus 360 Leadership Assessments.

KEY CORPORATE EXPERIENCE:

➤ Savage Management, President, (founder, 1993 to present, private, consulting, oil and gas management, coaching, leadership and negotiation training, negotiation mastery circles and leader round tables, conflict resolution and collaboration assessments),

> Prior to 2007, David held executive positions with BXL Energy, Marmac Mines Ltd., Sebring Energy, TriQuest Energy, Sommer Energy, Westar Petroleum, Total Petroleum, Ashland Oil, Bank of Montreal, and CIBC.

PUBLICATIONS

2003: David's Company to Company Dispute Resolution Council published the Let's Talk Handbook.

2011: Think Sustain Ability published Sustain Magazine.

2012: Ready Aim Excel: 52 Leadership Lessons

2016: Break Through to Yes: Unlocking the Possible within a Culture of Collaboration

2017: The Collaborative Podcast Series are;

Book 1: The Foundations For Collaboration

Book 2: The Collaborative Guest Podcasts

Book 3: The 10 Essential Steps

Book 4: Unlocking the Possible

Break Through To Yes Updated and Revised edition

2018: Break Through To Yes: Generating More Value with Collaborative Negotiation.

PURPOSE

Getting the right people, in the right places, with the right systems and the right resources to collaborate, innovate and figure out challenges together is the best way. And, if that is not possible, then guiding the parties to the right people, principles, processes and systems to ensure everyone's interests are heard and considered is my goal.

www.ingramcontent.com/pod-product-compliance
Lightning Source LLC
Chambersburg PA
CBHW060318200326
41519CB00011BA/1765